Princoirs

(pronounced prins'wärs) **VOLUME ONE**

OFFICIAL MEMOIRS OF PRINCE JOE HENRY, EX-NEGRO LEAGUER

Foreword by William A. Smith, Ph.D.
University of Utah, Department of Education,
Culture and Society/Ethnic Studies

COMPILED BY

SEAN R. MUHAMMAD

Princoirs
© 2008 by Sean R. Muhammad

Photographs © courtesy of Prince Joe Henry
All photographs printed with permission by the photographer.

First publishing by
Princoirs King Publishing
St. Louis, MO 63114
All rights reserved. No part of this book may be reproduced and/or transmitted in any form without written permission from the publisher, except by reviewers who may quote brief excerpts in connection with a review.

Library of Congress Cataloguing-in-Publication Data is available.

Layout & Design by Sean R. Muhammad
Additional Layout & Design by Natasha Moore
Editing by Professor Charles Wartts (Kitabu Editorial Services)
Distributed by R.A.G.E., Inc.

Princoirs

(pronounced prins'wärs)
OFFICIAL MEMOIRS OF PRINCE JOE HENRY, EX-NEGRO LEAGUER

Foreword by William A. Smith, Ph.D.
University of Utah, Department of Education,
Culture and Society/Ethnic Studies

COMPILED BY

SEAN R. MUHAMMAD

Princoirs King Publishing

St. Louis, MO

TO
"MAMA LU", T'LISA, T'ASIA, T'LIYAH, YUSEF, 'AQUIL AND BIANCA

In Loving Memory Of

Ida Henry ("Mama"), Grover Henry, Sr., Maggie Johnson,
William Henry ("Brother"), Grover Henry, Jr. ("Charlie"),
Essie Beatrice Stewart ("Bea"), Catherine McIntyre ("Cat"),
Richard Jackson, Joseph Henry, Jr. ("Joey"),
Melba Henry ("Denise") and Travan Hughes

Over the Years, We've Lost So MUCH but have Been Blessed with So Much MORE!
Peace be upon them, and may God be pleased with their efforts.

Besides God & Family, Special Recognition Goes to:

Mike Seely—Your work and support helped spark this Movement.

Tom Finkel, Krisitie McClanahan & The Riverfront Times—Thank you for offering a forum for OUR side of the story to be told.

Barak Corbett—Your words helped to bring this project to fruition.

Prof. William "B.P." Smith—Being under your tutelage helped me understand the value of taking advantage of a college "education".

Bro. Ajuma (AARM, Inc.)—Being under your tutelage helped me better understand the business end of being a "professional".

Ralph Muhammad—For almost 20 years, you have been an inspiration to me as spiritual counsel, mentor and friend.

Prof. Charles Wartts (Kitabu Editorial Services)—You are a Godsend, my friend, and your professionalism and expertise as an editor has taught me so much in just a short period of time.

Thank you Better Family Life, Inc. for giving me the opportunity to serve the people in a positive, cultural, corporate environment.

Thank you Natasha Moore (Apostolic Experience)—Your kindness, honesty, friendship and professionalism has been the most important part of this journey and undertaking for me in compiling this book.

Finally, I would be remiss if I did not (again) thank Almighty God and His Christ for The Honorable Minister Louis Farrakhan, who represents the Divine extension of Their Holy Grace.

To each of you...THANK YOU!!!

~Sean~

Praise for the Prince

"While with the Detroit Clowns, Henry - an outstanding third baseman - often donned a tail tuxedo and a raggedy top hat to entertain the fans. He was probably 'black baseball's' most prolific entertainer. He deserves more recognition for his contribution to the game."

-- *Larry Lester, historian and co-founder of the Negro Leagues Baseball Museum in Kansas City and author of Black Baseball's National Showcase*

"Books such as 'Princoirs', a historical review of the life and career of 'Prince' Joe Henry are vital."

-- *St. Louis American Sports Eye*

"Henry's showmanship at third base during two seasons in Indianapolis, a team that counts home run king, Henry Aaron, among its alumni and is often compared to basketball's Harlem Globetrotters, earned him the nickname 'Prince Joe'. As a youth, Henry was so good that he was quickly discovered by Negro League veteran catcher, Josh Johnson, who encouraged him to play baseball."

-- *Pitchblackbaseball.com*

"Today, his mind is still sharp, recalling dates and encounters from his career in the 1950s. Henry's stories will carry on long after [Major League Baseball's] ceremonial draft with 'Princoirs'. Such as work was inevitable for baseball's ultimate showman."

-- *Drew Schmenner of the St. Louis Post-Dispatch*

"It's no joke that Major League Baseball should do more for every living former Negro League Player. The game is making more money than ever, yet seems to cry poverty when it comes to helping players like 'Prince' Joe Henry."

-- *Alvin A. Reid of the St. Louis American*

The BLACK MAN'S Resolution ...

Three centuries and several years scores, our forefathers were transplanted in this country to start a new way of life. Conceived in Africa, they were forced to accept the proposition of becoming the white man's slave.

Now, "we" are engaged here in a hostile nationality conflict testing whether the complacent "Black Man" or the "Uncle Tom Black Man" – so conceived in this society – will cease prostitution of his dignity.

"We" are met on the battlefield of injustice. "We" have come to reverse that through Unity, as a final resting place, for those who gave their lives, so that one day this might become effective. It is altogether fitting and proper that we should do this.

But in a larger sense, "we" cannot falter..."we" cannot differ in pursuit of a common goal. "We" cannot tarry in carrying out this process. The brave men – both living and dead – while never enjoying their labors and who's intelligence was far below that of what we exemplify today, struggled to make this become a reality for us.

The white man will little note – but long remember – what we say here, but they will never understand what they have done to us since we have been here.

It is for us, who understand, to preach togetherness here and to reap the benefit(s) of our forefathers' laborious donors, while their bodies were racked with pain, thus far has allowed us to be nobly advanced.

It is rather for us to be here dedicated to the great task remaining before us that from these honored dead we take increased devotion to that cause, for they gave the last full measure of their own human energy, so that "we" here highly resolve that these dead shall not have died in vain, and this country – under God – shall have Liberty and the development of the Black man, by the Black man, for the Black man and shall NOT perish from the earth!!!

... Joe Henry © 1965

Ted Strong in an American Giants uniform, along with Joe Henry before a game. Strong, who was with the American Giants in 1951, was a complete ballplayer that could hit for both average and power and was a good infielder with a strong arm. During the off season, the six-time East-West All-Star was the western unit captain of the Harlem Globetrotters basketball team. *(Photo courtesy of NoirTech Research, Inc.)*

Foreword

I, too, sing America.
I am the darker brother.
They send me to eat in the kitchen
When company comes,
But I laugh,
And eat well,
And grow strong.
Tomorrow,
I'll be at the table
When company comes.
Nobody'll dare
Say to me,
"Eat in the kitchen,"
Then.
Besides,
They'll see how beautiful I am
And be ashamed—
I, too, am America.

Langston Hughes

Far too many People of Color, or the darker members of the human family, have a history of being sent to the kitchen to eat when company comes. The kitchen for us was supposed to be a place that was out of sight, as not to interfere with the personal business and racial taste of white folks. However, we developed the kitchen into a literal and metaphoric space, where all people eventually wanted to gather, socialize and learn the mastery, mystery and ingredients of our "culinary" culture within our presence. This culture was in part an extension from the remnants of a great African past, but cooked over the heat of racial oppression in the New World, which formed something unique and dynamic. Now, almost 400 years since the first people of African descent were forced into slavery to cook, clean, farm, toil, fight and also build the U.S. into a global superpower, there are still brothers and sisters who have to struggle with being relegated to a modern-day kitchen.

In this regard, professional baseball was no different. The great room would be considered the Major Leagues and only accessible to whites, while the kitchen was the Negro Leagues where Blacks were restricted. But – in actuality – it was the heart, soul and center of the talent, festivities, and entertainment in the house. The house of institutionalized racism in the United States of America and its deeply entrenched color line kept African Americans, Black Latinos and dark-skinned Mexican Americans out of Major League Baseball until 1947. Prior to 1947 there was not a single Black man on any Major League team. It would take the entire Negro League career of men like "Prince" Joe Henry (1950-1959) to come to an end before every Major League team had just one Black player on its roster. As a result, by 1959 this pattern of racial discrimination in professional baseball had not changed significantly. Even though the retarded promises of the Thirteenth, Fourteenth and Fifteenth Amendments offered "legal protection" from slavery or involuntary servitude; "equal protection" under the laws to all persons (not only to citizens) within their jurisdictions; as well as "banned" race-based voting qualifications, the actualization of a truly racially integrated league—free from the remnants of its racist past—was as slow as all other areas of race relations in this country. This is an important point to remember as you learn about the trials and thoughts of Prince Joe.

In spite of these obstacles, Prince Joe Henry and many of his Black comrades who played with or against him, as well as those important men from earlier

FOREWORD

periods like Andrew "Rube" Foster, responded to a rigid form of white supremacy by creating a system of their own – their own remodeled kitchen. I had the great fortune of meeting and learning about these struggles from Mr. Henry in 1993, while I was an assistant professor of African American Studies and Sociology at Western Illinois University. I also had the good sense to know that I was in the presence of a person of immense wisdom, and that practical or lived experience is sometimes a better teacher than any academic book. Mr. Henry is an inspiration and motivator. He made me proud to be considered his friend. More importantly, it was an honor to share the company of a Black person who had made extreme sacrifices, who had fought a tough fight so that I could have a place in the great room if I chose or live it up in my self-defined kitchen, where all of the action was. This lesson was also imparted to me early in my life, and coincidently through baseball.

Baseball was my first love. I grew up watching my favorite team, the Chicago Cubs, and players like Ernie Banks (1953-1971); Ferguson "Fergie" Jenkins (1966-1973); Billy Williams (1959-1974); and Bobby Bonds (1981). In Chicago, during the regular season, you can only be a fan of one Chicago team. The Cubs games were shown on WGN-TV channel 9, which was an always clear UHF (ultra high frequency) channel. After 1968, the Sox were no longer shown on WGN-TV, but moved over to WFLD-TV Channel 32, which was on the oftentimes fuzzy VHF channel (very high frequency), at least in my Black neighborhood, which was not close to the transmitter. This is the real reason I chose the Cubs over the Sox despite living closer to Comiskey Park on the predominantly Black Southside of Chicago where the Sox played. Despite this qualifier, my favorite White Sox players were Minnie Miñoso (1951-1957, 1960-61, 1964, 1976, 1980); Dick "Richie" Allen (1972-1974); and Bobby Bonds (1978). I loved to watch great Black players and then go outside and try to imitate them. I never knew then of their struggles prior to or since joining a Major League team, but those lessons were on their way. I was also fortunate to live in a strong Black community that supported its Little League Baseball teams. However, support most often meant that parents, family members, and friends would come to the games, cheer for their sons, daughters, and friends and grill in the park. This support did not extend to taking up a collection to improve the field conditions that their children played on.

Our baseball field was filled with scattered rocks and stones. We knew that our field was not as nice as the white kids' well manicured fields on the other side of town. Despite this, we fought through the awkward hops from the baseball hitting hidden rocks just beneath the dirt. We learned how to slide into bases and catch fly balls without getting injured. We would practice, and when we got tired, we practiced some more because our coaches reminded us that if we were going to be great at anything, we would have to be better than the white kids. In other words, we would have to compensate for the support that white supremacy gave to mediocre whites. Ironically, in this country's bicentennial year, these lessons came together as my all-Black team (Markham Manor) won the Illinois State Little League Baseball Championship. My role on this team and our win still stokes my self-confidence even to this day.

I went on to make the baseball team each year at my predominantly white high school. During the summer months, my best friend from my neighborhood, Bernard Holland, and I played for two teams – one, an all-Black team and another one where we were the only two Black players. On the all-Black team, we were just one of many very talented players. On the predominantly white team, we were two of the very best players. Eventually, our hard work and the support of Black men like our manager, Bobby Faulkner, allowed many of us to successfully play Minor League Baseball. Bernard and I also played college football at the same school. I pledged my predominantly Black fraternity, Omega Psi Phi, and he joined one with the colors of Black and Gold. As you can tell, athletics and friendship were major vehicles that kept me focused on my scholarship, health, hard work, perseverance, sportsmanship and what it meant to be a good teammate and an uplifting person. Now, I wonder how my opportunity to play baseball, to be mentored and coached by former Negro League players, and then to take that mental confidence and compete in equally racially segregated areas within higher education AND succeed, might have been hampered had individuals like Prince Joe decided not to punch holes in the walls of white supremacy and allow future generations of Children of Color to share their dreams.

Unfortunately, as you will read in this book, Major League Baseball is still sending former Negro League players to the kitchen. Mr. Henry was not among a group of 69 former Negro Leaguers whom Major League Baseball began paying inadequate annual pensions of $10,000 in 1997. In order to qualify for the pension, all former Negro Leaguers had to have played in parts of four seasons,

FOREWORD

with at least one coming before the 1947 season when Jackie Robinson broke the color barrier. If a Negro Leaguer's career began after 1947, he was excluded because the prevailing thought was everyone was now "on a level playing field." However, as I previously mentioned, it took until 1959 for Major League Baseball just to have one Black player on each team. Clearly, this is another knock against Prince Joe and other Negro Leaguers who played during this period.

To be sure, Major League Baseball is still struggling with race despite the apparent diversity on the field. Edward Rimer examined the experiences of Major League managers between 1975 and 1994 to determine whether the standards used by the teams were job related and the extent to which these standards were applied equally to all who became managers. The focus was on the hiring practices of the teams instead of the behavior of individuals seeking managerial positions. He examined the prior experience of these managers as Major League players, Minor League managers, and Major League coaches—and proved that Blacks had to possess significantly superior attributes to be hired as Major League managers.

Given this backdrop, you will be transformed by reading the wisdom and thoughts of a Black man who has seen and experienced many things since his birth in 1930. Prince Joe's life has extended over much of this country's most difficult periods of race relations since the Africans in America were emancipated. As a result, he is a walking racial encyclopedia. He is a teacher. He is a mentor. He is a father, grandfather and great-grandfather to more than just his kin. You will recognize that the thoughts he shares are peppered by what he has experienced through living during most of the 20th century. Most importantly, once you realize the significance of his story, his Princoirs, you will understand how beautiful he is "and be ashamed," because he, too, is America.

William A. Smith, Ph.D.,

University of Utah1 [1]

---

[1] Dr. William A. Smith serves as a Special Assistant to the President for Student Athlete Academic and Athletic Policy and Compliance at the University of Utah. He also is an Associate Dean in the College of Education and an Associate Professor in the African American Studies Program and the Department of Education, Culture, & Society.

The Gift

I have been working to compile this book for almost three years and as a result, I have come to see it as a labor of love that has afforded me the privilege of spending much time with "Prince" Joe Henry, my grandfather. During this special time I have had the opportunity to share in his wisdom and to see him from a different perspective. Recently, while searching for relevant materials to include in this timely collection, I was thumbing through some of the handwritten scribbles – sometimes very cryptic – that my grandfather had lying on or about the living room coffee table. In retrospect, I have discovered that these were some of the same writings and literary compositions he had authored as I was growing up in his household alongside the many other grandsons under his tutelage. A great number of these articles were written well before I was born.

At one point I came across a very tattered manila folder that housed a typed chapter of twenty-one pages, entitled "Separate But Equal," which he had written in 1972. This chapter was originally slated for his official autobiography. However, along with the Prologue and another chapter describing St. Louis' architectural structures, it now represents the introductory portion of this book. Affixed on the front cover of the folder were the words: "Gift – natural talent; genius."

I have always admired my grandfather's fascination with words—their etymology, their variations and rhythms, the colloquialisms or jargon—and ultimately the power relative to such. However, I began to wonder why this inscription was present. Had it been hastily tacked onto the folder with the intent of revisiting it later, possibly for further embellishment? The Oxford

English Dictionary defines the word "gift" as (1) a thing given willingly to someone without payment, a present; (2) a natural ability or talent; or (3) (informal) a very easy task or an "unmissable" opportunity. Further, it suggests the synonymous word present to be a thing given to someone as a gift. How ingenious and proverbial, I thought.

Likewise, this book's title, Princoirs!!! (pronounced PRINS´WÄRS), represents a unique play on words as unparalleled as the subject it represents – Mr. Joe Henry—better known as Prince Joe Henry, legendary ex-Negro Leaguer. It is derived from the combining of the words "Prince" and "memoirs," his way of giving the reader a furtive peek through an aperture of his mental window via his poems, essays, interviews and other artistic compositions. Phonetically, the reader may catch the idea contained therein, which suggests how great The Prince was – or how talented or astounding he may have been in his heyday. At present, Prince Joe resides in Brooklyn (or Lovejoy), located in Southwestern Illinois – a short journey east of St. Louis' Gateway Arch and the Mississippi River. Brooklyn represents the oldest village and perhaps one of the most historic townships in America. It is the home to Quinn Chapel A.M.E., which is noted to have been a part of Harriet Tubman's Underground Railroad system. As if that isn't ironic enough, the church's former long-time pastor, Rev. Leroy Henry, Sr., just so happens to be The Prince's younger brother.

Prince Joe – like so many other talented Negro Leaguers – willingly gave to the world of baseball to the delight and enjoyment of many who simply loved the game dubbed as America's "favorite pastime." One could even make a very strong and valid argument that the compensation they received for their services never matched the monetary value of those in the lily-white baseball league – the so-called Major Leagues. When one is capable of displaying exceptional natural ability (or talent), he offers a God-given gift to the world. It is indeed an opportunity "not to be missed," an opportunity for all to witness the greatness heralded by athletes sporting uniforms resembling those of heroic gladiators.

However, Major League Baseball (MLB) seems to have found a way to "miss" the perfect opportunity to finally recognize baseball's forgotten vanguard – its disposable heroes. In fact, it has thwarted the seemingly benevolent efforts it began almost a decade ago. In September 2004, MLB – along with a charitable foundation known as the Baseball Assistance Team (BAT) – denied Prince Joe's

THE GIFT

request to receive a well-deserved pension. Previously, it had awarded a handful of ex-Negro Leaguers a pension – either via a monthly stipend or a combined lump sum – based on their tenure. Perhaps MLB's requirements stiffened, because according to the organization's decision-makers, Prince Joe's income "exceeded his expenses." It wasn't until October 2007, after a team of us worked vigorously for several months to find "credible" documentation supporting Mr. Henry's participation in the Negro Leagues, that BAT finally conceded and awarded him four years worth of pension. The initial portion which issued in a lump sum (see "Prince Joe's Victory" by Chad Garrison at the book's close), and the remaining portion was/is to be given to Mr. Henry in monthly installments until approximately July 2008. Based on my research, though, I found that Mr. Henry serviced the Negro Leagues for approximately seven or eight years, whereas MLB and BAT – according to their "guidelines" to receive pension – he only played four.

However, upon examination, expecting anything less from an institution that has snubbed the likes of the late great Buck O'Neil by not inducting him into its Hall of Fame would be naive. The 2006 ESPN Baseball Encyclopedia refers to Mr. O'Neil as one who was "a slick fielding first baseman who hit for high averages." He would have celebrated his 95th birthday in November 2006. Moreover, Silas Simmons, the oldest ex-Negro Leaguer—and the longest living baseball player in American history—passed in 2006, shortly after celebrating his 111th birthday; he represents yet another ex-Negro Leaguer snubbed by MLB.

Outside of various independently-owned websites favorable to Negro League baseball history and memorabilia and sporadic footnotes occasionally displayed on ESPN's crawlspace ticker, I have yet to see anything celebrating the life of Mr. Simmons and very little recognizing that of Mr. O'Neil. In fact, I've yet to hear MLB's front man, Commissioner Bud Selig – in the midst of his campaign to "rid" the league of steroids – take the time to even mention either of them in any of his many sound bites. You mean, you couldn't even offer condolences to the respective families, Commissioner Selig??? Shame! Shame! Shame! on y-o-u and MLB. Perhaps Cooperstown, NY should rename its most prized historical shrine the Hall of Shame, because MLB appears to have a dirty little secret that is rotten to the core!!!

My quest here, however, is to present Prince Joe's unique perspective, which has always displayed the most vivid colors imaginable. His generosity also is legendary.

He has always given to friends, family, and ultimately to anyone in need without hesitation—and he has never asked for a dime in return. Prince Joe – along with his beautiful wife (my grandmother) "Lu" – has always set the best examples for me. Together they have exhibited every positive trait that a father and mother could ever offer.

In a world suffering from the ills and impediments of racism, sexism, materialism and nationalism, he has always demanded the best from his offspring. His message to us has always been this intrepid, well-crafted, yet simple message: "Be a thinker!" This, he coupled with the Golden Rule: "Treat others as you want to be treated." It is my prayer that my efforts in compiling these memoirs are in accordance with the above lines, for my genuine desire is to portray him as the great man that he is. Call it somewhat of a gift. I feel it is what he deserves. I hope his message is well received, because I know it will benefit the hearts and minds of all those who read it. In fact, its presentation is long overdue. Therefore, I humbly present to you Princoirs!!! Peace and enjoy!!!

Sean R. Muhammad

June 2008

Prologue

Born in October, I am a Libra; my zodiac sign is "the scales." Astrologists say this is the sign of "balance" and "equality," which both signify a factor bearing the same weight. One pan can be loaded with gold and another with iron pyrite (fool's gold), or even with human excrement. If the arrow points to the center, they are said to be "equal" – at least in weight.

A similar balance can be ascribed to history, which is a retelling of facts, and whether it be recorded or reconstructed, it is intended to immortalize the past, justify the present and extrapolate the future. American History – in particular – has been conveyed in such a manner as to justify the dominant society, i.e. white society ("His story" is an account of the past that consistently postulates a qualitatively imbalanced picture).

"His story" in America, particularly as it relates to the contributions of Black Americans, has systematically obliterated the important roles that Blacks have played – from a fledgling actress on the stage of world affairs to the leading lady (with all due frills and accolades) – in the gradual emergence of these "United" States.

Unlike their white counterparts whose laurels are all too familiar to students of American History – be they Black or white – Blacks, who indeed have made substantial contributions to America's rise to universal prominence and power, have been denied equal and proper "exposure" in the annals of "his story."

Hence, their achievements have gone unheralded or have been rationalized as "exceptions" and relegated to merely being a "credit to his/her race," rather than being rightfully categorized as a "credit to all Americans and to humanity."

As an illustration, let us examine the chronicles of history to compare and contrast the weight given to two famous Americans: Albert Einstein, the son of Jewish parents who fled Germany to escape Nazi annihilation and George Washington Carver, a Black man born in bondage on a plantation in Missouri. Take their respective contributions, place them on the "scales" of Libra, and let us see if they match the so-called "balance" of history.

Professor Einstein, while at Princeton University, conceived the world renown formula $E=MC2$, which was the trumpet that heralded the onset of the "atomic age," and which ultimately prompted two superpowers – the USSR and the USA – to point their highly developed, sophisticated nuclear weapons at one another's throats while attempting to ratify what has become known as the Strategic Arms Limitations Treaty (SALT II).

Thanks to Einstein, each nation has the (nuclear) potential to destroy the world as we know it. However, this era is yet unfinished, despite the chaos which erupted in the USSR following the proposed Democratic form of government, which is supposedly geared to upgrade the betterment of life for its people. Moreover, this carnage, which has befallen that particular region of the world, is very similar to the activity which has invaded the Black community since the Civil Rights Movement, a movement conducted to provide a better quality of living for Blacks.

The only difference between the occurrences in the two nations is that the menacing firepower that propelled the USSR to superpower status (when functioning as a unit), is still available somewhere to protect its citizens and its nation against outside forces, whereas Blacks in America – after developing in their own communities in a nation devised of two separate entities, yielded their personal belongings to White America in favor of the long-sought, false American dream concept – a swap that netted Blacks a self-induced, modern day bondage.

On the other hand, Dr. Carver who worked long and hard – patiently toiling in his primitive laboratory at Tuskegee Institute, a school founded by yet another famous Black man, Booker T. Washington – sought to create something to sustain

– not destroy – human life. His achievements? He took the lowly peanut, worked with it and produced hundreds of products such as peanut butter, shoe polish, cosmetics and plastics (just to name a droplet of 300 plus products credited to his innovative skills), which are now part of the mainstream or world life.

Both men are regarded as geniuses. Yet, if one was to question the average man on the street as to the comparative greatness of Professor Einstein and Dr. Carver, the answer would be most revealing. Very few will fail to credit Einstein with his greatness in making possible the "atomic age." However, few will have even heard of Dr. Carver, despite the fact that daily they enjoy his contributions to everyday life, which evolved from his research into the potential of the peanut.

Although the "under exposure" which Blacks have been accorded in American "His story" has affected all areas of Black involvement. Those who have participated in the world of professional activities – mainly considered as "sports" – have received far more exposure than their contemporaries in the fields of science, music, education and literature. This phenomenon is not too difficult to understand, however, when viewed in the context of "his story's" common assertion that Blacks are physically more astute than they are mentally. To perpetuate this myth, it is only natural that the accounts of Black contributors would reflect a greater emphasis on physical accomplishments than the more sedate arenas of cultural and educational achievement.

Perhaps the most glaring example of the ways in which the achievements of Blacks have been undermined by "his story's" lack of exposure, can be found in the saga of the Black baseball leagues, formerly known as the Negro National League (NNL) and the Negro American League (NAL). Nevertheless, these Negro Leagues were the spawning grounds for scores of prominent Black athletes, such as the likes of Jackie Robinson, Larry Doby, Roy Campanella, Willie Mays, Hank Aaron, Satchel Paige and literally thousands of lesser-known – yet equally as talented – professionals, such as Verdell Mathis, Willard Brown, Josh Gibson and Quincy Troupe, to name a few.

However, because the Black leagues were denied official recognition by "organized baseball" – by white so-called "organized baseball" that is – the achievements of the vast majority of these Black athletes have been mired in underexposed obscurity, eclipsed by the imbalanced recognition given their white American and National League counterparts.

Another important contribution of the Black baseball leagues, which has also gone unheralded in "his story," was the creation of thousands of jobs directly connected with the operations of the two leagues. Many skilled individuals such as drivers, mechanics and recording secretaries were hired to perform duties directly associated with the activities of the various teams in the NNL and NAL. In addition, there were numerous positions in allied fields: groundskeepers, concessionaries, bell hops, maids, waiters, waitresses and entertainers at the various establishments where ball players lived and often went to relax. Naturally, a host of businesses requiring the services of these people also flourished during the leagues' existence.

It has been said that there were no written rules or documents prohibiting the presence of Black players from the rosters of the white American and National Leagues' affiliations – only a "gentlemen's agreement." This was a set of racist policies (politics or "poly tricks" if you will) that moved only a step beyond the apartheid practices of South African notoriety, established many years prior to the election of Nelson Mandela, the country's Black figurehead president.

Ironically, it was the breakdown of this same "gentlemen's agreement," initiated by the late Branch Rickey during his introduction of Jackie Robinson into the formerly lily-white ranks of the white leagues, that ultimately led to the demise of the Black leagues. Rather than incorporate the teams of the NNL and the NAL into the white National and American Leagues – or evenly distribute the wide array of talented Black ball players among those existing league teams – the owners chose to systematically emasculate the Black leagues.

As ravenous prospectors once raided the California coasts, many white American and National League moguls realized that the untapped Black talent was worth their proverbial "weight in gold," and began to dig their picks and shovels into the veins of the NNL and NAL, mining what they considered to be the choicest nuggets the Black leagues had to offer.

Naturally, they were careful not to allow more than a token number of Blacks to play on any given team, for to have more than a handful would jeopardize the theory that only a few "exceptional" Blacks could excel in the field of competition with whites. Yet, those few who were chosen were sufficient enough to sever the lifeline of the Black leagues as more and more Black ball players began to shun the

NNL and NAL, seeking the "exposure" accorded those Blacks who had preceded them.

As a former member of the now defunct Black leagues, and in the interest of adding some semblance of balance to "his story," I feel that I must tell mine. Before doing so, however, there is one final point to make concerning the treatment (the "under exposure") received by Blacks in the pages of "his story." An examination of the previously mentioned examples of the imbalanced record of Black achievements in America (the story of Dr. Carver and the saga of the Black baseball leagues) reveals two basic ideological motifs that have permeated our nation since its inception: nationality and capitalism. In both instances, these two themes have played a critical role in determining the levels of "exposure" (or "under exposure") given Black achievers by white America.

In the case of Dr. Carver, his nationality – delineated by the color of his skin – was a constraining factor, limiting the full accolades merited by his extraordinary achievements. Ironically, the little recognition he did receive stemmed from the fact that his innovations with the peanut revitalized a dying southern agricultural economy by reclaiming for productive use thousands of acres of farmland. In other words, Dr. Carver was given "exposure" primarily because his achievements promoted the interests of those southern capitalist farmers seeking capital gain. Likewise, the teams and players of the NNL and NAL were denied proper recognition on the basis of the pigmentation of their skin. Yet, when "exposure" finally came to Black ball players, it was precipitated by the white parent leagues' discovery of their economic potential, which could be realized through the untapped source of Black talent.

The stories of Dr. Carver and the Black leagues are not exceptions to the Black man's lot in American society. Color prejudice and capitalism have been an integral part of our socio-economic structure since the days when George Washington "bought" and "sold" Black chattel. At that time, color prejudice and capital gain represented "de facto" national policy. However, as time progressed, they gained legal status and became inextricably bound in common wedlock – a marriage that produced the plantation system of servitude or enforced slavery.

Capitalism was not a phenomenon rooted in the plantation system, for its development in America preceded that of slavery. Nor was nationality per se an antecedent of the southern "human economy," for its tendencies were clearly manifested in the genocide of the Indians (Native Americans). However, one very distinguishable offspring of the "marriage" was that of "white supremacy," an all-encompassing "brain child" which has served to do the bidding of its "parents" since its conception and birth.

White supremacy – with its legacy of extreme paternalism; of brutal lynchings and burnings; of "Uncle Tom" and "Steppin' Fetchit"; of Amos and Andy; of Plessy vs. Ferguson; and of Law and Order – has propagated the interests of race prejudice in a way that has harmed both Blacks and whites. Obviously, it has served to impede the progress of Blacks politically, economically and socially. Less obvious – but equally as devastating – has been its effects upon the psyche of white Americans, particularly those in the lower social strata or the poor and working classes.

The legacy of white supremacy – as it is filtered throughout the capitalist system and with its accent on rugged individualism, lust for gain and fear of unemployment and poverty – has given the lowliest white worker a false sense of superiority arising from the existence of a contemptible pariah class below him. This false sense of superiority among whites has rendered them as enslaved to the system of capitalism as any Black man during the plantation era. Moreover, it has developed like a cancer that has been steadily eating away at the core of this country's social, political and economic foundation.

The tragic irony of white supremacy is that it has not only severely limited the extent to which Blacks can pursue the goals of the American Dream, but it has also removed the incentives of the majority of poor and working class whites. Rather than striving "to live and let live," many have found solace in their so-called "superior" status, as they worship and relish the thought of being "better" than Blacks.

As a result, white supremacy – the illegitimate child of color prejudice and capitalism – has failed to develop the nation's greatest source of riches: the full talents of its people. In so doing, it has all but written its own epitaph. If "his story" continues to repeat itself, as so often has been the case, we can expect the "cancer" to reach a malignant stage and our nation to meet an untimely death.

Herein lies the essence of my story: To critically analyze some of the major issues confronting American society in general and Blacks in particular, by relating

PROLOGUE

(sharing) my experiences as a professional baseball player – experiences gained while traveling extensively throughout the United States and Canada.

Much of this manuscript involves a mental recreation of the personality and character of the "color monster" devised centuries before my own birth, but which continues to lurk in the shadows of my lifetime. While my story's aim is to focus a spotlight on the Black baseball leagues, it is unfortunately a chronicle that begins with the leagues' demise. Nonetheless, it is a truthful account that will serve the purpose of exposing the hoax surrounding the "mainstream" crystal ball by reconstructing the past, addressing the present, and forecasting future events regarding Black and white America.

The phrase, "A Big Niggah Catchin' And A Li'l Niggah Pitchin' " was derived from an incident that took place in the state of Mississippi in 1950 involving two Black baseball clubs. The incident occurred just prior to the game when an ignorant white southern announcer blared out the aforementioned words as he sized up the team's pitcher and catcher, whom he first addressed as "the battery."

Although this unscrupulous gesture occurred some forty-five years ago, the same statement – with a slight change in the characters' positions – was deemed appropriate for a book title describing certain activities carried on within the Black community. In portraying a better understanding of this transformation, a "big niggah catchin' " becomes "a big niggah pitchin'," while a "li'l niggah pitchin' " becomes a "li'l niggah catchin'." In both instances, however, the underlying factor relates to employment or jobs.

During the waning moments of the Black baseball leagues' existence and at a time when both northern and southern Blacks were accorded little or no respect at all from whites, Black entrepreneurs – mainly baseball or franchise owners – booked games throughout the nation to provide paychecks for their hired hands. Because white society was "off limits" to Blacks, owners and their hired hands alike were met with much ridicule and denial. However, nothing was so important as to erode the mutual respect between employer and employee.

With the crumbling of the Black baseball leagues and with the introduction of the so-named Civil Rights Movement, which brought about job opportunities for Blacks, a new era had begun. And with it came the revised book title, A Big Niggah Pitchin' And A Li'l Niggah Catchin', because many Blacks assumed positions of power they had never before enjoyed and began treating other Blacks – whom they deemed to be less than they – in the same disrespectful way as did whites. Blacks retaliated angrily, feeling they were the recipients of a double dose of rudeness. Thus, as a result, the amended version of the aforementioned title became A Big Niggah Pitchin' AUTHORITY And A Li'l Niggah Catchin' HELL!!!

Due to the said reaction, the bleak political situation, the proposed welfare reform, the move to revise the Affirmative Action Program, the separation of the Black Church and the evolution of the crack industry (which enriched the coffers of many of its pushers and caused others to get killed or become incarcerated as the effects of their products mentally enslaved and/or killed its users, both Black and white), the Black community in its present state faces the brink of destruction. Thus, the Black community personifies the victimization of the country's institutionalized and cancerous bigotry, which produced its condition.

My story contains many aspects of "his story," but it takes reality a step further by attempting to show how race prejudice and capitalism have contributed (and continues to contribute) to our nation's steady demise. It is hoped that the telling of my story will heighten the consciousness of its readers and sharpen their awareness of the adverse pattern of America's development. Perhaps the malignancy that threatens the life of America, as well as its component – the Black community – can be controlled and reduced to benign.

-- Joe Henry

Circa 1975

★★★★  ★★★★

The Frederick Douglass Distinguished African American Citizenship Award

Mr. Joseph Henry

For your **_Distinguished Leadership_** in the field of **_NEGRO BASEBALL LEAGUE AFFAIRS_**. This prestigious award, in honor of such a great African-American Leader of character, dignity, intellect, and devotion; Mr. Frederick Douglass – "the most important African-American leader and intellectual of the 19th Century", is presented to you for your civic/cultural contributions in your lifetime and because your "good works" reflect the model of Distinguished Citizenship.

Thank you for being as our Ancestors;
Distinguished, Dignified, and Devoted . . . .

_____ _____
Nathaniel O'Bannon – Chairman   Darnell Thompson, Events Co-Chairman
Village of Brooklyn Heritage Council   Thompson Institute and Commonwealth
July 9, 1999

Mr. Frederick Douglass was the "Father of the 14th Amendment/U.S. Constitution" that gave ex-enslaved Africans, 'American Citizenship'; July 9, 1868. He viewed political liberty as the means to economic independence and social equality.

INDIANAPOLIS CLOWNS

Last season the Indianapolis Clowns sent eight of the teams stellar players up the baseball ladder. This season with an eye to developing more such finds the Clowns have a youth movement that finds an interesting group of youngsters that can hold their own in any competition.

Princoirs

SEPARATE BUT EQUAL

"All Major League clubs will have a wary eye cocked on the nation's first baseball school of Negroes run by Negroes when it opens in Greenville, Mississippi on February 27th. With the Negro now an accepted part of the big league pattern, baseball men realize they must have a source of supply for future players. This school, to be under the direction of Homer "Goose" Curry of Memphis, is the start in that direction. It will be known as the "Delta Negro Baseball School."

Excerpted from the book, *Get that Nigger off the Field*
by Art Rust, Jr. – United Press (Memphis), 1950

"Testin'…Testin'…Testin'," drawled a low voice quietly on a hot, humid evening in 1950, as it echoed through the makeshift ballpark in Silver City, Mississippi. The white announcer – assuring himself that the public address system was in proper working condition – continued, "Good evenin', ladies and gene'men." A hush slowly descended over the confines of the ballpark, hardly more than a converted cow pasture.

He continued, "Tonight, the Chamber o' Commerce o' Silver City is mo' than proud to bring these two fine cullud teams of the Nigra American League to ah city. We sho' are mighty obliged to see such a large turnout and certainly do hope y'all will have an enjawable evenin!!! Also, ah'd like to add that sandwiches and other refreshments can be bo'ght directly beneath the gran stans, and there is uh special section reserved fo' ah nice cullud friends, if they desire somethin' to eat."

I slipped the glove off my left hand, folded it and placed it under my right armpit as I walked back to the edge of the grass behind second base. From this position, I had a clear view of the fans and the park as my teammates went about their pre-game warm-ups. Behind the first and third base lines were the stands – wooden seats arranged in a stair step fashion. The superstructure – also constructed of wood – was covered by a roof of tin. In front of this "grandstand" was a screen of cyclone wire erected to prevent the fans from being struck by errant balls. All seats along the first base line and behind home plate were labeled for "White Only" and were completely filled. The seats behind the third base line had been designated as those for "Colored." In order that there would be no mistake as to where the "nice cullud friends" were to sit, there was a large sign located at the entrance to the stadium which read "Colored," accompanied by an arrow pointing to the designated seating area.

The wooden fences encircling the outfield were painted with advertisements from some of Silver City's leading business enterprises. Because the game was a sellout, there were two to three rows of spectators standing in the outfield, nestled against the painted fences. The grass in both the infield and the outfield was far from being in good condition. In fact, a ballpark of this nature could best be described – in the vernacular of a baseball player, or in another sense, as an adverse referral to whites – as a "cracker box."

As I stood on the edge of the grass, kicking at the turf with my spikes, it occurred to me that the twilight of my second decade of life as a Negro in America was rapidly coming to an end, and the dawn of a third, more complex era, was about to begin. The atmosphere of "separateness" in my immediate surroundings was almost overwhelming.

From my childhood, I had been aware of this nationality dichotomy formalized by statutes laid down by officials of the "law" and dutifully executed by supportive constituents in an effort to preserve the "color line." Although I was born in a small predominately Negro community in southwestern Illinois, and had never personally encountered the strict Jim Crow laws for which the South was notorious, I was nonetheless exposed to "the proper etiquette" since it was populated primarily by whites. Such communities sectioned off certain parts of town, generally those in the most dilapidated condition, and relegated Negroes to reside in these areas and submit to the laws and mores of their segregated society. My only other contact with the laws of separation occurred during a brief stint with the United States Air Force. Although most of my social activities were limited to the base installations in Texas, Florida, and Virginia, I occasionally ventured to some nearby towns via public transportation, and was required to take my pre-appointed seat in the rear. This was a new experience for me since, in the environs of my hometown, I sat where I desired.

Here in Silver City, Mississippi I was being introduced to two separate and distinct lifestyles, which represented the nation's principal issue – socially, politically and economically – the doctrine of "separate but equal." This doctrine produced an adverse pattern of strange mental behavior. There were two separate syndromes – one "White," one "Dark." One was obsessed with a false sense of inhumane omnipotence, while the other was forced to submissively adhere to a state of social and economic degeneracy. Yet, both were purportedly created equal, at least according to the bold ideals set forth by the Founding Fathers. It was difficult to reconcile the blatant inconsistencies and ironies, which constantly besought my subconscious mind.

This was my first visit to Mississippi. Previously, I had read and heard a great deal about the South's infamous crimes against Negroes. Of all the states guilty of such atrocities, however, Mississippi's notoriety stood at the helm. In its enforcement of Jim Crow Laws, the Southern state implemented a policy of "either/or" – "either " you abided by laws laid down for you, "or" you were dealt with harshly. "Harshly" often meant unjustified arrests, brutal beatings, burning of homes, raping of women, and the lynching of innocent men. The same techniques, designed during the days of bondage to encourage the development of the American culture, were being employed against those who dared to deviate from the norm. All of this was done to keep the Negro in his "proper place."

Recalling the earlier sign designating the "proper place" for "Colored" patrons in the ballpark, I couldn't help but wonder how people could continuously live under such conditions and still maintain some semblance of stability – of dignity. What I was later to learn was that "dignity" was a characteristic that whites did not expect of their "nice cullud friends." I had often heard the expression, "When in Rome, do as the Romans do." Although Silver City, Mississippi was a far cry from Rome, I felt compelled to undergo a social metamorphosis in order to adapt to my new environment. This dramatic change in my lifestyle involved developing a keen awareness of my "place" as a Negro in the Deep South. I soon learned that to know my "place" was to know to obey signs designating "Colored" or "White"; to answer, "Yes sir" or "No sir" and "Yes ma'am" or "No ma'am." To do otherwise was to expose oneself to verbal as well as physical abuse. Fortunately, I had long ago been taught by my mother and father to respect individuals in positions of authority – be they my elders, teachers, policemen or business people. Since it was soon apparent that whites in Mississippi were without question in the position of authority, I found no great difficulty in conforming to the acceptable manner of addressing them without compromising my integrity or self-esteem.

Reminiscing about my parents' instructions reminded me that Mississippi was their native state. My father had left home to defend his country in France during World War I. Although he was not among the "combat" troops, he nonetheless served with distinction. Ironically, he was wounded in a senseless, unprovoked gas attack launched against non-combat troops and subsequently received an honorable discharge from the United States Army. I mused as I recounted my father's stories about the war, especially those relating to the treatment of Negro soldiers. One account, which stood out foremost in my memory was that of a ridiculous rumor spread among the French allies by our white American counterparts – that the Negro "service" troops were not quite human, and that in fact, they were just a step above monkeys and literally had tails! He told me that there were a few naïve French men and women who believed this outlandish rumor and actually asked to see the tails, which were allegedly under their uniforms.

Upon his return to the United States, my father discovered that little had changed relative to his status as a Negro in the Deep South – and despite his service and his wounds – he was once more relegated to his "place." Unwilling to continue to submit to the rules of Jim Crow – and with intent on raising his family with dignity and respect – my father migrated North to Illinois and settled in a small hamlet known as Brooklyn, the place of my birth.

Brooklyn, Illinois was a virtual island as far as the nationality composition of it inhabitants was concerned. Although there was a triad of Caucasian, Jewish and Chinese merchants who owned the bulk of Brooklyn's businesses, the actual residential population of the town was overwhelmingly Negro. The vast majority of the business owners resided outside of Brooklyn's boundaries. Consequently, our hometown contained no restrictive barriers, and the attitude of the respective nationalities was one of mutual respect.

Despite being free from the rigid Jim Crow dogmatism practiced in Dixie, Brooklyn was not without its own unique set of internal social problems. Ironically, it was not the bigotry of a white power structure that victimized its townspeople, but rather the despotism and tyranny of the town's Negro mayor, supported by an equally brutish and mainly illiterate police force. In much the same self-righteous style as our white adversaries in the Deep South, Brooklyn's Negro mayor dealt swiftly and harshly with those holding opposing views to his own political and economic program – fully condoning vicious attacks of brutality executed by his police force against the local electorate. It was this environment, replete with its social ironies and contradictions, in which I was instilled with a strong sense of dignity and self esteem by my conscientious parents.

My father, in particular, played a large role in influencing my habits and attitudes throughout my life. It was my father from whom I developed my initial love for sports. I recalled the numerous times he and I would sit hunched by the radio, listening to broadcasts of football, basketball, baseball or boxing. When we weren't involved with listening to sporting events on the radio, my friends and I occasionally spent time attending baseball games at Sportsman's Park, home of the St. Louis Browns and Cardinals. In addition to exposing me to the world of sports, my father also served as my personal professor of Negro history. I suspect that much of the accumulation of knowledge, from which he could expound for hours on end, was gained during his years in the military, having been exposed to men from all walks of life. Whatever the source, I was the beneficiary of a wealth of information on such notable Negro figures as Marcus Garvey, Frederick Douglas, Richard Wright, Mary McLeod-Bethune and Harriet Tubman.

Initially, I did not fully appreciate my father's intentions in tutoring me to a broader view of my ancestors. However, I was always careful not to allow him to know my true feelings on his enlightening words of wisdom. Although I would sit appearing to listen attentively as he related one story after another, his words would go in one ear and out of the other. Because of my obsession with sports, my interest in NEGRO history was limited to athletes, such as Joe Louis, "Goose"

Tatum, Jesse Owens and Leroy "Satchel" Paige. Ironically, my father would never live to witness the tremendous impression his history lessons were to have on me in my later years.

While standing there in deep meditation, the umpires had come onto the field and the game was about to begin. The drawling voice of the announcer exhorted all to stand for the singing of the National Anthem, accompanied by a man using what seemed to be a battered trumpet. As the closing words "O'er the land of the free and home of the brave" were being sung by the enthusiastic crowd, my wandering mind's eye took a glance backward into a small classroom in Lovejoy High School, an all-Negro school located in my hometown of Brooklyn, Illinois. I recalled our daily ritual of reciting the "Pledge of Allegiance," a routine mandated by the school administration. As I pondered the scene of students standing at attention with the palms of their right hands covering their hearts, I couldn't help but dwell on those last few words of "One Nation, under God, indivisible, with liberty and justice for all." Somehow, these words rang hollow in my mind as I recalled an incident that occurred upon our entry into Silver City, which served notice to me in no uncertain terms that this was not one nation but two distinct and separate nations, where liberty and justice was not available to all, but was reserved for those wielding power.

Only six hours earlier, our blue and white bus, emblazoned with our team's name, Memphis Red Sox, on both sides, had approached the outskirts of Silver City. Although I had never been there before, I knew we had reached the town by the various welcome signs from the "Kiwanis," the "Lions Club" and the "Chamber of Commerce." We had not eaten since leaving Memphis, and were all quite hungry. Fortunately, our driver, Sam Thomas, whom we affectionately called "Chauff" – an abbreviation for chauffeur – knew how to handle himself in unfamiliar surroundings. He pulled up at the nearest filling station and was met by a young white male who appeared to be about seventeen years old. As the bus came to a halt, the youngster began questioning Chauff. "What y'all need, boy?" It was immediately obvious to me that the minor had not been properly instructed by his parents to respect his elders. His mode of addressing Chauff shocked me. After all, Chauff was nearing his mid-fifties and was old enough to be his father. Chauff stood approximately 5'10" and weighed almost 190 pounds and bore a striking resemblance to "Jersey Joe" Walcott, the venerable boxer who would later win the heavyweight championship of the world at an advanced age.

Nevertheless, Chauff only smiled and calmly replied, "Fill 'er up, sir!" adding, "Where's the colored section in this town?" Without responding to Chauff's question, the youth began to pump the gas – his eyes fixed on the gauge until the tank was full. Slowly, as he removed the spout of the hose from the gas tank, he looked up and said, "Oh, y'all the boys what come to play ball tonight?" Following a brief pause, he continued, "Y'all cross the railroad tracks and there's the cullud section…cain' miss it, ya know." How often was I to learn in subsequent years that in order to find the "colored section" in any town, all one needed to do was to find the railroad tracks and cross over to the "wrong" side. Interestingly, I was soon to learn this dividing line was not limited to towns in the Southern states, but was very much in evidence in places North of the celebrated Mason-Dixon line.

Chauff thanked the youngster for his directions, paid him and then put the bus in gear. From my favorite seat on a water cooler in the front of the bus, I was able to observe the entire exchange between Chauff and the abrasive white youth. There was a deceptive smile on Chauff's face, one that an untrained observer could easily interpret as being docile and submissive. However, Chauff was a crafty character who was anything but an "Uncle Tom." Due to his wit and innate insight into people, he repeatedly succeeded in manipulating his self-appointed white "superiors" into conforming to his way of thinking, ultimately accomplishing his purposes.

Amused and somewhat puzzled by his peculiar style, I began to needle Chauff about the incident that had just occurred at the service station. "Chauff," I said, "you sure know how to talk with these white folks down here!" He turned in my direction smiling brightly and nodded in apparent agreement. "Joe," he began slowly, deftly swinging the bus into the left lane to pass a slower moving vehicle, "you got a lot to learn. You're a youngster, and I think you have a good future in baseball, but when you're in the South, as we are now, you gotta know how to handle 'the man.' You gotta make 'em think that you've joined them and don't want to fight. That way, you get what you want, what you need, but remember this: things won't always be this way. One of these days, we'll be able to stand up and face this same 'man' and tell him to go to hell. Right now, we can't do it, but if you know how to play your cards right, you'll still be able to get your way. You gotta take advantage of his confused emotions. You see, deep down in his subconscious, he knows that he depends on you and realizes that he has been negligent in giving you justice. Even though he recognizes that he can gain much by utilizing your talent, his intense desire for superiority clouds his vision and undermines his pursuit of his own financial interests. In spite of his endless attempts to keep us down, he reluctantly senses a change – a change that will move the obstacles that have blocked our advancement. You see, one of these days – and it's not too far from now – you'll be able to meet him face to face…won't have to ask where the 'colored' section is…won't have to let no snotty-nosed brat call you 'boy.' Oh yeah, times will change!!"

It was then that I realized that Chauff didn't fall in the category of an "Uncle Tom," rather that of a shrewd psychologist who knew how to get what he wanted by patronizing his unsuspecting white "superiors." My only desire was that I might someday develop this same quality.

As the trumpeter blurted out the final high-pitched note, the National Anthem came to a close, and we took the field. The announcer began to introduce the starting line-up of our opponents, whom he erroneously referred to as co-members of the "Nigra American League." The game had been billed as a match-up between the Memphis Red Sox of the "Negro American League" and a semi-pro "all star" team. The truth was that our opponents were aspiring young ball players from the Delta Baseball School that hoped to one day play in the Negro National or American League. The school was conducted out of Greenville, Mississippi and was sponsored by Homer "Goose" Curry, our manager.

Following the introduction of our opponents, the speaker began to call out the names of our team, beginning with the regular starting line-up. Lastly, he came to the pitcher and catcher, known in baseball as the "battery." Our catcher stood 6'5", while our pitcher barely reached 5'5". The tremendous contrast was quite obvious to all observers, and the announcer took full advantage of the situation to make a startling comment. Suddenly, with a slight touch of humor in his voice, he blared into the loud speaker as he regained the attention of the large crowd: "Ladies and gene'men, the battery fo the Memphis Red Sox tonight will be a big niggah catchin' and a li'l niggah pitchin'." He also added, "Y'all boys can play ball now." The announcer's rude assessment of our pitcher and catcher set the mood for the remainder of the evening.

In the first inning, our pitcher retired the opposing side in order. I was the first batter to stride to the plate and there was fear and anxiety in my every bone. Fortunately, the opposing pitcher walked me. Upon reaching first base, I glanced briefly into the stand to my left. There was nothing but white faces – a virtual sea of whiteness. All at once, a voice rose above the raucous crowd, "C'mon, steal!" But I had been given no sign from my first base coach and made no move. Stepping off the bag to take my lead, I watched the pitcher intently – analyzing his style – trying to find some little flaw, which I could use to my advantage. The fan, who continued his uninviting coaching from the grand stand, did not know how close he came to making me head for second base, if only to get away from his strident, unnerving voice. I bluffed a moved to second base and danced back and forth as the pitcher threw to the plate. The catcher made a futile snap throw to first to try and pick me off, but I safely slid back to the base. As I stood up and dusted myself off, my grand stand coach hollered out once more above the hullabaloo of the crowd, "C'mon, Sambo, steal!!! Don't tell me you don't know how to do that!!!" There was a roar of approval from those sitting about him. A peculiar mixture of humility and hostility welled up within me – humility, because I was a Negro, and he was implying that all Negroes were thieves – and hostility because I was unable to defend myself against the remarks of this self-appointed coach. I had no choice but to swallow my pride – if only in silent answer – while the heckler's companions seemed to enjoy my discomfiture.

While standing on first base, my subconscious mind once again drifted to the past. Like a mental time machine, it began reducing weeks into days, hours into minutes and minutes into seconds. Perhaps I should have heeded that telegram, which conceivably could have changed my life. It was a wired message from A.S. "Doc" Young, a sports writer for the Chicago Defender who had gone to Los Angeles, California to cover special sports events. On learning that Leroy "Satchel" Paige had been signed by the Cleveland Indians, coupled with the breakthrough of Jackie Robinson, I contacted Mr. Young. I figured that if "Satch" could make the roster of the Indians at his age, certainly I had a chance to make some big league roster at the robust age of twenty.

During my early years, I began developing an avid interest in the weekly Negro newspapers such as the Chicago Defender, Pittsburgh Courier and St. Louis Argus. Although all of these "weeklies" carried excellent accounts of current events in Negro sports, I was particularly attracted to the column written by Mr. Young in The Defender. I especially relished his sports editorials, which seemed to reflect a deep concern for the struggles of Negro athletes in their quest for recognition and advancement in their chosen endeavors. Because of his apparent dedication to the cause of the Negro athlete, I had written him to express my interest in playing "organized baseball," hoping he would be able to direct me along a path that could help me find a beginning.

As it turned out, Mr. Young's dedication and concern was even more than what I initially thought it to be. Upon receiving my letter, he must have set to work immediately, assuming that I was serious and determined. And that if I wished to become a professional baseball player, he would do everything possible to make it a reality. Instead of writing me a letter, as I had done him, he sent me a telegram, perhaps deeming the mail too slow. The message was sent to Mr. Joshua Johnson who served as principal and athletic director of the all-Negro Dunbar High School in Madison, Illinois – and who was also a former standout catcher in the Negro American League.

In my letter to Mr. Young, I had spoke of knowing Mr. Johnson, of having worked with him in playing softball. When he received Mr. Young's wire, he drove the mile and a half distance separating his school from my home in Lovejoy, Illinois and delivered the good news. The telegram read as follows:

Have Joe Henry pack his grip and have fare to California. Once there, he will be given a tryout with Los Angeles Angels of the AAA League, open classification, which I have arranged. If he doesn't make it with the Angels, he will be farmed down to a lower classification. My address is enclosed. Will meet him and take care of the rest.

Good Luck!

A.S. "Doc" Young

The telegraph to Mr. Johnson was also a complete surprise to him, as I had told him nothing of my intentions or of my letter to the columnist. He had long been trying to persuade me to stop wasting my time playing every infield position on a 12-inch fast pitch softball team. When he learned that my interest in baseball was sufficient to warrant my choosing it as a career, he gave me another option: enter the Negro American League, where he had once starred with the Pittsburgh

Crawfords. He was also a very close friend of Mr. Homer "Goose" Curry, manager of the Memphis Red Sox, and offered to endorse me to him.

All of a sudden, I had two choices to consider in my desire for a career in baseball. Mr. Johnson and I discussed the matter at length, weighing all possibilities. It was not a snap decision, but in the end we decided that among other things, Memphis was so much closer than California, and since Mr. Curry was such a close friend to Mr. Johnson, I would be more than assured of a good tryout with his team. It was a decision that I have never regretted. There is, however, one regret that I do have. So great was my elation about the events that had recently transpired, that I forgot to render the courtesy of notifying Mr. Young of my decision not to come to California. Despite the fact that I have never seen nor met Mr. Young, I always felt a warm spot in my heart for him for his efforts on my behalf. Here was a man – a Negro who had never heard of this anxious twenty-year-old Negro lad who had written to him asking for directions, and whom he did not turn down. This man had such confidence in my ability that I was literally shocked when later, upon reading his column in the Chicago Defender, I saw a statement printed by him about me. In essence, he admonished the readers to "watch out for a twenty-year-old youth from Lovejoy, Illinois named Joe Henry, who will be hitting the sports pages very soon."

My reverie about the beginning of my career was brutally interrupted by a sharp warning from the first base coach. I had wandered too far off the bag, and the pitcher attempted – in vain – to pick me off. Next up to bat was a left-handed batter who was notorious for taking powerful swings at the ball. For some reason, on this night, whether because of the heat or due to nervousness, he took a vicious cut at the ball, missed, and let the bat slip from his hands. It sailed along the first base line in front of the wire fence where several white people were standing. I later learned they were dignitaries from the Chamber of Commerce who wanted to be "seen" on the field. When it reached the crowd of white onlookers, it struck a man on the head and he went down as if pole-axed. I ran for second with the pitch, and as I rounded the base on my way to third, a loud moan came from the stands. As the man went down, my eyes switched to the area of third base to pick up a signal from the coach. It was then that I witnessed a grand exodus from the "colored" section of the stadium. The stands were being emptied. Patrons were running for the exits – some climbing fences in their anxious desire to get out of the place where a "Negro" had hit a "white man" with a baseball bat, albeit inadvertently. Fortunately, the man was not seriously injured. In fact, he refused to go to the county hospital, received first aid and remained until the game was over. But for us, it truly was OVER, although it had just begun. We played like robots, mechanical men, not taking any chances on anything that might provoke an incident.

My mind drifted back to the earlier scene following our leaving the gasoline station, where Chauff had received instructions on how to get to the "colored" section of town. We had left the wayside station and proceeded ahead about a mile and a half when we came to the railroad tracks – the outskirts of Silver City and the entrance to the "colored section." There was a large wooden sign painted in foot high letters, which read: "MISSISSIPPI LAW-----STOP!!!" It was a statement, an exhortation that you were literally going into another world when you crossed that line. As we entered, the otherwise dead town came alive, teeming with the sound of laughter of the townspeople and their children.

There was an overwhelming sense of squalor – complete with ramshackle, unpainted homes – some so rickety that they seemed to "kneel in prayer." There were no sidewalks, merely beaten paths of packed earth leading up to the dilapidated houses. Occasionally, we came across a more respectable looking residence, usually a brick house encircled by a recently painted fence with a neatly trimmed lawn in front. This was by far the exception to the rule.
It was several hours to game time, and we were hungry. Baseball players burn up a lot of energy, and it's hard to play nine innings of baseball on bologna sandwiches and Coke. It was Chauff who had the answer. He stopped and asked directions of a small barefooted lad. Clad in ragged pants and a dirty T-shirt, he stared at our bus in awe. Then, overcoming his adulation, he told us that "Mom's" was the best place in Silver City. We later learned it was the only place where Negroes could get a decent meal. Following his directions, we soon pulled up in front of a wood-framed structure with a sign hanging precariously at an angle, threatening to fall any minute, proclaiming it to be "Mom's Place." As our bus came to a halt, hordes of children – mostly boys in their early teens – swarmed about shouting, "The Memphis Red Sox! The Memphis Red Sox! They here! They here!" I smiled, then grinned at their exuberance, recalling my own exaltation when I was their age. I had followed the Indianapolis Clowns and my idol, Reece "Goose" Tatum, never imagining in my wildest fantasies that I would later play on the same

team with him. The cheers of these youths also gave us a moral lift...a feeling of being wanted, recognized, and accepted. We felt we had arrived! Seemingly, we were their idols.

My glowing enthusiasm was soon dimmed as we entered the diner. There were but four tables, and we would have to eat in shifts, but we could at least eat! The long wait did give us a chance to mingle with the growing crowd, which had been attracted by our silver and blue bus, and to scribble a few autographs. Finally, we got our chance to eat. The meal was simple but well-prepared – strictly "down home." There was no printed menu and no choice of entrees. Pork chops, sweet potatoes, collard greens, grits and mounds of biscuits were the order of the day. To supplement our meal, there was coffee and milk in abundance, syrup, and real butter that tasted as though it had been freshly churned.

Everything was to perfection. The only thing lacking in making me feel totally at home was my hometown brand of syrup known as "Sho Is Fine." The bottle carried a degrading advertisement on its label depicting two very dark Negro kids in ragged, cut-off shorts with one licking his fingers while the other looked on with bulging eyes. A quote above them read, "Sho Is Fine."

The plates were of China, some cracked and chipped, but they were clean, not greasy. The wooden floor was bare, with cracks appearing in places from which an occasional cockroach would crawl to feed on crumbs that had fallen. Flies buzzed about, coming through the door whenever someone entered, but it was Silver City's best...for Negroes that is.

As we were eating, two patrol cars pulled up – one from the Silver City police station and the other from the Mississippi State Police. The officers in the state police car could easily be distinguished by the large beige Stetson hats they wore. There were four of them. Without saying a word as to their purpose, they waddled into the restaurant and began a thorough search. One went into the kitchen, another behind the counter and a third into the one restroom, which served men as well as women. The fourth milled about our tables – billy club in hand – pounding it into his free palm as though he were itching for an excuse to bounce it off the head of some non-conforming Negro who failed to answer his questions properly. At first they seemed to pay us no attention, limiting their questions to the employees. Then, one approached Chauff, who was clad in a Memphis Red Sox jacket. "You the boys who come from up nawth to play?" he queried.

"Yes sir," Chauff replied. "We're from Memphis – the Memphis Red Sox." I was amused to think that he considered Memphis "up nawth." "Does any of y'all have a knife?" He looked menacingly – harassment clearly written in his lined red face. As we inferred that we did not, he went to the other men, who gave negative shakes of their heads. Then all four proceeded to the door. As they opened it, one turned and said, "You boys stay out of trouble," and then they left. Over and over in my mind, I saw the images of some of the Negro law enforcement officers from back home – badges flashing, hands on guns, terrorizing the townspeople with open acts of intimidation, but then I recalled the wooden sign I had seen – "MISSISSIPPI LAW-----STOP!!!" Yes, I was indeed in Mississippi.

The game continued in the same pattern that had been established up to that point, with shouts of "Look at tha' nigger run!" or similar insulting jibes when a player made a spectacular play or struck out a man in scoring position. Finally, the game ended with our team prevailing. Once again, we were back on the bus en route to Memphis. The all-star team and some regular members of the Memphis Red Sox rode together. We were still in an early phase of spring training, and all of the other members had not yet reported to camp. Having left our fears and anxieties behind, the bus became a stage for entertainment. One of the older players of the Red Sox riding with us told about a game once played in a park similar to the one we had just left. He said the only difference between Silver City's park and the one of which he spoke was that it was enclosed with seats. He related to us how one of his teammates once hit a line drive to the right field seats, striking a white woman seated in the crowd. As the batter trotted toward first base – knowing that the ball was going out of the park – he began to pick up speed as he turned for second. Hearing someone in the stands holler that a white woman had been hit by the ball, he increased his speed en route to third. And the announcer – befuddled by his sudden burst of speed – blared to him through the loudspeaker that the ball he hit was a homerun. The runner – now at his apex of speed – supposedly retorted, "And that's exactly where I'm going!!!" As I was subsequently to learn – after games played in towns such as Silver City – the best solution was to board the bus and get the heck out of there.

Joe Henry

Circa 1972

Editor's Note: The following comments, entitled, "Black Preachers Undermining Truth" from Prince Joe Henry were in response to this personal note sent to him by mail.

Hey Joe: Although I am no longer a pastor, I have to agree with you about the voice of the Black church. The church was more vocal back in the day of "that old time religion." My mother raised six children in that era. When I was a pastor, if a family had a broken refrigerator, I might have been the one delivering a new one. I survived, but I never got rich. I was more of a hands-on pastor. What would I look like trying to influence my congregation to vote for Reagan or Bush and most of my congregation made minimum wage. Like my mother... give me that old time religion. If it was good enough for mother it was good enough for me.

In His Service,

Everett

Black Preachers Undermining Truth

Most Black preachers – both men and women – are guilty of undermining the truth about American slavery by failing to address the issue as prescribed in the Bible. Sadly, truth of the matter is they know not what they are doing. In Atlanta, Georgia rests the tomb of Dr. Martin Luther King, Jr. In Kansas City, Missouri stands the Negro League Baseball Museum. Each year, hundreds of thousands of people – both Black and white – visit these national sites. The reason being that they represent a period of American history, one denoting a separation of nationalities in Christianity and the other in professional baseball. The advent of both stems from institutionalized racism – a direct violation of God's Law.

Strangely – despite their social differences – both have something in common in the area of civil rights. Although other famous Blacks of lesser visibility had fought for the same cause earlier, the nation was awakened by the sensationalism surrounding these two events. Though the beginning of this historical, modern day era commenced with Jackie Robinson and Branch Rickey, the former a college graduate and the latter a white team owner. However, had it not been for Rube Foster, the great Black baseball player and Negro League organizer, the occasion could have very well been prolonged. Due to this foundation, the meeting of

Robinson and Rickey was made possible.

As the story goes, Robinson was playing baseball with the Kansas City Monarchs, one of numerous powerful baseball teams of the Negro Leagues that he was compelled to retreat to after leaving an unparalleled athletic career at the University of California at Los Angeles (UCLA). This was the case because of Blacks being disallowed by white law to play in the white leagues. As a result, from the Kansas City team arose the connection of Robinson and Rickey, which led to a dialogue between the two in relation to the racial breakdown of baseball that lay ahead.

The process consisted of Rickey posing such questions to Robinson regarding what he would do if he were spit on and called insulting names by opposing, hateful white baseball players while sliding into different bases. Following a series of these hypothetical questions, which Robinson answered with the philosophy of "turn the other cheek," Rickey knew he had found the man who would not fight back until the appropriate time. Thus, the psychology used to make the experiment work was the beginning of the Civil Rights Movement.

Although not nationally recognized as such, it can truly be said that Jackie Robinson pre-dated the social exploits of Ms. Rosa Parks and Dr. King by at least a decade. Robinson, following his college days, became a lieutenant in the military. One day while riding a post bus driven by a white civilian, he was ordered to take a seat in the rear, which he refused to do. This incident occurred because he was sitting beside his friend's wife, who was of a light complexion, and who the driver perceived as white. For this disobedient act, he received a military court martial; however, the Black press made a national scene of this gross injustice.

Later – shortly after joining the Brooklyn Dodgers – Robinson began breaking barriers in hotels who had earlier refused Black patrons. Much folklore has since been spoken surrounding the collaboration of Robinson and Rickey. Some say Robinson was chosen by Rickey because he was educated. Others suggest he was simply the best player. Fact of the matter is that the Negro Leagues was an organization comprised of college and non-college players, and many other players who – before and after him – were equally good if not better.

In a spiritual context, the breaking down of unjust laws in baseball by Robinson and Rickey is analogous to the relationship between God and Moses. God – during the time of Moses – could have chosen any Hebrew to perform the task at hand. Ultimately, He chose Moses. Not because he was the better man, but because he was the man God wanted. When Moses went down into Egypt land, he went with God's Message to tell Pharaoh, "Let my people go!" – a clear-cut indication meaning all oppressed people under God's Power should be devoid of discrimination. God has no nationality ties. He is ruler of the Universe.

Though, I do not mean to say Branch Rickey was God, but rather to reflect upon similarities. He – like God – who sent Moses to Egypt land, sent Robinson into the white baseball leagues for the purpose of signaling their end. In so doing, he defiled the sanctity of his people, who beforehand believed that Blacks were inhuman. Robinson – in this ordeal – only possessed God-given talent. Unlike the staff Moses carried, which was empowered by God, his weapons were bat, spikes and a glove. With these tools to fight his battles, he performed miracles on the baseball field before the very eyes of disbelieving whites who previously believed that it was impossible for a Black to excel on the same field with whites. His demonstrative revelation destroyed the myth that Blacks were inferior to whites, thus proving themselves to be human as well as equal.

His performance also proved Man can only control certain things. Bondage is a case in point. Then, whites controlled Blacks both physically and mentally, but not their inborn talent. This was a gift bestowed upon them by God that was suppressed during enforced slavery, which occurred after being kidnapped from African shores and being brought to the country called "America" where they were stripped of their native culture and forcibly named "slaves."

While serving in this capacity, they were forced to adhere to self-appointed slave masters, who – by submitting to such pernicious titles – were in reality masters of a slave mentality. However, it took the coming of President Abraham Lincoln to break the stranglehold of bondage, for which he was murdered by his own kind. However, the system of slavery was established by his predecessors, historically known as the "Founding Fathers" – a group of men that initiated The Constitution, following the destruction of the Native Americans, the original inhabitants of the land that later became America. The Constitution, as it was set up to establish law by assuring white rule, revitalized the ruling spirit of Pharaoh during the time of ancient history.

But God's Law was different, and it was meant to overthrow dictators. The Constitution, though, was designed for man-made rule – a subject that most Black preachers refuse to address. Conversely, white preachers are members of the ruling class and are students of American History. In this context, they have witnessed the fate of Abe Lincoln for defiantly practicing the Golden Rule, which states, "Do Unto Others As You Would Have Them Do Unto You."

Lincoln's execution is a prime example of the deeply ingrained hatred that consumes whites, even to the point of killing their own simply for being kind, especially when feeling that these whites favor Blacks. The source of this mentality stems from the hate-mongered Constitution, which has given even the lowliest white a false sense of superiority. According to American History, Christopher Columbus "discovered" the country in 1492. From this point on, man separated it from God's Law by devising The Constitution. The Ten Commandments – as recorded in the Book of Exodus – covers the whole topic. The Evidence can be found in the ashes of Native Americans and Blacks.

 Arising from these ruins was the Holy Bible containing a story, before reaching America, that had been spiritually executed, chronicled and settled – both factually and absolute – occurring after the death of Christ. But once Native Americans and Blacks were subdued in America, it became symbolic of Christianity. Though, before this reached fruition, the Native Americans were natives of land owned by God, who ruled the Universe. Therefore, The Bible – being a finished product – needed "nothing added nor taken away."

Christianity too, however – like Blacks – once brought to America, underwent a social metamorphosis. The change, in this instance though, related to the word believe, a term used by Christ in His rallying cry to the multitude. As He walked the land among them, he often counseled that if only they would believe in Him, they would have "everlasting life," as recorded in the text of ancient history. However, thousands of years later, the territory once inhabited by Native Americans was destined to undergo progressive change, supposedly of a civil nature – an idea formulated by white settlers after Native Americans befriended them and after these "settlers" took advantage of their neighbors' kindness by perceiving them as "uncivilized" in a land supposedly discovered by Columbus. Finally, in their native land, they were placed on reservations, eventually to utter these famous words, "The White Man speaks with forked tongue." Historically – in relation to the three aforementioned nationalities – the statement made was true.

American History – along with the inclusion of "Indian reservations" – defines the fate of Blacks, especially regarding words like "slave," "slave quarters," "breeding," "domestication," "chattel," and the like. The history of Blacks in America is further defined by the animal-like chores that Native Americans refused to do. Although many Native Americans were killed, they were familiar with the land they roamed and charted a course of escape. Blacks had no such recourse for they were victims in a strange land and had no choice other than to become submissive. Ultimately, both were stripped of their respective native cultures.

Due to these circumstances, white settlers of both British and English persuasion, with superior firepower, capitalized on the opportunity that occurred after the whites' flight from their own native homelands to escape oppression, while bringing along The Bible. This group was later believed to be thugs. At the time, America was in its primitive stage and was in no way linked with Ancient History. The Bible by that time was written in English rather than the original Hebrew. Consequently, devoid of interference by Native Americans and Blacks, who spoke in their native tongues, English settlers reproduced The Bible to fit the occasion at hand. In so doing, they renewed the word believe by spiritualizing it to appeal to the incoming colonizers, like Jesus did with the Hebrews in order for the idea to grow – thus reversing Christ's original meaning of the word as He walked the land in Biblical days and replacing it with a new meaning for the purpose of confusing the minds of their parishioners.

But God's primary plan was designed to overthrow dictators. In order to fulfill this goal, He chose His son, Jesus as His candidate for the purpose of seeing it through. During His son's sojourn, He set out to prove His Father was Almighty. He did this by performing miracle after miracle before the watchful eyes of many doubters, hoping for them to believe in Him so they could have "eternal life."

So, in all actuality, The Bible, before reaching the land that would later be called "America," had already been perfected. Christ accomplished this miraculous feat by proving that God was God. Following his death, however, The Bible's prophecy was fulfilled – or in other words, it was closed. It then was His followers' sole witness. Consequently, it removed all doubt. Thereafter, nothing was to be added nor taken away. Due to the revelation of God's Power, the word believe was transformed into the word know, because it was known that God was real. Later, The Bible was acknowledged as "The Word."

Evidence supporting such a contention is found in American History. It – like ancient history – represents two separate but distinct times, which consist of different stories. Ancient history, which encompasses the evolution of God and Christ, relates to such places as Egypt, Rome, Babylon, Syria, Israel, etc. – nations where God's Law was manifested. In other words, within these locales His Word was made perfectly clear without inclusion of America.

Conversely, American History differs; it was created out of the architects' own volition. It coverssuch topics as The Mayflower, the so-called slave ships, the Pilgrims, Paul Revere, colonists, Founding Fathers and Stars & Stripes – along with adoption of the Christian doctrine, which pertains strictly to The Bible. However, Native Africans – after departing the so-called slave ships – were portrayedas "uncivilizedbeings," thesamefatethatwasmetedouttoNativeAmericans. Categorically, both stories bear significant meaning.

During the time of Christ, the Message He sowed was a seed of Righteousness, such as "If the people 'believed' in Him, they would have Everlasting Life." By doing this, all doubters were offered a choice, which pertained to Heaven or Hell. As a result, those choosing to receive Him were rewarded with His Blessing, otherwise, those who refused opted to perish. After making His point, The Bible was closed. This did not necessarily eliminate doubters, such as was the case with the architects of America.

Truth of the matter is, before America was America, and before The Bible was translated into English, God's Law was Law – beginning with His transformation of Moses and climaxing with the man beside Jesus on the cross, whose sins He forgave for surrendering unto His Will. Therefore, there was no such logic as "adopting the Christian doctrine" because either Christians were Christians or they were not, and history records that the architects of America were not.

As a consequence, when The Bible arrived in America, it was known at the time by its architects as God being real. Had they followed His Word, it would have been a utopian nation or one void of sin. Then, everyone would have had the choice to chart his or her own destiny. But rather than adhere to the Word of God, man granted himself the Supreme Power to construct a corrupt society. The basic element of his immorality commenced with The Holy Bible, which pertained to two words.

Although Christ never walked upon American soil asking people to believe in Him, professed Christians – during the development of the American culture – were led to believe it was so. This occurred through visual imagination, a gimmick created by illusionary vision when portraying the image of Christ. Preachers have mastered this art for better than 500 years from the friendly confines of their pulpits. This they have done in a subtle manner by switching the words know and believe.

During ancient history when Christ walked the land, the dominant word was believe, a term He used during his soul-saving campaign, while performing miracle after miracle to prove He was the Son of God. For instance, such was the case of the woman with the blood issue. Her faith in Christ was so strong that once He was near her, she remarked, "If I could only touch the hem of His garment, I will be made whole." Immediately, following her outcry, no sooner was it said than done. Thereafter, no longer did she have reason to believe, because now it was known. This was His way of doing things; therefore, from this point hence, the dominant word was know. Upon His death – following proof of God's Wonders – The Bible was complete because God was not a God of incompleteness.

However, when the same standard is applied to American History, the entire scenario changes. This is due to the reversal of the words know and believe. While the latter indicates uncertainty or doubt, the former represents knowledge and understanding. By replacing it, The Bible was rendered incomplete, thus taking away from the ancient Bible and adding to the one translated in English – which violated the Word of God's Law – ironically, in this respect, rewriting the chapter of Pharaoh. Only in this case, man appointed himself as the "omnipotent administrator," or in other words, God. Therefore, man had to answer to none but himself. All of this transpired as a result of resurrecting the word believe to fit his purpose – which as yet has never changed. In fact, it was here that the seed of unrighteousness was sown.

Evolving from this idea was the dismantling of Native American sovereignty, enslavement of Native Africans and a distorted interpretation of The Bible. Supporting such immorality was The Constitution, a document designed for whites to control descendents of Africa forever. So, once Native Americans were relegated to reservations, Native Africans were confined to slavery. For the following 400 years, white members of the Christian church were wrongly educated about The

Bible. Specifically, they were taught a Dr. Jekyll and Mr. Hyde mentality, in this case a love/hate relationship between human beings and God. On the one hand, members were taught to seek salvation through God, and on the other they were taught to denounce Native Africans, claiming they were children of Ham. As evidenced by the outcome, this belief prevailed. At this point, the American culture was born.

Accordingly, the nationalities were separated. Due to the nature of the situation, it produced an adverse pattern of strange mental behavior, which created two different syndromes – one white, one dark. The former was obsessed with a false sense of inhumane omnipotence, while the latter was forced to submissively adhere to a state of social and economic degeneracy. Yet both were purportedly created equal, at least according to the bold ideals set forth by the Founding Fathers.

But these men were those who embraced The Constitution, which not only legitimized the cruel and inhumane treatment heaped upon Native Africans, but also advocated separation of church and state. Though, as a result of this infamous activity, as centuries progressed, the label "slave" – as was applied to Native Africans – gradually changed to Colored, Negro, Nigger, Black and then Afro-American. The title "Black" was chosen by Blacks themselves, to express a sense of pride rather than the whites' original meaning, which was used in a derogatory manner.

Emerging from this division was two nations – one of the ruling class and the other of subservience. The former were the beneficiaries of religious freedom, social justice, educational institutions and political asylum, while the latter was denied access to all. Never in the history of mankind has human beings undergone such drudgery, which was akin to that accorded animals, a condition that existed until the Civil War, a battle waged between the North and the South over the belief of right and wrong, while the organized church remained neutral.

Following this phase of American culture, Native Africans graduated from country servant to "politics." In this case, an acronym meaning "People Oppressed, Livelihoodless, Isolated, Tormented, Insignificant, Castrated Subjects." These were evils upheld by The Constitution – a concept derived of man and – in short – a document permeated with hatred. This hateful document legitimized statutes laid down by officials of the law, which were then dutifully executed by supportive constituents in an effort to preserve the color line, a blatant divide that included serving God in separate churches.

Unfortunately, by the time Robinson and Rickey executed their incredible feat, the country was governed by the doctrine of "separate but equal" – a phrase supposedly meaning separate but equal treatment for both Blacks and whites under the law. This wording alone was proof that God's Law was never followed. As a consequence, both Robinson and Rickey faced overwhelming odds. Robinson's fate stemmed from a hostile white society whose inbred hatred of Blacks had long ago been validated by a stamp of approval from both the Church and Constitution.

Rickey's dislike among his people stemmed from the notion that he betrayed them by associating with Blacks. Truth of the matter is, Rickey cared no more about Blacks than Abraham Lincoln, whose move was made to save the Union. Rickey's act was done to upgrade the quality of the so-called Major Baseball Leagues. As a team owner, he hired Robinson to jumpstart the job, therefore, defying two laws – the law of "separate but equal" and a so-called "gentlemen's agreement" among white team owners designed to keep Blacks out of their leagues. Additionally, white players on Robinson's team and those on others, planned to strike if he was allowed to play, claiming this would threaten their jobs.

Rickey, while hated by whites for his courageous deed, was revered by Blacks. But revering a person such as Rickey was not uncommon among Blacks. Abraham Lincoln, Elijah P. Lovejoy and John Brown – just to name a few – are prime examples. These humanitarians refused to concede to the immoral law of conformity. Other than the Black Church– to which Blacks were relegated – people such as the aforementioned raised a beacon of hope among Blacks, which was first shone by the Black church.

Prior to the existence of the Negro Leagues, the Black Church was well established following many years of bondage. By this time, however, the damage had been done. Bondage destroyed all principles of The Bible, especially those which consisted of God's Commandments – past, present and future – as written by the Scribes in a variety of ways, pointing out His Laws for man to live by. Bondage was excluded from these Laws; it was a creation of mankind.

In the Book of James, although every chapter and verse are of paramount interest, two verses in particular stand out vividly to illustrate the state and the condition of

Native Africans before and after reaching America. The verses in question pertain to horses and the tongue. In reference to horses, James admonished his brethren with the following statement: "Behold, we put bits in the horses mouth that they may obey us; and we turn about their whole body." His purpose for this parable followed the Teaching of Christ. Specifically the statement Christ made to those who wanted to stone the harlot by saying, "He who is without sin cast the first stone."

According to The American Heritage College Dictionary, a "bit" is defined as the metal mouthpiece of a bridle, serving to control, curb and direct an animal. The "bridle" is defined as a harness, consisting of a headstall, a bit, and reins fitted about a horse's head and used to restrain or guide the animal. Attached to the bridle were "blinders," a pair of leather flaps about the horse's eyes to obscure side vision and deny clear perception and discernment. However, before applying the bridle, the horse had to be captured from the wild, corralled and broken – or in other words – tamed. Likewise, from a human standpoint, this was the case of Native Africans after reaching America.

Africa, during ancient history, was the cradle of civilization. It was a continent that encompassed locations such as Nubia, an ancient kingdom in The Nile. This bit of information concerning it only scratches the surface. Its history concerning kings, queens, educators, rich resources, etc., if researched, is unparalleled. Further, Egypt was a dynasty within this continent. Ironically, centuries following ancient days, a few of these self-serving African kings – lusting for financial rewards – sold their people to Europeans, who then transported them to America. As a result, an indeterminate number of them were chained and shackled to the hulls of ships and carted off. This act was the beginning of the country's sin due to the kidnapping and cruelty imposed upon those who hailed from the continent where Moses encountered Pharaoh.

Once in America, they suffered the same treatment as the horse, which James warned his self-righteous brethren about concerning the bit, especially those who considered themselves sin-free. In comparison to the relation of the horse and the African, the spirit of both had to be broken before domestication. The horse, a product of the wild, had to be tamed with the aforementioned gear before responding to man's orders. Africans were of the human element; they had to be broken of their natural culture before transformation to chattel. This process began with the chains and shackles that pinned them to seats within the hull of ships. Upon entering the country – following the devastation of Native Americans – they were free of American sin. This was due to the introduction to a "new world," which was akin to the likes of a newborn child.

Horses (either by horseback or otherwise), during Biblical times, represented a mode of transportation. Their attention was gained with whips, the prime tool oppressors used to break the spirit of Africans whose chores were multi-purposed – jobs consisting of every domestic task conceivable. To compound this transgression of God's Law, they were forced to have children out of wedlock for the purpose of being bought and sold, which duplicated the cycle. Such activity, in its primitive state, was the first steps of capitalism.

In order for this method to reach fruition, Africans were harnessed in America, corralled in slave quarters and bridled by people bearing deep-seeded hatred. They were remanded to the custody of self-appointed slave masters who used the whip – instead of the bit – to bring captives under control. Blinders for them were an unneeded item because they were blind to the differences in language. Bondage, since its inception, has been Blacks' only equal opportunity employer, and that was because the work performed was charge-free.

Several thousand years before American slavery, the same existed in Egypt, at which time Pharaoh was dictator. Moses, a servant of God, was sent to Egypt to have him abolish slavery. Pharaoh refused to obey. Moses' only weapon was his staff, which was empowered by God, and Pharaoh's weapon was his army. During the debate that developed between them over the situation's outcome, Moses' staff and Pharaoh's magicians became the deciding factors. However, after much confrontation in this power struggle, Moses' staff prevailed. The Power of God's miracles, as displayed by it, was greater than Pharaoh had ever witnessed. Reluctantly, Pharaoh set his captives free, but this failed to diminish his ego. Accordingly, he directed his force to overtake them, which occurred near the Red Sea. Moses, sensing the impending danger, called out to God for help because he and his people were trapped between Pharaoh's army and the Red Sea.

God said to Moses, as revealed in the Book of Exodus, *"Lift up thy rod, and stretch out thine hand over the sea, and divide it."* By him obeying, the water parted. The divided portions, both on the left and right sides, formed walls of protection for the people, so they could be led across on dry land to a location God had prepared before their arrival. Accompanying them were donkeys bearing clothes, food and numerous other necessities. Their personal possessions consisted of things such as silver, gold and also jewelry, which came from Egyptians whom Pharaoh despised joining their bandwagon. With the Pharaoh-led army in the middle of the sea, while following closely on the dry land, God said to Moses, "Stretch out thine hand over the sea, that the waters may come again upon the Egyptians, upon their chariots, and upon their horsemen." By Moses obeying, the waters returned and covered the chariots, the horsemen and all the hosts of Pharaoh that came in the sea after them. But Pharaoh, before perishing in the water, acknowledged that the people's God was God. By Moses leading them out of Egypt, their bondage – more than 400 years – ended.

However, despite the death of Pharaoh and despite the seemingly untiring sacrifices of Moses to set his people free, they were soon to lose faith in him – occurring after leading them out of Egypt on a danger-free course that God charted through the wilderness onto The Red Sea. Thereafter, He directed Moses' course during their journey to Mt. Sinai, by way of the wilderness, where they wandered for 40 years. Prior to reaching Mt. Sinai, which was located between the wilderness and the Red Sea, they traveled through several locations. It was in the wilderness where they became disobedient to God and took their spite out on Moses, who – in God's infinite Wisdom – was chosen to carry out His orders. For this he was ostracized – the primary reason being selfishness – because of his refusal to cater to their every beck and call. Consequently, he was inundated with complaints regarding food, water, etc. – with shoes, clothes and sickness being exceptions. But he did not respond to their bickering; he did it on God's terms.

In addition, they accused him of leading them there to die, while suggesting also that they would have faired better in Egypt. However, in relation to their complaints about water, before Moses went up on top of Mt. Sinai to receive The Ten Commandments, he had tempted God – or in other words angered Him – occurring when the people experienced bitter water and he was told by God to smite the rock with his rod in order to render it drinkable. But Moses did it his way rather than God's. God also was displeased with the people's bickering, which developed into a wilderness of sin. Therefore, when Moses went up to the mountaintop to remain for 40 days, they were forbidden to follow.

During Moses' lengthy stay, however, the people presumed he was dead and built their own god, symbolic of a golden calf and structured from the Egyptians' gifts. But Moses' people were of a rebellious breed, not only against him but also against God, because He directed Moses' path. They witnessed his wonders at the Red Sea when the water parted to set them free, and then they believed. However, since this occurrence, their belief was upgraded to knowing, and had they followed Moses' instructions, which God commanded him to do, they would have acknowledged no other God, just as did Pharaoh before perishing.

By the time Moses returned with The Ten Commandments, they were all broken because of the people's iniquity. So angered was Moses that he broke the slate rock bearing them. Eventually, those guilty of committing sin died out in the desert, but their offspring carried on. Moses – as revealed in the Book of Deuteronomy – later died on one of the mountains. Before his death, he lectured to them about obeying God's Law in order to inherit The Promised Land – a place he said he was denied because of smiting the rock wrongfully and breaking the slate of Commandments. Though before his death, he was the first and last prophet to encounter God face to face. His message to the people was that there be no other God before Him – along with love and obedience.

Accordingly, beginning with the Book of Exodus, every book in The Bible reflects stories based upon the aforementioned principles. Therefore, The Bible was structured of historically, prophetic books, like Exodus, whose Biblical legacy pre-warned people against sin as well as the predetermined fate of offenders. In other words, God's Ten Commandments set the standard. Though, before the statutes were established, Israel was granted a choice between right and wrong. Alternatively, after marveling over all his wonders, Israel chose to forsake Him, while knowing He was God – a truth even Pharaoh refused to deny, which dispelled the word believe.

Strangely, better than 2,000 years after the above occurrences, everything old became new again – this time in America, which became the ghost of Egypt, especially in relation to bondage. Her slave quarters was the Egyptian ghetto. The Constitution devised by The Founding Fathers became the modern-day Pharaoh. Europeans – similar to the golden calf – appointed themselves as God, thus feigning a Christ-like image. But Jesus said – as revealed in the Book of John when speaking to Doubting Thomas – *"I am the Way, the Truth and the Life: no man cometh unto the Father, but by me."* Further, He said, *"If ye had 'known' me, ye should have 'known' my Father also: and from henceforth ye know Him, and have seen Him."*

Nonetheless – unlike God – who parted the Red Sea to free Israel from bondage, these transgressors of His Law transported Africans across the water and forced them to become their slaves – an act completely devoid of Christ, whose purpose on earth, when sent by God, was to teach man the Christian way of life before sacrificing His for their sins. Though, despite His reason, as recorded in The Bible, these false standard-bearers of Christianity, by originating a segregated society, reconstructed a wilderness of sin by annihilating Native Americans and systematically emasculating Native Africans – or in other words castrating them, which was anti-Christ and contrary to the Will of God. During the time of this transition, all parties spoke in different tongues. Thereafter, these Euro-Americans advertised Africans as immoral reprobates and the worst product ever to set foot on American soil.

By the time the Black Church evolved, the Black family was destroyed and completely dehumanized – victims of identity loss – both culturally and religiously. The will of their oppressors had been imposed upon them, and they were prone to obey. Accordingly, they began serving God on a separate basis, as was the case in all other affairs, which The Constitution upheld. In other words, a separation of church and state steeped in racial overtones that prohibited love between Blacks and whites because it was against the law. Therefore, it was man not God that separated the church. God's Law demanded unconditional love and He loathed disobedience.

Unlike Moses who was denied the Promised Land for the aforementioned reasons, but was yet received into the bosom of Abraham – these transgressors of His Law created their Promised Land in America and forced Blacks to help build it. After bondage, however, Blacks were promised 40 acres and a mule, which they never received. Consequently, the only manner in which they served God was at the direction of their oppressors, a matter in which they had no other choice but to submit. But while they submitted to the oppressors' will, the oppressors submitted to the will of The Constitution. In other words, it became their Pharaoh; thus, their self-made god served their self-made demon.

Finally, after more than 300 years of dog-hearted treatment, Blacks were permitted to have The Bible. In addition to following the oppressors' daily orders duly enforced by The Constitution, they were also denied scholastic rights, which rendered them ignorant. So the Black Church, once established, and they were permitted to attend, became their sole recourse. Then, under the strict supervision of their white oppressors, freed "slaves" were able to release long pent-up emotions by taking their burdens to The Lord. At that time, the Black churches were run by a variety of Black preachers, commonly called "jack legs," or in other words, those lacking academic skills.

Conversely, during the same era, white preachers taught white churchgoers in a two-fold manner. These were to seek salvation through the Love of God but to hate Blacks because they were the descendants of Ham, as was revealed in the Book of Genesis. This philosophical theory by white preachers has been followed for generations. Black preachers, despite much ridicule, have taught their parishioners the philosophy of "turn the other cheek and wait upon The Lord." This has long been the case traditionally. Therefore, these Black preachers, in a psychological manner – without them being aware of it – avoided imminent danger. In both cases, though, this superior/inferior rationale affected the mentality of their followers. While whites endorsed both hatred and Christianity, Blacks bowed out gracefully. In reference to the previously-mentioned tongue, as revealed in the Book of James, the words as recorded are as follows: *"Even so the tongue is a little member, and boasteth great things. Behold, how great a matter a little fire kindleth; And the tongue is a fire, a world of iniquity: so is the tongue our member, that it defileth the whole body, and setteth on fire the course of nature; And it is set on fire of Hell. For every kind of beast, and of birds, and of serpents, and of things in the sea, is tamed, and hath been tamed by mankind: But the tongue can no man tame; It is an unruly evil, full of deadly poison."*

Ironically, by the time the Black Church was granted autonomy, Black churchgoers had undergone the whip used on the horse and the sting of the oppressor's tongue. They, along with their predecessors, had been baptized in American culture and had developed a subservient mentality. Therefore, the Black church, when first organized, adopted the pattern of the White Church but served God separately. In addition to it being a sanctuary to praise God, it was also a therapeutic center that served as doctor, psychologist and psychiatrist, as well as a safe refuge from whites, whom they felt would leave them alone if they were being obedient. Consequently, there stands good reason why Blacks idolize Abraham Lincoln, John Brown, Elijah P. Lovejoy and numerous whites who helped to form The Underground Railroad so Harriet Tubman, the great Black heroine, could lead Blacks out of bondage.

In revisiting Jackie Robinson and Branch Rickey, Robinson – long before his acquaintance with Rickey – had already experienced the fate of being Black in America – the most vivid occurring while he was a commissioned military officer who was confronted by a white civilian bus driver, whom he refused to obey.

Memphis Red Sox (from right to left)

Casey Jones (whose son, J.J. Jones was backup quarterback to Joe Nameth of the New York Jets football team), Jose Colas, Gibert Verona, Marshall Bridges (who also played for the Cardinals team, Cincinnati, and was on the World Series winning New York Yankees team; he finished his career with the Washington Senators), Prince Joe Henry, Orlando Varona, Vebert Clarke, Pedro Formrenthal and Isaiab Harris.

The other five players' names could not be remembered by Mr. Henry at press time.

The Pauper Prince

THURSDAY, FEBRUARY 24, 2005
UPDATED: FEBRUARY 28, 11:17 AM ET
BY MIKE SEELY
SPECIAL TO ESPN.COM

Charley Pride is the Jackie Robinson of country music, having long ago obliterated Nashville's good ol' boy barricades through sheer force of will and the voice of a dark angel. But it turns out music superstardom was merely Pride's safety valve.

"I didn't intend to be in the hall of fame for singing," says Pride, who still performs regularly at venues nationwide. "My thing was baseball: I wanted to be the next Babe Ruth."

Throughout six seasons with the Negro League's Memphis Red Sox in the mid-'50s, Pride, an outfielder and pitcher, resembled both rugged Ruth the slugger and young Babe the hurler, baffling hitters with a three-pitch arsenal that included a fastball in the low 90's.

"I remember leaving New Orleans Saturday morning for a Sunday doubleheader in Indianapolis," recounts Pride.

"I was getting paid $100 per month and two dollars a day eatin' money. I drove the first shift on the bus until after midnight, went back and slept, and then finished off the driving," he says. "I stopped at a convenience store and got some Saltines and Pepsi, and that was my meal. I then went out and beat the Indianapolis Clowns 3-2 (as the starting pitcher) and then played outfield in the second game and hit a three-run homer."

Such exploits should have put Pride on a collision course with his big league dream. But while Jackie Robinson broke the color barrier in 1947, it is rarely noted that three teams -- the Philadelphia Phillies, Detroit Tigers and Boston Red Sox -- had yet to sign a Black player by the time Robinson retired in 1956.

"Segregation and the color barrier didn't turn over at 12 o'clock midnight on April 15, 1947," says Negro League historian Larry Lester. "It was a gradual transition.

It took a couple decades to balance out in the minor league and Major League levels."

And so Charley Pride never got his shot, the victim of imperfect timing and a recurrent bum shoulder. Enter Plan B, which saw Pride tackle the similarly stratified world of country music, achieving the sort of lofty success that eluded him on the diamond.

"Reporters used to ask me, 'How does it feel to be the first colored country singer?'" says Pride. "Then it was, 'How does it feel to be the first Negro country singer?' Then, 'How does it feel to be the first Black country singer?'

"Now they ask me, 'How does it feel to be the first African-American country singer?'" continues Pride. "And I tell them, 'About the same as it did when I was colored.' "

Joe Henry missed being Pride's teammate in Memphis by about a year, having moved on to play integrated baseball in Mississippi after the 1952 season. A dexterous, all-star second baseman in the Negro Leagues, Henry was knocked out of the game, seemingly for good, by knee and arm injuries.

But Henry resurfaced in 1955 as a third baseman with the storied Indianapolis Clowns, the team with which a young slugger named Henry Aaron cut his teeth. Hobbled but still moderately effective as a player, Henry re-emerged as a flamboyant court jester, earning the nickname "Prince Joe" for his brash antics on the field.

"I was doing in 1955 what Reggie Jackson would come up with years later: hittin' a home run and watchin' it go out," says the 74-year-old Henry. "I'd slap the catcher's hands, slap the umpire's hands and then run around the bases."

Henry's playing days ended with Detroit's Negro League franchise in 1958, and he eventually moved into a "luxurious mobile home" on 7th Street in his native Brooklyn, Ill. The 14-by-65-foot trailer, where Henry still lives, ain't so luxurious anymore. Nor is Brooklyn, a mostly Black, economically ravaged Southwestern Illinois community whose sole economic engine is a handful of strip clubs at the western edge of town.

Henry, who suffers from diabetes and rheumatoid arthritis, passes the better part of his days on a ripped maroon couch in his living room, surrounded by newspaper clippings and mementos from his athletic past. He lives on a fixed income of $16,839 per year, thanks to Social Security and a small pension from his post-baseball years as a union shop steward.

Neither Pride nor Henry was among a group of 69 ex-Negro Leaguers whom Major League Baseball began paying annual pensions of $10,000 in 1997. To qualify, these players had to have played in parts of four seasons, with at least one coming before Robinson broke the color barrier in 1947. Negro Leaguers whose careers began after 1947 were excluded, the rationale being that they arrived at a time when players of all races were welcome in Major League Baseball.

"Had those guys been good enough, they would have played (in the big leagues)," opines 93-year-old Buck O'Neil, a former teammate of Jackie Robinson and Satchel Paige with the Kansas City Monarchs whose Negro League career spanned three decades. "We didn't play because they wouldn't let us."

Others, like Lester, take a more nuanced stance, reasoning that the post-Robinson playing field in the '50s was far from level for players like Henry and Pride. Such a sympathetic perspective prevailed upon Major League Baseball commissioner Bud Selig this past spring, when it was announced that Major League Baseball -- in conjunction with its charitable arm, the Baseball Assistance Team (BAT) -- would distribute approximately $1 million in quasi-pension payments to 27 former Negro League players who had been excluded from the original group but played portions of four or more seasons before 1958. They'd get $40,000 each, paid over a four-year period.

Pride is on this list, which has since been expanded to include five more players. But Prince Joe Henry, despite indicating the required service tenure on his BAT application, has not been as fortunate. To wit, in a letter dated July 20, 2004, BAT executive director Jim Martin rejected Henry's application, noting that Henry's expenses (which he estimated at $1,000 per month) did not outstrip his monthly income of $1,403.

"For B.A.T. to provide assistance, a financial need is required on behalf of the applicant," Martin wrote. "In reviewing your application, your income exceeds your expenses."

"He can't afford any expenses," says Lester, who's currently working with the National Baseball Hall of Fame in Cooperstown to develop a definitive history on

Black baseball. "A lot of ballplayers live like Joe does. I know what shirt they're gonna wear at the next reunion, because they only have one."

Upon being rejected, Henry responded with a five-page written appeal, which was again dismissed by BAT. But this time, Martin's organization cited a different criterion: that Henry's Negro League tenure fell short of the service requirement.

While no one disputes the legitimacy of Henry's first three Negro League seasons in Memphis, his 1955 season in Indianapolis remains a point of contention. University of Delaware historian and author Neil Lanctot and, evidently, Major League Baseball do not consider the barnstorming Clowns to have been part of the official Negro Leagues that season, thus putting Henry one season short of the required tenure.

"My sense is, compared to where we started back in '97 with the broader program and how we've kind of broadened the eligibility with the second program, I've got to believe we're in the 90-plus percentage in terms of whom we've captured," says Jonathan Mariner, Major League Baseball's executive vice president of finance. "If there's a player out there who has approached us who could not substantiate their eligibility through their existing records, we'd be happy to use the [Negro League Baseball] Museum if they've got records to substantiate that."

The Kansas City museum, it turns out, considers the 1955 Clowns to be bona fide. "Officially, they did not renew their membership in the league in 1955, but were considered an associate team," says Lester, who co-founded the museum in the early '90s. "They were part of the league schedule, and played many, many games against league teams. The Clowns were much like the Kansas City Monarchs in the '30s, who abandoned league play to barnstorm across America. The Negro Leagues were not of a perfect world at the time, and were simply trying to survive the raid of their players by Major League Baseball.

"All in all, this is a gray area, and should not keep a player like Prince Joe from receiving a pension." On this point, Lanctot concurs: "There was a shallower level of talent in the mid-'50s in the Negro Leagues. I'd say anyone who played before '52, give them something."

Such a list would include Don Johnson, who played in the Negro Leagues with the Baltimore Elite Giants, Philadelphia Stars and Detroit Stars during 1947-1952.

Like Henry, Johnson does not receive an MLB-BAT pension, despite seemingly boasting the required tenure.

Clifford Layton, who played for the Indianapolis Clowns during 1951-1954, also falls under the purview. Johnson, a utility infielder who was cut by the Reds in spring training in 1947 for reasons he believes were racially motivated, is in similar financial straits as Henry. "All I get is Social Security," he says.

Now 78 and living in Cincinnati, Layton's still in good enough health to work four-hour shifts as an instructor for the Cincinnati Recreation Commission. Johnson coaches varsity girls' basketball at Woodward High School and varsity boys' baseball at Jacobs High School, from which he draws seasonal stipends of $1,000 apiece.

"I need help, too, because all I'm doing is helping kids," says Johnson. "I have to pay a $508 mortgage every month. I just try to carry my life on. Whatever they're doing ain't benefiting me any. It should."

For his part, Pride -- who's using his $833 monthly stipend to assist his brother, Mack, also a Negro League veteran -- takes a more comprehensive stance, asserting that all former Negro League players should receive remunerations from Major League Baseball, length of tenure notwithstanding.

"I really didn't need [the money]; but since they decided to do it, I call it guilt money," says Pride. "I look at it from the situation of Japanese internment. I think everybody that ever played -- whether they played one or two weeks -- ought to get something, as far as I'm concerned."

Former MLB commissioner Fay Vincent agrees, and has put his money where his mouth is: In 2002, Vincent donated a portion of revenues from his book, "The Last Commissioner," to every living former Negro Leaguer, of which some 130 remain today.

"I had Cooperstown give me a list of probably 250 guys, and I gave them $300-$400 apiece," says Vincent. "I got to know a number of them over the years, and I realized they got the worst deal.

"The country gave all Blacks a bad shake, but baseball was particularly tough," he added. "Whatever can be done for them, I think we should do."

1952 M.O.V. All Star Team

Editor's Note: The following article originally appeared in the St. Louis Post-Dispatch/St. Clair-Monroe Post section on September 26, 2002 and was written by Michael Shaw. Reprinted by permission.

Brooklyn Man Recalls Years As Player in Negro Leagues

The phone calls from old friends aren't as frequent anymore at Joe Henry's home in Brooklyn. "A lot of these old guys are dead now," he said. "I'm nearly there. I'm 73 now."

Still, once in a while, he'll get a call from someone wanting to reminisce about their days as players in the Negro Baseball Leagues or pass on some news about former teammates. Last week, a fellow former Negro Leaguer from Jacksonville, Fla., phoned and told him that Congress was honoring players such as themselves. More than 100 players, including Willie Mays, went to Washington for a special event.

Henry wasn't sure what the political event was about and couldn't make the trip. But talking about it did trigger a flood of memories. "It was the greatest experience of my life," he said of the time he spent playing. "Every time I went to a new town, I made it a point to find places where great Blacks walked. This was important to me."

Henry joined the league in 1950 just as they were wrapping up, three years after Jackie Robinson broke baseball's color barrier as a player for the Brooklyn Dodgers. Henry grew up in the small Illinois town of the same name, Brooklyn, catching Cardinals games at Sportsman's Park. It was his talents at fast-pitch 12-inch softball, however, that caught the attention of an area high school principal. The principal convinced him to head to Memphis for a tryout with the Negro League team there, the Red Sox, Henry said.

The stories roll out of Henry like fastballs from a fresh arm - stories about the players he encountered on their rise to fame, such as Hall-of-Famers Satchel Paige and Ernie Banks. Each story triggers another. At the time he was playing, Black players were still using the Negro Leagues as a steppingstone to the Major Leagues.

"When I went up against Satchel Paige, I struck out four times," Henry said of the only time he faced Paige, when the pitcher had gone from the Cleveland Indians to the all-Black Chicago American Giants. "The fifth time, I hit a little dribbler back to him. And I was so happy. I called my daddy and told him I hit Satchel Paige!'"

Henry's season in Memphis led to tryouts at two integrated farm clubs for Major League players. But injuries kept him from going any farther. He tore his knee on a play at second base, what he described as a deliberate attempt by a white player to hurt him. Henry, who played all over the infield, has no idea what his batting average was in his years playing ball, because no one kept accurate statistics. "You knew who could play and who couldn't," he said.

It was Henry's work after being injured that brought him some notoriety. He went to play for a team called the Indianapolis Clowns, and he brought a measure of showmanship to the game. "I would wear these big pants and put about 20 bats in them," he said. "I'd get up to bat and take two or three of them out at a time, swing them, put them down, take out two more. The crowd went wild."

Henry doesn't move like an infielder any more. He has severe arthritis, exacerbated by the construction work he did after leaving baseball. He played until 1959, but by then, there were few teams that survived. "I don't care too much for baseball these days," he said. "I watch it if there is nothing else to do during summer. Now it's one dude trying to make more money than the other."

He added: "When Jackie Robinson went into the Dodger organization, that was the end of the Negro Leagues. That was the beginning of the Civil Rights Movement."

Ask a Negro Leaguer

Editor's Note: With respect to the reprinting of the questions and answers that follow – originally published in the St. Louis Riverfront Times newspaper – some names of participants have been changed in order to protect their privacy. Furthermore, many of these reprints have been purposefully placed out of chronological (dated) order to group similar subjects, issues and answers (etc.) together.

INDIANAPOLIS CLOWNS TEAM ROSTER

(Subject to Change)

26—JONES, SS
28—McCOY, LF
24—HENRY, 3rd Base
31—WEST, RF
20—DRAKE, CF
22—FEABRY, 2nd Base
30—MONTANO, Catcher
34—NATURE BOY, 1st Base
29—BLACK, Pitcher
25—COBBIN, Utility
33—MASON, Pitcher
35—SMITH, OF

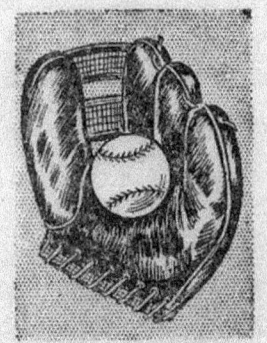

★ ★ ★

KING TUT and SPEC BEBOP of CLOWNS' Diamond Fun Show

VERDES DRAKE
Most Sensational Fly Chaser in Negro Baseball

Do you know of any young players between the age of 17 and 23 that you feel can play ball of the same calibre as the Indianapolis Clowns or New York Black Yankees? Here is how they can try out. The next time the teams play in your park have the player report to the ball park at 6:30 P.M. and ask for Ed Hamman at the office. Have player bring uniform, glove and shoes, and he will be given a chance to display his ability.

Week of July 20, 2005

Hey Joe: I own a mobile home in West Alton and I'm going to be installing a Jacuzzi. Would you recommend installing the tub inside or out? And what music would you suggest I play to attract the ladies to my tub?

K.S.

> I've never really cared for mobile homes, although I've lived in one for better than 30 years. But if I had the option between installing a Jacuzzi on the inside or outside of my home, I would certainly have it installed within. My type of music would include Marvin Gaye and Lionel Richie. It is no secret that women have "punked out" over the sound of these two guys.

Hey Joe: Which pitcher would you rather have start Game Seven of the World Series: A) Dock Ellis, high on acid; B) Doc Gooden, high on coke; or C) Dontrelle Willis, high on life?

Steve "Boy and Howe"

> Regarding Ellis and Gooden, while I refuse to endorse drugs, I have grown up in a society from an early age that referred to pharmacies back then as "drugstores." Therefore, America has been -- and still is -- afflicted by addictions. Prime examples are alcohol, cigarettes, steroids, Viagra, Cialis, etc. -- with the worst possible addiction being racism.
>
> However, if I were to choose a pitcher for the seventh game of the World Series, it would be none of those three. I would narrow my list to Denny McLain, Dizzy Dean and Satchel Paige. McLain, a former Detroit Tiger, and Dean, a former St. Louis Cardinal, were two of baseball's best pitchers during their abbreviated heyday. Seemingly, both were unbeatable at the time. But "Satch" -- like Old Man River -- kept on rolling along.
>
> Unfortunately, McLain wound up addicted to gambling, eventually to serve time in prison. Dean suffered an injury to his toe from a line drive hit back at him off the bat of Earl Averill of the Cleveland Indians that ended his baseball career. Subsequently he became a broadcaster of Cardinal games, though white schoolteachers tried to put an end to this. The reason being: In describing advancing base runners, he would say, for instance, the guy

"slid" into the base. Teachers claimed he would destroy school kids' English. But in spite of all, he was the most popular announcer in the booth. I dug his dirty drawers because he got his point over.

Regarding my starting pitcher, it would have to be Satch. All the other guys had a chance at a young age. Satch never did. Ultimately, the moral behind this story is: We all have undergone adversities.

```
Week of July 27, 2005
Hey Joe: Do you feel like Barry Bonds properly respects
the game of baseball, given his perceived arrogance and
alleged steroid abuse?
John Tomachefski, Arnold, Missouri
```

Bonds is one helluva baseball player, but no baseball player has ever been more arrogant than the late Ted Williams, the former Boston Red Sox great. Usually power hitters tipped their caps in response to fans' ovations after connecting on long ones; Williams never did. After hitting a home run, he would jog around the bases, and after crossing home plate, he'd seemingly spit in the direction of fans. Despite being one of the greatest players ever, his most humanistic gesture was when he made the statement that the "Hall of Fame" was in all actuality the "Hall of Shame," due to the fact that great Black baseball players had not at the time been enshrined. I have a deep love for both Williams and Bonds. Both have exhibited their own personal manhood. In reference to steroids, Bud Selig and Congress ought to quit.

```
Hey Joe: What do you think of Tony La Russa's customized
lenses? What do you think of wearing sunglasses at night
in general?
Corey Hart Fan, Death Valley, California
```

Recently, an ardent Cardinals supporter approached me concerning this past World Series. So disenchanted was he over the Cardinals' poor performance that he attacked Tony's shades. "Maybe if La Russa would relieve himself of those Stevie Wonder-like glasses, he could see what's going down," he bellowed. "Or maybe he keeps them on so he can't make eye-to-eye contact with the spectators, because he hasn't brought a World Series championship to St. Louis."

During Casey Stengel's successful years with the New York Yankees, they were so good that a manager was unneeded. Really, all Stengel had to do was name the next team in line for the butt-kicking. Stengel eventually bowed out in a blaze of glory as a managerial wizard. Meantime, the Giants left New York for San Francisco and were replaced by the New York Mets. Ol' Casey was coaxed back into baseball as their manager. As of the last count, he hasn't won a game since.

Following his brilliant managing career in Oakland, La Russa's stock has slowly diminished, much like Stengel's. Granted, he has kept the team up top most times in their division, but fans can no longer afford the luxury of waiting for him to win a World Series, like people have waited since Ted Williams for another .400 hitter. As for my opinion about dark glasses, I can't see a thing during the day with nothing covering my eyes.

Week of August 3, 2005

Hey Joe: Baseball purists have long maintained that it is bad form to have sex the night before a game. What has your experience taught you about this bit of folklore?

Jackie Treehorn, Wood River

Boxing purists held the same belief about boxers not engaging in sex the night before a fight -- feeling that if they did, it would sap their strength. So strongly did they hold this opinion that fighters were alienated from the general public and carted off to some desolate location to do their training weeks before a fight.

During the early '50s, I was assistant boxing trainer to a stable of aspiring Golden Glovers in my hometown of Brooklyn, Illinois. Of the various weight classes, we had a novice heavyweight who exhibited great potential. He was a virgin, stood six-foot-five, weighed 230 pounds, had a head like a Rockefeller cantaloupe and could hit harder than lightning could bump a stump. On the night of his first fight, we had him in tip-top shape. His opponent was a rather large white kid.

Once the bell rang, the white kid bolted from his corner into the corner of our fighter (as if jet-propelled), stuck his head in the chest of our fighter and commenced throwing lefts and rights to his body until he spit out his mouthpiece and hollered for us to come get him. Our fighter hit the canvas like a fallen California Redwood. When we arrived back in Brooklyn, I had to ride him around town 'til the wee hours of the morning because he was afraid to go home. He said if his father knew he lost the fight, he would kill him. Therefore, he wanted me to go home with him. I promised I would. Before I did, however, I concocted a big lie about the fight being taken from him. This is what I told his daddy while standing by the open door. So my feeling about this opinion of boxing purists is that it's hogwash.

Now, on to the baseball purists: Having sex the night before a game is as common as apple pie. I've known guys who, after having sex three hours before games, hit the ball so hard that their teammates hollered out to infielders of the opposing team to have their married men play deep, so they wouldn't get hurt. My philosophy about this is the same as the Isley Brothers, the group that recorded the song about, "It's your thing; do what you wanna do. I can't tell you who to sock it to!" So, therefore, I couldn't care less if he stuck [his wang] in a deep freezer.

```
Week of August 17, 2005
Hey Joe: A friend of mine who works in the office wanted
to know if you knew Ivan Johnson of the Kansas City Mon-
archs. That was her uncle.
Diana Ware, Normal, Illinois
```

I am not aware of Ivan Johnson. Matter of fact, I'm not aware of many former Negro Leaguers. However, there is a book authored by Robert Peterson, entitled Only the Ball Was White, which has been on the market for numerous years. It contains an index that lists players from many years back in the 1900s up until '50 and '51, which might be of great help.

```
Hey Joe: What is your opinion of the proliferation of
churches in African-American areas?
Hammer, Oaktown
```

Traditionally, as far back as I can recall, including my travel throughout most of the country during the time I spent playing ball, the church has been an integral part of the Black community. For example, in my Brooklyn hometown, I grew up in a community of 2,600 people and 14 churches. Today, there are supposedly 700 residents and also 11 churches.

The source of these multiple sanctuaries stemmed from selfish Black so-called preachers -- who claimed to be called by God -- assuming the title "preacher" after vacating churches they were unable to head. Ultimately, they organized their own, which in most cases created occupations and a measure of prestige that satisfied their egos. Due to this kind of mentality, divisiveness permeated the Black communities because of no cohesiveness. Rather than administer the Bible as prescribed, most have complicated it. Unlike men of the cloth -- such as the late Dr. Martin Luther King Jr., Rev. Jeremiah H. Wright and the late Rev. Adam Clayton Powell, etc., who refused to take a backseat to truth -- nothing positive can be said about spineless, self-proclaimed "reverends."

Most devastating is the mere fact that a sizable majority of their parishioners don't even know what happened to Pharaoh. Conversely, in defense of their Christianity, when faced by people who opposed their Christian views, immediately they are characterized as being like Paul, especially before Christ changed him. It has been this type of spiritual jargon coming from the various churches that saturate the Black communities. For those who don't know what happened to Pharaoh -- and the preachers likewise -- God killed him for being wicked. Although this is my personal opinion, you're not mandated to accept it. Read the Book of Exodus.

```
Week of October 5, 2006
Hey Joe: What do you think of the fuss that's being made
about the Hooters they want to put in Florissant? Do you
think the restaurant is in good taste or is it just kind
of slutty?
Prudie McSpinster, University City
```

I've always heard that behind every successful man was a good woman. I'm not a betting man, but I am willing to bet that the fuss over the Hooters restaurant stems from complaining wives.

Case in point: The ruckus there is similar to the kind that occurred between a man and his wife over a lady walking past their home every day on her way to work. This caused the guy and his wife to be constantly at each other's throats. (The crux of their fights stemmed from the way she swished.)

The lady, with her good looks and sexy appearance, created an uproar between the couple each time she passed their house. The husband would try to sit on the porch to watch her walk by, and his wife would try to stop him. Finally, his wife had the lady arrested for reckless walking. Upon the judge hearing the wife's story, he asked the lady in question to walk to the back of the courtroom. While she was on her way, he bellowed, "Case dismissed! Case dismissed!" The guy's wife hollered, "Ain'tcha gonna fine her?! Ain'tcha gonna fine her?!" He retorted, "You can bet your life I will, before daybreak in the morning."

If this is the case in Florissant, the wives should reconsider. Women have been made sex objects throughout America. The bottom line? Money. Therefore, there is nothing slutty about the restaurant. The same rule has to apply to television. Both feature skimpily dressed women and bikini attire, and I don't guess there is a law against reckless eyeballing. Once I was told that there were two guys walking down a street with a shapely lady walking ahead of them. One of the guys was so busy watching her that he forgot that his buddy was talking to him. His friend quickly picked up on what had a hold on the other guy's attention. Suddenly he broke his buddy's concentration by telling him that if he kept watching the lady the way he was, he would go blind. His buddy replied, "I'm gonna take a chance on one eye."

Thank God for eyes! Hooters is just as legitimate as any restaurant in the country. The women add an extra attraction. I am unable to give a snap opinion because I've never been to one. Maybe I'll visit a Hooters soon. My only worry is hoping I don't get run over by the male rush, because I'll be in my wheelchair.

```
Week of July 13, 2006

Hey Joe: Do you think St. Louis has gotten warmer in your
lifetime? If so, what do you think the causes are?

Al - Nashville, Tennessee
```

Not really. During my childhood, coal-burning stoves were used for all seasons of the year. In the winter, they were used for cooking and heating and for the other seasons they were used only for cooking. During summer, the only cooling system was screen doors and windows. Not many electrical fans were en vogue. There was no such thing as global warming. Most people were compelled to adjust to the weather. The only air pollution at the time was smoke that emitted from coal-burning stoves and smokestacks near businesses located in and around East St. Louis and downtown St. Louis, which caused the location to be dubbed "The Pittsburgh of the West." Then came war with Japan and the atomic bomb whose explosion formed a mushroom-like cloud.

In recent years, the idea of weapons of mass destruction has cropped up. It's a theme that has grown extremely popular within the George W. Bush administration and a topic that Tom Tomorrow illustrates vividly through his This Modern World cartoons in the RFT. In doing so, he points out the negative side of the president's cohorts that's directed toward anyone who disagrees with Bush's political philosophy, all the while noting that Bush claims to be a devout born-again Christian and has a large following of Christians of all denominations. I wonder if they have missed what I have found in the pages of the Bible during my short research of it. There, found in the Book of James (3:5-8), is the answer to why there is conflict abroad and division within this country.

These verses relate to the tongue. I think the most dominant is James 3:8, which states, "But the tongue can no man tame; it is an unruly evil, full of deadly poison." This warning occurred during ancient history, better than 2,000 years before America became known as the "modern world." However, the prophecy was right. Evidence is found in the lie that Bush told Americans, which initiated this ongoing mayhem. Bush's tongue was the real weapon of mass destruction. Those tongues that speak in support of him are also weapons of mass destruction. Further, James 1:8 states, "A double-minded man is unstable in all his ways." I seriously think that people should stop playing Christians and instead begin acting the part.

Week of August 10, 2005

Hey Joe: Would you rather be a Hall of Fame player, rich beyond your wildest dreams but never a part of a championship team (à la Karl Malone, Dan Marino or Barry Bonds), or a role player who has had moments of greatness, is rich but not excessively rich, but has won championships (like "Big Shot Bob" Robert Horry, Jermaine Wiggins or Craig Counsell)?

F. Bishop, Seattle

> The two guys named last -- Wiggins and Counsell -- must have starred quietly in their respective athletic circles, because I have never heard much about either -- not to say that other people haven't. Now the playing field is level. Well, if I must make a choice, I'd choose to be like Malone, Marino and Bonds. I'm not a betting man, but I'd be willing to bet that none of these guys ever missed a meal because of not playing in a championship.

> These three will certainly be inducted into their respective Halls of Fame, but I refuse to bet that the role player will be as successful. Yes, I suppose winning a championship is nice, but not nice enough for me to give some of my hard-earned money back in exchange for a championship ring. In reference to legends, rookie athletes perceive Malone, Marino and Bonds as such now.

Hey Joe: What factors have caused Latinos to overtake African-Americans as baseball's dominant athletes of color?

Tito, Joplin

> This question mirrors the greatness of the Negro Leagues in relation to the phrase "Liberty and Justice for All." Not only did it pave the way for Latinos, but also white promoters and white team owners during a time when such collaboration between Blacks and whites was prohibited by the law. Ironically, the only Latinos accepted in the white leagues were those

with a complexion comparable to that of my best friend, Gene. However, in Cuba -- or other places similar -- one brother might have a color like Gene while another might be as dark as Edgar Renteria because there was no color line.

Blacks traditionally have been forced to pursue areas in American life where the most money was accessible, because it was their means of survival. Boxing was a prime example. For those outside boxing, it was the Negro Leagues. Once it was destroyed by unmerciful white baseball moguls, nothing was left for the scouting of Black talent in baseball other than sandlot and semipro teams. By this time basketball and football had gradually opened their doors to Blacks. Thus, places such as the Dominican Republic were ripe for baseball scouts to solicit talent. Today the versatility of Blacks is magnified. They are the dominant force in basketball and football.

Week of August 24, 2005

Hey Joe: It looks like they will be voting to accept Negro League players in the National Baseball Hall of Fame in 2006. What other Negro Leaguers do you think deserved to be enshrined in Cooperstown?

Jamie Krock, Canton, Illinois

I'm sorry, but even as a former Negro Leaguer, I am not qualified to answer your question. So says Bud Selig, commissioner of Major League Baseball, and Jim Martin, executive director of the Baseball Assistance Team (BAT) -- two guys who, if asked to review the history of the Negro Leagues, would be green as goose doo-doo around a country pond. In 1997, Ol' Bud and BAT, an organization fronted by MLB, did a wonderful thing by providing charitable pensions to former Negro Leaguers who played before 1947. Excluded from this group were many players who played from 1948 until 1960.

Last year a local newspaper revealed that the pension was being extended for players in need who'd played parts of at least four years. I contacted BAT's office, was sent an application, submitted it and was rejected.

Suddenly the rules had changed. In spite of being disabled, I was told I didn't have four years, but neither did Willie Mays, Ernie Banks nor Hank Aaron -- all Hall of Famers. Between 1948 and 1951, I played against Mays and Banks while I was with the Memphis Red Sox and Mays was a Birmingham Black Baron and Banks a Kansas City Monarch.

With the exception of Ernie Banks, who in 1953 stepped off the Monarch bus in Chicago and went straight to the Cubs' locker room, I followed the rest into the white minor leagues. While there I sustained a career-ending knee and arm injury and subsequently joined the Indianapolis Clowns -- Hank Aaron's alma mater -- in 1955.

To make a long story short, Ol' Bud and BAT decided to compensate twenty or more handpicked players with pensions. Unfortunately, other Negro Leaguers who played until 1960 were denied, including me. Had Jackie Robinson, Mays, Banks or Aaron fallen into the above category, they would have been denied too. For the above reason, I took offense, called the press and made known my intention to expose it.

For the time being, Congress should table the steroid stuff and investigate Bud Selig and BAT for misleading the American public. After all, players of color in the majors today are by products of the Negro Leagues. In 2006 my vote for an inductee into the National Baseball Hall of Fame is cast for the Negro League Baseball Museum, which houses all the invisible stars, including the late Ted "Double-Duty" Radcliffe, the league's most charismatic, celebrated figure.

Week of August 31, 2005

Hey Joe: I was always interested as to which of the two men, Josh Gibson vs. Babe Ruth, was: 1) The best hitter? 2) The best player overall? 3) The best role model for up-and-coming players? I wish that they could have had real playoffs against the greatest teams of both the Negro Leagues and the Major Leagues.

J.E. Horst, Dittmer

Questions 1) and 2) will be forever debated without answer, thanks to a Black and white society that was separated at the time. In answer to question 3): In 1950, when I tried out for the Memphis Red Sox -- the team I started with in the Negro Leagues -- every regular member was my "role model." My focus on them was as baseball players and not their personal lives. Again, in regard to Gibson and Ruth, society then prohibited such fraternizing.

However, the subject surrounding the Negro Leagues and the Major Leagues is a pretty good topic. If I recollect my historical memory correctly, there was only a Negro League and a white league. The so-called Major Leagues never became major until after 1947, the year Jackie Robinson broke the barrier. That's when the best ballplayers in the country -- Black and white -- began collaborating. But then, the late Curt Flood, a Black former St. Louis Cardinals outfielder, took it a step further. He did it by hammering away at the reserve clause previously monopolized by white team owners, until the walls came tumbling down, which ushered in free agency -- thus making ballplayers millionaires and the game of baseball big business.

Hey Joe: Most of my baseball-knowledgeable friends tell me they think Bret Boone was using steroids in 2001, though he denies it. I like Boonie and want to believe him when he says he wasn't. My (slim) argument has been that everyone on the team did great that year -- for Pete's sake, they won 116 games. Am I just engaging in wishful thinking?

Melissa, Seattle

In most cases, even the guiltiest of offenders denied charges filed against them until proven guilty. As yet, Bret Boone is innocent because nothing pertaining to the allegation has been proven. Anyway, from reading your question, I gather that your knowledgeable baseball friends say they think he used steroids. The word "think" won't hold up in any court of law. Until you find out definitely, there really isn't a case, because your information is only hearsay.

Week of September 7, 2005

Hey Joe: How come white women, even when they ain't desperate, are always so quick to drop their towels for a Black man?

T.O., The Bahamas

> Love cannot be legislated, at least not by God's standard. His Love is unconditional. Thankfully, I enjoyed such Godly creation within my family. Among these are nieces with white husbands and nephews with white mates, which -- from these bonds -- have brought forth several offspring. At each meeting, I see nothing but in-laws and blood relatives, of which there is no distinction, as previously legislated by man.
>
> America, however, dating back as far as bondage, has separated Blacks from whites. Seemingly, the central focus from this division was Black males and white females. In this respect, the country has a legacy of lynching Black males for allegedly assaulting white females. The most vivid illustration pertains to Emmett Till, the fourteen-year-old Chicago youth who was killed in Mississippi while visiting relatives, for allegedly wolf-whistling at a white female. Unless these relationships assimilate the movie Driving Miss Daisy, foul play is suspected. At my family gatherings, I see what America has shunned, which is the true essence of unconditional love.

Hey Joe: There are several Negro League catchers that never get noticed. Josh Gibson is the big attraction solely for his ability to hit. Aside from Gibson, rank the top catchers of the Negro Leagues. I have three: Biz Mackey, Bruce Petway and Louis Santop.

Roger Webb, St. Louis

> Regarding Louis Santop, in spite of my intense research, I was unable to learn much about him. In addition to the aid of a large, thick, encyclopedia-like book entitled Black Baseball's National Showcase, I solicited help from two former Negro Leaguers, whose knowledge of him was also a bit shallow. They were Gene Smith, a native St. Louisan, and Reggie Howard, a Negro League historian and now a resident of Memphis,

Tennessee, who was able to reveal that Santop played with numerous teams from 1906 through 1926 and, at times, served as catcher, outfielder and manager. However, both support your position regarding Josh Gibson, a onetime teammate of Smith. After bringing to memory the names of several catchers, such as Biz Mackey, Bruce Petway, Larry Brown, Pepper Bassett, Frank Duncan, "Double Duty" Radcliffe, Casey Jones and the like, it was decided that Mackey was the best candidate for the second spot behind Gibson.

Week of June 21, 2006

Hey Joe: Why are you such a seemingly outrageous bigot?

Whitey Jones, Laguna Beach, California

You remind me of a souvenir I received many years back. It was a miniature W.C. Fields look-alike with a tuxedo, top hat — the whole bit. Inscribed on it was, "Oh, what a beautiful day. Now just watch some bastard louse it up!" Anyway, thanks for the compliment.

Hey Joe: What do you think about the Smith/La Russa saga that has caused Cardinal Nation to turn on Ozzie like one of his MLB record 1,590 double plays?

Benny C. Lewis, Ozzie Smith Diversity Scholarship Recipient

It seems only yesterday that the Houston Astros embarrassed the Cardinals in last season's NL Championship Series. Ray King, one of the Redbirds' top relievers, loved St. Louis the same as Ozzie did. The media admired him for his post-game interviews. He was witty, had a pretty good sense of the game and was dedicated to the team. Then came his demise, all because he voiced his displeasure about La Russa not pitching him in the series, due to Tony thinking Ray's performance wasn't up to par. Even if true, there was no reason for King to be released for speaking his mind. The whole team performed poorly, but this was King Tony's opportunity to exercise his ego. Somebody had to be the fall guy and King was his man. While in Houston, prior to Pujols' home run (bringing the team back from certain disaster), La Russa raced onto the field to save face by belittling the umpires in the event his team lost.

In 1996, his first season as Cardinal manager, he created what would become a long-standing problem between Ozzie Smith and himself by pitting Smith against then-rookie shortstop, Royce Clayton. Smith has been the greatest shortstop I've ever seen. Check baseball's Hall of Fame to see if I am wrong. He went after balls the average shortstop would've only waved at.

Despite his wizardry at his position, his greatest attribute was his dedication to St. Louis. At the time that La Russa wanted to bench him, he wasn't ready to retire. Now the subject reappears in 2006. I am not interested in who defends Tony's position, but the way he handled the situation was classless. Smith should've been given the courtesy of making his own decision about retirement rather than being platooned with Clayton as he was. Because of this, undue pressure was placed on both he and Clayton, and there was the possibility of this causing much dissension between them. As an end result, Ozzie handled it gracefully. Personally, based upon his overall character as baseball player and person, I would love to see him return to the field — but this time as manager of the Cards. He is entitled to this and would fare as well as La Russa's replacement (he seems to cling to the job).

Week of August 24, 2006

Hey Joe: Were you affected by the recent St. Louis area power outage? Do you think Ameren responded more slowly to Black customers than to white customers?

"The Rev." - New York

Coincidentally, on the day I received your question, a power outage occurred during another threatening thunderstorm. Afterwards, the day's projected temperature of 101 degrees dropped considerably. However, any outage that extends beyond three hours (as was the case on this day) affected me as well as every other homeowner or renter. Therefore, the longevity of the two most recent major outages, attributed to thunderstorms, affected all involved.

During both of these calamities, I wound up at a motel for several days.

Thankfully, my insurance policy covered most of the damage — quite unlike others without coverage. In both instances, however, I was so distraught I never considered whether Ameren responded slower to Blacks than whites. However, many years before Ameren arrived on the scene, there was suspicion in Black communities about utility companies jacking up rates. As a former utility employee, I agree with such feelings.

Ameren is another story. During the past three or four years of its control, there have been more power outages than during most of my lifespan. I'm sure many former Union Electric customers feel likewise. This leads me to believe that Ameren cares less about whether a customer is Black or white. So devastating have these outages been that once thunder is heard, the fear of God wells up within people living under such circumstances. It prompted a next-door neighbor to remark, "Damn! Every time a person farts too loud, out goes the lights."

Unfortunately, there are others who might disagree with my philosophy. This was indicated approximately three weeks ago by some panel members on KETC-TV Channel 9's Donnybrook, who seemed to sympathize with this greedy terrorist giant, which has monopolized the industry while leaving its customers helpless and virtually subdued with no recourse. The rationale was that the company did a yeoman's job in restoring services to the seemingly endless list of victims after they had undergone a destructive storm, which they classified as an act of God. Granted, the problems encountered were an act of God.

Perhaps these panelists voiced their opinion based upon the damage left by the recent thunderstorms and not a person such as myself who has contended with this power company for the past three or four years. During this period of time there has been outage after outage. The cases are so numerous that I, along with hundreds of thousands of others, dread summer or winter's arrival for fear of power outages.

I learned long ago that complaining to the company about high rates is an exercise in futility, and it is impossible for these bills to be viewed as an act of God. Three consecutive times, my bill was over $400 per month. When inquiring about this, I was told an assortment of things such as, "We have no control over it," "Speak with your state senator," and "We only get a small percentage of the money." Since then, as customer of Ameren, I have become very fearful of their actions. When fear overcomes a person because of frightful reasons, the entity that caused that fear has become a terrorist.

Week of August 3, 2006

Hey Joe: I've enjoyed your poems lately. Ever written any regarding Blacks?

Ms. Maya, New York, New York

I wrote a poem about Blacks in 1964 called "The Negro." I got a check for $100 from Dick Gregory Enterprises Inc. for it. On the back, the check said: "For all uses and all rights of a certain poem known as 'The Negro' of which the payee is the author by way of description but not by way of limitation in a certain book entitled Nigger, of which Dick Gregoryis the author and Dutton and Company the publisher." I never cashed that check.

Through all of my life I have followed a trend

Of laws laid down by egotistical men,

Though human structures are basically the same

Pigmentation of my skin has been the blame.

Year after year I have been denied,

But would rather die than lose my pride.

I've been instrumental in enriching this land,

But I'm still considered less than woman and/or man.

When entering to eat in some restaurants,

I've been told to sit in the back.

"It's the owner," I'm told by the waitress, "Your face is Black."

Also hotels, I've been told, when in need of sleep,

"I'm very, very sorry, but we're filled this week."

I've been stopped at doors of clubs and confronted by some guards
"This is a private club, sir, you need a membership card."
I have graduated from colleges with a chosen degree
But the chances of getting the job I want is slim after they see Me.
We try to tell other countries we do not discriminate,
But I can't begin to count the years that I've been separate.
I've been accused of unlawful doings, though Innocent I be.
I've been taken from jails, mutilated or left hanging from some Tree.
I've tried to help alleviate this dense jungle of nationality fog
By advocating non-violence only to be bitten by dogs.
On sit-in demonstrations, I'm often thrown in jail.
I feel these are the steps I must take so I won't accept a bail.
While trying to buy a decent home, I found this to be corrupt
That once known I am a "Negro," automatically the price goes up.
And if I choose some school I prefer to attend
If not escorted by the "Federal Guards" I won't be permitted in.
I've been pushed around in every town which is unbearably hard,
But it never once discouraged me from winning Nobel Awards.
I've proven myself in every field once given a chance to do,
But still I have to be qualified, because the other facts haven't gotten through.
I've been a credit to this country from the Olympics to here in the Ring.
My feet are full of rhythm and my voice of harmony when I sing
I'm very conscientious and love doing things I feel
In other words, I have to say, I've been an ambassador of Good Will.
In view of this daily and rigorous toil,
I've left my blood on distant soil,

Trying to uphold this so-called "democracy,"

Yet experience all types of hypocrisy.

After passing years this should come to an end.

Let's practice humanity and release downtrodden men

By mending this wrong, we will understand

That Liberty and Justice for all can really exist in this land!

```
Week of September 7, 2006

Hey Joe: Do you think it's a good idea to live "in sin"
with someone before you marry them?

Jessica, Hollywood
```

I assume you mean "intimately." I consider it to be one heck of an honor for you to ask me a question of such magnitude. In this respect, we have something in common. Many times I have asked the advice of others in helping me to arrive at a fair determination. After weighing the pros and cons of the advice offered, I take full responsibility of providing the appropriate answer, which in your case is: no. Whether you realize it or not, as limited as my Bible knowledge is, you have touched upon a biblical subject — one stemming back to ancient history better than 2,000 years before America's existence.

According to the Bible, God laid down His laws after He sent Moses to Egypt to lead Israel out of bondage. It is clearly recorded in the Book of Exodus that after Moses accomplished this goal, he went up onto Mount Sinai to receive God's ten commandments, thus leaving Israel behind until his return. Upon returning, he found that the group had broken every commandment listed. After the compilation of the Bible, it was closed. Nothing was to be added nor taken away. Enclosed, in addition to the five books written by Moses, are many other books written by men the likes of Moses.

The Book of Genesis, along with the general makeup of Hebrew families, reveals the beginning of the story surrounding Adam and Eve. First Corinthians, Verse 7, sheds more insight into the question asked, which was very intelligent, especially when in search of truth. My turning to the Bible, which began over a year ago, stemmed from the same reason: I wanted to know the truth about the outcome of Pharaoh, a question not many preachers nor church members were able to answer. For this reason, I began reading the Bible for myself. Initially, Exodus was the book that struck my fancy. It related to this evil man called Pharaoh, who enslaved the Israelites.

Because of such control, God sent Moses to tell Pharaoh to "Let His people go." "His people" meant those who wanted to serve Him. Pharaoh refused his request. On several occasions Moses delivered the same message, only for Pharaoh to continue his defiance. Not until God exhibited His omnipotent power did Pharaoh concede — even then defying God until God killed him. However, the legacy left by Pharaoh did not faze the orchestrators of America. The system of slavery God destroyed in Egypt was renewed in America. I've often wondered if those who structured the country felt it was OK with God. If so, Hebrews 13:8 states, "Jesus Christ the same yesterday, and today, and forever."

America chose God; God did not choose America, though she had the opportunity to be what God wanted Israel to be, which was a holy nation. She flunked. Moses demonstrated what is called commitment by doing God's will. For every wrong committed, the Bible tells how it can be rectified. Matthew 7:8 says, "Ask, and it shall be given you; seek, and ye shall find; knock, and it shall be opened unto you." Most preachers aren't preaching the truth, they are preaching around it.

Week of September 14, 2006

Hey Joe: Did you happen to read the August 31 RFT story "Hang Tuft"? What did you think about it?
GEN.EX, St. Louis

At first notice, one would immediately surmise the phrase "Hang Tuft" is slang talk. The only difference is the word "tuft" versus "tough" (or "tuff"). But the former is the last name of Carolyn Tuft, a committed news reporter for the St. Louis Post-Dispatch, whose editors are out to hang her.

It all started with two 2005 investigative reports into the financial empire of televangelist Joyce Meyer. Tuft's stories followed the fight the ministry was having with Jefferson County Assessor Randy Holman to keep its $30 million headquarters tax-exempt. In June 2005 the Post-Dispatch punked out and apologized for the stories Tuft wrote, as if she was wrong. Following a suspension without pay, she was granted arbitration to prove her innocence, which now leads me to the Bible.

God spoke to Israel through Moses and Jesus. Both God and Jesus formed a split personality — God was a disciplinarian, Jesus an angel. God loathed anybody or anything that created competition for Him. Jesus was always personable. God and Moses, after leading Israel out of bondage in Egypt, received their thanks by the Israelites creating a golden calf to worship rather than God. Jesus was killed for standing up for righteousness.

In America people call the Bible "the Word." But there is no God, Jesus, Moses, Paul or Abraham to police these so-called pastors directly. They view God as Israel viewed the golden calf; many claim they were called by God. This is known to be a lie, because God made Moses do what He wanted him to do, even with Moses' reluctance.

Meyer has proven her godliness by using His name in vain to amass her earthly wealth. She controls it like Pharaoh controlled Egypt. Many so-called preachers follow suit in various ways, maybe because the only thing to police them is their own conscience. (And from all indications, it's in their appendix, and their appendix was removed.) In Hosea 4:6, God says, "My people are destroyed for lack of knowledge: because thou has rejected knowledge, I will also reject thee, that thou shall be no priest to me: seeing thou hast forgotten the law of thy God, I will also forget thy children."

Most preachers throughout America have never started from Genesis and walked parishioners through each proceeding book, so they could better understand. Instead they jump from book to book like a checkers game, carefully choosing book and verse to dramatize and emotionalize to such a pitch as to work their audiences into a frenzy. Carolyn Tuft should be glorified, the Post kicked by the wayside (and RFT writer Malcolm Gay should be congratulated for the magnificent way he detailed such a story).

Week of September 21, 2006
Hey Joe: Why aren't I married?
Sam Malone, St. Louis

This question brings back memories of a love affair I had at a very young age. My heart had gone all-out for a very attractive young lady in my hometown. Then word came from a buddy of mine that she was fooling around with a fellow from a neighboring township. Upon hearing this, it buckled my knees. I thought to myself that there was no way she could be doing this, as nice as she treated me.

Anyway, each time my buddy and I conversed, he always posed the question as to how my lady and I were doing. After a while, this began sticking in my craw. I became very suspicious of her but could never find anything she was doing wrong. Based upon this, the next time my buddy and I dealt with this subject, I told him not to bring this mumbo-jumbo to me again. He acknowledged my wish but he asked if I would do him a favor.

The favor was if I would go see the aunt of Miles Davis, the nation's greatest trumpeter. She supposedly was a fortune teller. My reply was, "Hell, naw. I don't believe in that kinda junk!"

Strangely, I found myself knocking at her door. I can't recall her last name, but it was Madame Something. After a warm welcome to her home, I found myself in a chair, explaining the reason I was there and all the things my buddy told me about my girl. After listening intently, she said the young lady I'd fallen in love with was the sweetest, most innocent person I would ever meet, and the only person I should worry about was me. I gladly paid her the $3 or $5 she charged and was on my merry way.

So happy was I that I decided to pay my girl a surprise visit. En route to see her, I picked up a love card for her, while waving and speaking to everybody who crossed my path. I finally arrived at her door. After a few knocks, the door opened and a guy came out so fast that he ran over me, knocking the love card one way and me the other. Following this encounter, I could better understand why Madame X told me I only had myself to worry about. From this point on, my buddy never heard about this, because I started ducking him.

Now, every time I see Sylvia Browne — the psychic who appears on The Montel Williams Show — I feel sorry for those people who ask her weird questions about their lives, which she addresses without knowing anything about them.

Getting back to your question: You gave me nothing to work with, just, "Why aren't I married?" Maybe you need Sylvia Browne. Otherwise, there are many reasons you are not married, such as bad breath, funky hygiene or maybe you have something against women. Or it could simply be that nobody wants you. Did you ever have an experience like mine? Check yourself. Nobody can answer your question better than you.

Week of July 26, 2006

Hey Joe: Do you think a sixteen-year-old girl should be allowed to marry that guy from the West Bank who she met on Myspace?

B. Costas, St. Louis

I think that a sixteen-year-old girl can do what she wants, provided that it is legal.

Hey Joe: What is your body fat index?

Mr. Mandel, Brentwood, California

I have no idea. But whatever it is, it's incorrect. I refuse to adhere to any medical TV ad that's supposedly a cure for it.

Hey Joe: Why does every network feel the need to add a female sports reporter to every coverage team? I originally thought it was to add diversity, but since they have pretty much fired every Black male sports reporter to make room for all the ditzy blond and/or Jewish female reporters they've hired, I would have to say that true diversity has nothing to do with it.

Lesley Mabrey, St. Louis

The "separate but equal" era should shed light on your question. In the first place, it was a lie. No matter what it was intended to mean, whites were not enslaved with Blacks. For this reason, the whole concept of it was destroyed. During post-bondage years, the real meaning surfaced with signs bearing the words "Colored/White," which directed both parties to their respective areas when patronizing public accommodations. These signs throughout the South left no doubt as to where their place was. Throughout the North, because of no such signs, Blacks had to guess what places would tolerate them. In other words, the signs represented a play on words.

Since you have excluded Black males from the jobs and focused upon white females, I have the right answers for you. During the Civil Rights Movement, when demonstrations applied pressure on white establishments to hire Blacks where they had never worked before, whites scrutinized Black applicants until they found the kind of Black that was thought to be acceptable. Because of this, many Blacks whose applications more than proved their capabilities retaliated by calling the Blacks they employed "tokens." Subsequently, they joked among themselves by saying, "If you're white, you're right; if you're brown, stick around; but if you're Black, get back." In reference to the white females, the late, great Black comedian Jackie "Moms" Mabley made it more understandable. Standing before the mirror primping one day, she said, "Mirror, mirror on the wall, who is the fairest of us all?" The mirror answered by saying, "Snow White, and don't you forget it." Blacks are yet being played upon by such sayings as "America the melting pot," "multicultural society," "minority," "diverse" and the like.

```
Week of June 28, 2006
Hey Joe: The only thing bigger in baseball than steroids
is my ego. Are egos all that bad? Did you like Muhammad
Ali?
"M-Brad", Oakland, California
```

    Not at first. But here's a poem I wrote about him some 40 years ago:

February twenty-fifth of sixty-four

Is the night for young Cassius to hit the floor.

He'd bragged about being the Champ at twenty-one

But a year has passed and the time had come.

He screamed and hollered until no one could rest,

Trying to make people believe he was the best.

He got so cocky he would predict the round

Of the fighters he fought and when they would go down.

He called them "bums" and slandered their names,

While proclaiming he was the greatest fighter in the game.

He made statement after statement without a slip,

And he was dubbed by sportswriters as "The Louisville Lip."

He beat "Aging Archie," who was worn and aching,

Ducked Zora Folley, Williams and Eddie Machen.

His campaign was great to gain him fame,

But his ability wouldn't let him live up to the name.

He called Sonny Liston "The Big Ugly Bear,"

Although Sonny was champ and really didn't care.

Sonny used him as Chester who plays with Matt Dillon

Letting Clay have the show while he made a million.

Now it's Sonny's night to have some fun,

His intentions are to put Clay to rest in one.

When in mid-ring with Clay, Sonny stood and stared

And could tell right away that the "Lip" was scared.

Clay's pockets will be crammed with money from the fight,

But he wonders if he has really treated the Champion right.

If all those words that were said, he could eat.

He has talked himself into boxing's largest gate,

But if Sonny scarred his face, that he would hate.

He had ridiculed Sonny and called him a tramp

But was now facing the man who would be our greatest champ.

Many, many people were curious to know

What kind of fighter to Liston Clay will show

Will he try to outslug him or turn on the fan

When he realizes he's in the ring with a dangerous man?

How happy I am the night has come

Because I have predicted Clay will go in one.

He will get his dream and a very large fee.

If he gets by the first — I say no later than three.

I wish him success and all kinds of luck

Although he is educated in making a buck.

But on his way back to his home in the South,

He's learned fighting is serious and not all mouth.

His talents aren't limited exactly to the ring.

He writes a little poetry and, I hear, he can sing.

Hang on to your money and you can leave these alone.

So don't be disappointed about the Heavyweight throne.

```
Week of October 12, 2006
Hey Joe: My boyfriend's parents are coming into town for
a week. They've never been to St. Louis, and I'm trying to
think of things to do with them. Any ideas? Would a trip
to East St. Louis be worthwhile?
Sally O'Single, St. Louis
```

Being that Blacks and whites are products of a so-called separate-but-equal society, it would be difficult for me to answer this question without some form of clarification. Based upon the way it is asked, I take for granted you are white. The reason being is that, historically, Missouri has been in the limelight as a so-called slave state. And seemingly you feel more comfortable about your boyfriend's parents coming to St. Louis, although you say they've never been there before. In reference to East St. Louis, because of it being predominately Black, you seem to feel a bit doubtful about it.

However, prior to East St. Louis becoming a mostly Black community, it was like any other city or town in both the North or South regarding treatment of Blacks. Those in East St. Louis, who lived in areas called the "colored section," were forbidden to patronize white movies or hotels, couldn't patronize yellow cabs or, in short, anything that intermingled the two races. The only difference between the North and the South was that Blacks in the South knew where they stood regarding public transportation and the like, but most places in the North, they had to guess. Politically, as far back as I can recall in East St. Louis, Blacks could only get as high as precinct committeemen for both national parties. But it must be remembered that this city was the scene of the 1917 Race Riot.

During the '60s, however, when Blacks started moving from the colored section into areas previously dominated by whites, "white flight" took place. By the time the city elected its first Black mayor in the early 1970s, it was financially strapped. From this point on, it continued to spiral downward. Though at the time East St. Louis upheld the separate-but-equal law, other towns in Illinois, such as Anna, Red Bud and Granite City, had their own ways of dealing with Blacks.

The name "Anna," it is said, is an abbreviation for "Ain't No Niggers Allowed!" In Red Bud, a sign was supposedly posted bearing the words, "Niggers, if you can read...run! If you can't read...run anyway!" Although Blacks shopped and did domestic work in Granite City, they went there with the idea of not letting dark catch them there. Regarding the part of your question which asked if a trip to East St. Louis be worthwhile — well, East St. Louis would be just as worthwhile as St. Louis, because both have tourist attractions. Gateway Racetrack and the Casino Queen are both on the east side. In fact, one is located in East St. Louis and the other is partially located there. And don't overlook the golf course, which is located nearby in Madison, Illinois.

```
Week of July 20, 2006
Hey Joe: What's your definition of success?
Li'l "Yusey" M., St. Louis
```

I think it's this poem given to me some 30 years ago; the author is unknown:

A smile that time shall not erase, and a song within your heart;

The courage to meet life face-to-face and the will to do your part;

The strength to hold on when the going's tough and clouds are as dark as night;

The confidence never to cry "enough," the grit to stand up to the fight.

The faith to believe in your fellow man and the sense to protect you from guile;

The spirit that says, "I will" and "I can." The mind that does things worthwhile.

The charity that kindness gives and a cheering word for a dole;

The hope unconquerable that lives in an indomitable soul.

No matter what the score may be, it needs no more, no less...

You shall have won to victory and sought and found success!

To some, success means money, but what shall money avail?

The gold of Midas shall not abide us when we come to the end of the trail.

We are all like birds of passage, flying, soaring and roaming,

Winging away 'til the passing of day brings us to our last rest, homing.

Then why all the striving and struggles? Peace, avarice, poisons and blunts.

Remember this thought: Love cannot be bought, and we only pass this way once.

Success! A kind word in the giving; a smile as we go on our way.

The good we can do as we're passing through to bring happiness today.

These are the only efforts that shall stand the final test.

These He shall weigh on the final day, and He shall discard the rest.

No! Success lies not in the gaining all for yourself while you live.

The REAL success, or I miss my guess, depends on what you give.

```
Hey Joe: What's your favorite column in the Riverfront
Times?
Malcolm Gay, St. Louis
```

It isn't a column, but I love Tom Tomorrow's This Modern World cartoons because they are so outspokenly truthful.

```
Hey Joe: I cheated on my wife with both of her sisters.
Should I tell her, or should I just enjoy the ride?
Matty McDuke, Swansea, Illinois
```

Ordinarily I would say let your conscience be your guide. Obviously, though, based upon what is stated, you don't have a conscience. Therefore, why hurt your wife deeper? Just try to change your ways and hopefully allow time to heal all wounds.

```
Week of August 10, 2006
Hey Joe: You're referred to as "Prince" Joe. When I listen
to baseball games on the radio, that Shannon fellow re-
fers to Pujols as "Sir" Albert. Wouldn't "Prince Albert"
be catchier? Were there any Prince Alberts in your Negro
League locker room?
Pierce Weiner, St. Louis
```

Although I'm no Mike Shannon admirer, I think he made the right choice in calling Pujols "Sir Albert." Ever hear of this case where this guy has filed a multimillion-dollar lawsuit because he says people are mistaking him for Michael Jordan (I see no resemblance there)? Well, there's no resemblance between Pujols and the Prince Albert tobacco company. But a lawsuit could certainly generate publicity for the tobacco industry. Greed seems to dominate our lives today. No, there was no

PRINCOIRS

Prince Albert in Negro League locker rooms.

Hey Joe: Do you think a former prison chef or deli manager could, in a few months' time, raise his or her culinary game to the point where he or she could assume the reins of a five-star restaurant in Vegas?
Gordon Ramsay, Los Angeles, California

> Yes, if they had enough funds for advertisement. Aunt Jemima's pancakes and Uncle Ben's rice did it, although they had no part of the advertising process. Their thing was a creation of someone else.

Hey Joe: It's hotter than a deep-fried turkey and we got no a/c. I say mass quantities of iced-down Busch Light make it easier to fall asleep. The wife disagrees — right upside my head. Any tips on staying cool?
Joe Sixpack, Pontoon Beach, Illinois

> During the mid-'40s, the late Harry Caray was the radio broadcaster for St. Louis Cardinals baseball games. During the same period of time, an alcoholic beverage named Griesedieck, which he advertised, was among the area's most popular beers. Caray had a thing of saying "Holy cow!" behind every exciting play or occasion that took place during the course of a game. Unfortunately, due to some unknown reason, he and his wife parted ways. So the standing joke among people concerning their breakup was that there was too much "holy cow" and not enough Griesedieck.
>
> In answer to your question, the fact that your wife went upside your head suggests that from now on, no matter how hot it gets, you should keep your mouth closed. Or, in slang terminology: stay cool.

Hey Joe: Where all de white women at?
Cleavon Little, Squaw Tit, New Mexico

> Even Mortimer Snerd wouldn't have submitted such a question. Regarding "de white women," my answer is: "Damned if I know!!!"

Hey Joe: I'm what you call a Latino. I don't look like a Negro. Sometimes I watch baseball and I think a player is a Negro, but no, he's Latino, too. And he's pretty good! What's your take on the Latino baseball player? Is Latino the nuevo negro? Or are the Latinos and Negroes just better players than the white guys?

Jesús, Hazelwood

> I just became a legal immigrant myself. What about you?! If you are in doubt about your nationality, check to see whether you are in the majority or minority. In reference to baseball, had there been no Negro League, most Latinos would have been locked out of the white baseball leagues. I suggest you decide for yourself about who are the best baseball players.

Hey Joe: One of my friends just got engaged and asked me to be in her wedding. I think her fiancé is an ass and that they shouldn't get married at all. Most of our friends feel the same way. Should I tell my friend how I feel – and risk losing her friendship – or should I shut up and be in the wedding?

Carry & Mike Cox, Los Angeles

> Find yourself a way out of the situation and allow your friend to find out herself about the man she plans to marry. This way, you maintain your friendship.

Hey Joe: In answering a recent question, you wrote, "Although I'm no Mike Shannon admirer...." Whatever your problem with Mike Shannon, couldn't you leave it alone, given what he's going through these days? (He's been absent from the Cardinals broadcasts because his wife is battling cancer.)

A Mike Shannon Admirer, Iowa

> I'm very sorry to hear that Shannon is undergoing such a stressful period in his life. However, so I can make myself perfectly clear on that issue, I'll tell the whole story about my truthful feelings. I haven't cared for a Car-

dinal broadcasting team since the days of Gabby Street (nicknamed "The Old Sarge"), France Locke, Dizzy Dean and Harry Caray. I'm sick of these other jokers making gods of the Cardinals and some of their broadcasters. Had you not responded in the way you did, then it wouldn't have reached this point.

Week of August 17, 2006

Hey Joe: What do you think of the Cardinals' addition of Ronnie Belliard – can he help them lick the competition in the NL Central? And what's the deal with the dude's tongue when he comes to bat? Ever seen anything like that?

Colonel Angus, Paducah, Kentucky

A sandlot player would have fared just as well. The National League Central has proven to be just a bunch of patsies. In fact, any team winning the National League pennant awaits their turn to get an American League butt-whippin'. As for Belliard's tongue, I've never paid any attention.

Week of October 19, 2006

Hey Joe: Lil' Bow Wow is my favorite rapper. Who's yours?

T'Asia Mandesa, St. Louis

I'm not too familiar with rappers. I do know they are very creative, but I've never been able to understand everything they are saying. That's something that youngsters can pick up immediately and afterwards repeat the words verbatim. Though for some reason I really like Snoop Dogg. I've seen him several times on television, appearing on Jay Leno and Jimmy Kimmel. I find him to be quite amusing. I also hold Nelly in high regard. I follow his contributions to the inner city and think they're very thoughtful.

But most well-known rap artists have also proven to be shrewd business people. I am so glad I learned this, because prior I was turned off by the derogatory statements directed toward women. Devoid of this, their method of devising such entertainment is the mark of a genius. But rap enthusiasts must remember that everybody can't be a rapper but most can become geniuses in school. Therefore, if you can't become successful in one category, you definitely can succeed in the other.

Now, you say you like Bow Wow, or as I understand it, "Lil' Doggy Bow Wow." There is nothing in the world wrong with that, provided that he isn't using slanderous sayings against women and/or using profane language. Imagine you reaching the height of Bow Wow without the necessary schooling to protect your finances. Then in all probability you would have to pay someone to do these things. And if a person isn't trustworthy, there is a chance you might end up broke. This is the situation Bow Wow could experience had he not prepared himself academically. The same holds true for celebrities in all walks of life.

At your age, if you are able to follow the words of Bow Wow, you can do likewise with schoolwork. Nothing beats knowledge, and once you become successful, having knowledge makes it better. I always keep in mind this saying: "A wise old bird who lived in a tree, the less he heard, the more he would see. The more he would see, the less he heard. That's why he lived to be a wise old bird."

In the world in which we live today, you must be wise in order to survive. This is due to its competitiveness. The competition usually boils down to jobs, and without a job, it is very difficult to survive. Therefore, it is essential that you get academically prepared. In these days, a high school diploma is required to land a job digging holes. The more technology advances, the more difficult it is to find a job. As a result, it seems the more knowledge gained, the more that's needed to escape the process of elimination.

`Week of October 26, 2006`

`Hey Joe: You say you don't really care about baseball anymore. Why's that?`

`Joe, St. Louis`

Baseball was never my thing — not even after becoming a member of the Memphis Red Sox in the Negro Leagues. I played it because the Negro Leagues gave me the opportunity to travel far and wide throughout America. What I mean about it never being "my thing" is that I did not eat it and sleep it, like I have seen and heard so many other guys do. I could take it or leave it.

My thing at the time was stickball, a game played with the long handles of old mops and brooms used as bats. With these, we had three choices of ball-like objects to swing at. They were a rubber ball, small Pet milk can or tops from beer or soda-pop bottles. The latter game was called "tops." With the rubber ball, no catcher's mask was necessary. Usually two or three guys played it at the same time. Imagine: playing games like this when on both sides of the Mississippi River and in other areas, semi-pro baseball teams were in abundance.

In addition to being "hooked" on stickball, the same applied to twelve-inch fast-pitch softball, a game I played until after Jackie Robinson joined the Dodgers. Prior to this occurrence, I followed baseball on the radio and even attended games at Sportsman's Park for free, as a knotholer. I was never enthused about paying to see a game, and if I did, it was after Blacks became a part of it. My previous idea concerning the game was that it was off-limits to Blacks. Not until joining Memphis did I become educated about the great history of the Negro Leagues.

The beginning of it commenced when I began meeting great players like Willie Wells and Oscar Charleston. Baseball was so far out of my mind at a young age that I was oblivious to the great Black players and teams right across the bridge from me. After my baseball career, not in my wildest dreams did I suspect that a few decades later the Negro Leagues Baseball Museum would emerge. From this humble beginning, pensions would be eventually given to former players, which highlighted the league's existence. The contribution stemmed from the Major Leagues.

From the initial group of men who engaged in this historical undertaking, one was named John "Buck" O'Neil. He headed the Negro League banner. With a spokesman's persona, he carried the message about the Negro Leagues across America. He emphasized the great stars of the league. He spoke of how Blacks and whites worked together back then, when the country said it was forbidden. Buck left no stone unturned. He generated love and was loved.

So loved was he, that dislike throughout America was voiced in many different forms about him not being elected to the Baseball Hall of Fame. Buck left us recently, hopefully to arrive at a Heavenly home. Since I've known Buck, I can think of but two milestones he fell short of: the Baseball Hall of Fame and ensuring that every former Negro Leaguer received a baseball pension.

My personal feeling: I'm sure that one day he will be voted into baseball's Hall of Fame, and I am also sure that Bud Selig (unless he changes his mind about giving former Negro Leaguers pensions) will live in the Hall of Shame for cutting short the history of the Negro Leagues by refusing to give pensions to all former players.

Week of September 14, 2005

Hey Joe: Ted "Double Duty" Radcliffe died August 11 here in Chicago at the ripe age of 103. As you know, Radcliffe earned his nickname by playing both pitcher and catcher -- sometimes on the same day. Did you ever play against him? Can you give us a story about him that we can't find in his obituary page?

Thomas Francis, Chicago, Illinois

Oftentimes I've wondered: "Who didn't know 'Double-Duty'?" Because wherever he landed, his mark was always left there. Regarding me playing against him -- in all honesty, I did. But at the time, he was old as dirt. Such an historical moment occurred in July of 1950. Information documenting the occasion was contained in a newspaper, which I received recently from South Bend, Indiana. Found in a section of its sports column, among other sports activities of the day, were two box scores of a baseball contest between the Memphis Red Sox and the Chicago American Giants. Revealed was that "Duty" went two for five and I did likewise for Memphis in a game we won 10 to 4.

Before that game, which was my first time playing against the Chicago American Giants, I was completely unfamiliar with "Double-Duty." Obviously, especially after the game, he remembered me. Upon his team's visit to Memphis, he found my room at Martin's Stadium and informed me that the New York Giants had purchased the contract of Willie Mays from the Birmingham Black Barons. He then asked me to come with him to Canada. "Duty," at his advanced age then, joined by numerous other Black players, was representative of enormous durability. Had Jackie Robinson not joined the Dodgers at age 29, which created positions for Blacks in the white baseball system, players like myself -- unless very special -- would've caught particular hell trying to land a job in the Negro Leagues. These guys were forerunners to guys like Julio Franco, the Atlanta Braves first baseman.

Hey Joe: What is your opinion on the designated hitter?
J. Marsh, Neola, Iowa

Pinch hitters in certain instances have been a lifelong component of baseball. But I've known of pitchers and regular players that took being lifted for a pinch hitter as a personal insult. Since baseball has become so dramatically streamlined, showbiz is the name of the game. However, unlike most original Negro Leaguers who played well beyond their youthful years, designated hitters -- in reference to money -- make more for doing less.

Week of September 21, 2005

Hey Joe: In light of the current gasoline crisis and the abandonment of the urban core by affluent whites and Blacks alike, do you think suburban carpetbaggers who enter the city for sporting events and concerts should be charged a toll at the city limits, with the toll money being returned to the city's crumbling tax base?
David Brooks, New York, New York

I take for granted the city you speak of is New Orleans. If so, seemingly I have this penchant of daydreaming for the best. I did it every Sunday when I was a little boy, while gazing at the pictures of Christ and the beautiful scenery surrounding Him, which was displayed in the pages of my Sunday school pamphlet. I wished that I was there with Him. I had no such adoration for most preachers, nor was I a student of the Bible. During recent months, however, because of the gigantic commercialization of God for money by big-time Black and white TV evangelists, I decided to study the Bible for myself. For some strange reason, I became imbued with the hymn, "Go Down Moses, Way Down in Egypt land/Tell Ol' Pharaoh to Let My People Go." With this song in mind, I delved into the Book of Exodus. My finding: God killed Pharaoh for upholding separatism between Egypt and Israel and for constantly going back on his promises to end it.

In the wake of Hurricane Katrina, I've constantly daydreamed that it is only a nightmare. Though when the news first broke, and I saw all of that water, I thought about many things -- the foremost being Pharaoh. I visualized him and his army perishing in the Red Sea, especially his army because of following the fool. When the blind lead the blind, they all fall in the ditch. Pharaoh, whose spoken word of righteousness was absolutely no good, violated the three principles of God's Law. They were: There shall be no other gods before me, love and obedience. In doing so he sealed his own doom.

In following the national TV coverage of the event, I saw two preachers, one Black and the other white, announcing to the nation that all denominations were coming together for a common cause, when in fact the church is the country's single most segregated institution. I feel that such fence-straddling clergymen should clean their own house to set examples, while millions of people from all walks of life are left to exhibit Christian traits, whether in church or out, void of political motive. Benevolent contributors will demonstrate that in spite of some coming on slave ships -- while others came on the Mayflower -- Hurricane Katrina has proven that we are in the same boat now. Something that Larry Rice, a white St. Louis minister, has strived to do for years.

```
Week of October 12, 2005

Hey Joe: What about the statement of Bill Bennett in re-
gard to aborting Black children as a means to reducing the
crime rate?

Rev. James A. Buckels Sr., Madison, Illinois
```

Had Minister Louis Farrakhan indicated -- even remotely -- that the best way to eradicate racism in America was to murder all white babies, white preachers and the white community -- along with most Black preachers and most residents of the Black community -- would have been ready to castrate him both verbally and physically. Bennett, in all probability, takes a front seat in a church pew every Sunday of the Evangelical faith, or that of Pat Robertson. Both of their attitudes coincide with bondage.

Bondage put the "C" in crime. Young Black men and women were brought to America for the purpose of -- in addition to millions of other things -- reproducing children. If not, then why weren't women left alone? Without reproduction, bondage would've died out. Up until now it has been America's worst crime. Every criminal offense listed in America's law books has been committed during bondage, including laws listed in the Ten Commandments. Had the Bible been followed from the beginning, all crimes committed against it (and Blacks) would never have occurred. Pastors of the white church, during 300 years of Black enslavement, taught their parishioners to seek salvation through God but hate Blacks because they were children of Ham -- a pattern followed for generations. But over the same period of time, millions of godly white members refused to buy that jazz.

In both cases, educationally and Christianity-wise, Blacks have been mentally devastated. Educationally, they have been denied access to their greatness. In Christianity, they have been misguided. The beginning of both commenced during bondage, where their case was similar to Israel in Egypt regarding serving God, and continuing through the death of President Abraham Lincoln. By the time the Bible reached the hands of Black preachers, they were referred to as "jack legs" -- in other words, "ignorant."

Had there been no bondage, America would be without a history (i.e., the Civil War, civil rights, Dred Scott, Abraham Lincoln, Dr. Martin Luther King Jr., etc.). Then America would have been an Aryan nation. Then, in addition to Blacks' countless contributions to America, there wouldn't have been any Black babies to grow up into men like the Tuskegee Airmen, Jesse Owens and Joe Louis, who teamed together to save America's name and destroy Hitler's ambition. Wake up, Bill Bennett, and smell the roses -- you and Pat Robertson.

Week of October 19, 2005

Hey Joe: One of my frustrations with the classy strip joints in Sauget is that none of the strippers will finish me off, even for a C-note. I'm told that the ladies of Brooklyn might be more willing to go the distance, especially at massage parlors. Can you verify this? And what is the general opinion of Brooklyn's adult-entertainment presence among longtime residents such as yourself?

Hugh Jardon, Centreville

> Guys like you make these places possible. Brooklyn, a community of 2,600 people, is the most historical community in America. Nearly five decades past, Black children from communities such as East Carondelet, Centreville and the like were bused from their hometowns through East St. Louis to Brooklyn and Venice, where they attended Lovejoy and Lincoln high schools because of being disallowed to attend white public schools. This meant crossing many railroad tracks along Route 3.
>
> Of Brooklyn's seven major east-west arteries, five bear names of presidents. Numerically, the north and south thoroughfares are Second, Third, Fourth, Fifth, Sixth and Seventh. Route 3 is Second Street. The town never had a First. Every street and block throughout the town -- including space behind railroad tracks -- was replete with a variety of houses and businesses. The phrase "separate but equal" as applied to Blacks in neighboring communities was unheard of in Brooklyn. There were no such junk words as "majority" and "minority." Although Blacks were in the majority, all residents were regarded as townspeople without regard to nationality. In addition to the town being surrounded by railroad tracks, it was also surrounded by American history.

Hey Joe: What are your thoughts on the Millions More Movement in Washington, D.C. this year?

Earl McDowell, East St. Louis

> Here's my answer: "MORE MILLIONS!!!"

Hey Joe: Did you ever play against my grandfather Jim "Lefty" LaMarque? He was a pitcher from the KC Monarchs. If so, was he tough to hit off of? I never got to talk much baseball with him before he passed away.

Thanks,

David LaMarque Smith, Ellisville, MO

> Yes, he certainly was difficult for me to hit, but many other guys experienced the same.

Week of January 19, 2006

Hey Joe: As far as you know, are the Negro Leagues and Major League Baseball working together to help promote Negro League history?

Mike Spatz, Ellicott City, Maryland

> Nationally, the only source I am aware of that currently promotes Negro League History is the Negro League Baseball Museum in Kansas City. If not for it, I am almost positive that the history displayed there wouldn't be available elsewhere. The only time Major League Baseball promotes the Negro League is when a former player — after having been denied the opportunity of performing in the white baseball league — is inducted into the Major League Baseball Hall of Fame in Cooperstown, which I regard as tokenism.
>
> Truth of the matter is, there was no Major League during the time of the Negro League's existence. There was only a white baseball league and a Negro league. The so-called Major League only became "major" after Negro Leaguers became a part of it. Shortly thereafter came the Negro League's demise: Thus an institution within the Black community was destroyed without remorse. White baseball moguls made every excuse conceivable for their destructive actions once their teams reaped benefits — claiming that the Negro League was in the zone of rackets because several Black team owners were policy kings — while at the same time overlooking the fact that the white baseball league was in the zone of racism.
>
> The only reparation I recall from MLB's destruction of the Negro League

was a few pensions to existing members, which took place in 1997 because Bud Selig said racism ended in 1947. Therefore, he and a group called the Baseball Assistance Team (BAT) provided yearly benefits of $10,000 to players who played up to then. Nothing could be more racist: an organization fronted by MLB coming together to hoodwink the American public as if their goal was to help former needy players, after Negro Leaguers not only made the white baseball league "major," but also big business.

The racist element about it is, after the 1947 cutoff date, Willie Mays, Ernie Banks and Hank Aaron have been used since to immortalize the greatness of the Baseball Hall of Fame, while overlooking players such as myself, who played against Mays and Banks. Due to them playing in the league during the '50s, every existing player from 1947 through the 1950s should be receiving a pension. In 2004 Bud Selig and BAT decided to handpick twenty more players for pensions and end the history of the Negro League in 1957. So rather than promote its history, MLB destroyed it.

Week of December 15, 2005

Hey Joe: As far as you know, are the Negro Leagues and Major League Baseball working together to help promote Negro League history? Or is the MLB trying to push it under the bed, to try and erase all the memories many have about the bad side of the Negro Leagues, like the racism and biased attitudes white people had for Black players?

Michael Spatz, Baltimore, Maryland

My baptism in racism occurred in 1950, shortly after the conclusion of the first and only Black baseball school, known as the Delta Negro Baseball School, held in Greenville, Mississippi, which I attended and which was conducted by Homer Curry, manager of the Memphis Red Sox.

Later, players that attended the school would become a part of the Red Sox spring-training season. During this phase Goose booked an exhibition game mainly between these players and a few regular members of the Red Sox. The game was billed as "The Memphis Red Sox vs. A Semi-Pro All-Star Team" and was played in a ballpark in a small Mississippi town.

The park was jammed with whites. All seats along the first-base line and behind home plate were labeled "For Whites Only." Seats near third base were designated as those for colored. Seated behind home plate was a white announcer. He related how proud the town was to bring "these two 'cullud' teams" of the "Nigra American League" there to play.

Scheduled to pitch and catch for the team billed as the Red Sox were two of the team's regular members; the same applied to the semi-pro all-stars. I was assigned to the Red Sox. Following the introduction of our opponents, the speaker began to call out the regular starting lineup. Lastly, he came to the pitcher and catcher, known as the battery. Our catcher stood six-foot-five, while our pitcher barely reached five-five. The announcer took full advantage of the situation to make a startling comment.

Suddenly, with a slight touch of humor in his voice, he regained the attention of the crowd. "Ladies and genel'men, the battery fo' the Memphis Red Sox tonight will be a big niggah catchin' and a li'l niggah pitchin,'" he said, adding, "y'all boys can play ball now."

The announcer's rude assessment set the mood for the evening. To make matters worse, a bat slipped out of one of our player's hands and hit a white man. He went down as if pole-axed. Blacks seated near third base exited the park by jumping the fence, because a Black man had hit a white man, albeit accidentally. This was the beginning of many such incidents during my baseball career.

Week of December 22, 2005

Hey Joe: Do you have stories about the differences between clowning and playing NLB teams? Some say this wasn't legitimate baseball, but my research indicates that it was simply a different way of approaching the game and earning the needed revenue to keep the team operating.

Kate Sutter, Lebanon

In 1950, when I joined the Memphis Red Sox, the Negro League was composed of ten teams. In addition to Memphis, there were the Kansas City Monarchs, Cleveland Buckeyes, Chicago American Giants, Birmingham

Black Barons, Baltimore Elite Giants, New York Cubans, Philadelphia Stars, Houston Eagles (who later became the New Orleans Eagles) and the Indianapolis Clowns. The Clowns and Monarchs had white owners.

By 1953 the league had dwindled to four teams. In 1955 the Indianapolis Clowns abandoned the league to become independent. Later they traveled with the New York Black Yankees — similar to the Harlem Globetrotters' relationship with the Washington Generals.

As great as the players were, Black owners shared the same likeness, especially in reference to business. At the time of Black owners' existence, they filled teams with the money. The Black baseball league was as legitimate as the white baseball league. The only illegitimacy was prohibiting Blacks' inclusion. Had this not been the case, Blacks would have invaded the white baseball league then, as they have the NBA and NFL. Not one time do I recall a Negro League baseball team parading up and down streets to attract fans to the ballpark, as was depicted in the movie The Bingo Long Traveling All-Stars & Motor Kings.

At a very early age, I was attracted to a radio program called Amos 'n Andy, a show in which two white men amassed a fortune by mimicking Blacks as ignorant, easy marks. I could hardly wait for the show to air so I could laugh at myself. Many Blacks did likewise, though there were others who were quite disenchanted. Most whites took this for granted. This seems to be the crux of the question, because of the name Indianapolis Clowns. Before I joined the Clowns in '55, all clowning was on the sidelines, similar to the Cardinals' Fredbird, which also pertained to white entertainers like Bobo Nickerson, Max Patkin and Ed Hamman. The only time infielders joined in the fun parade was during the famed "shadow ball act," which was faking infield practice without the ball.

Due to a serious injury that occurred when I played in a white league, I was unable to perform 100 percent, which I hoped to do once I joined the Clowns. Therefore, I undertook clowning while playing and originated many things seen in the majors today.

Week of December 8, 2005

Hey Joe: What do you think of the behavior of Terrell Owens of the Philadelphia Eagles?

Sean Breit, St. Louis

I'm a firm believer in practical sayings. I learned long ago that if I made my bed hard, I would have to lay in it. Owens is doing just that following his recent suspension. Frankly, I feel it should have come sooner.

For the past two seasons I've observed his selfishness. In more than one instance what happened to him was usually the outcome once the boundary is overstepped. Granted, he is one heck of a receiver, but not good enough to pass a ball to himself and then run fast enough to catch it. He seems to feel that each time the ball leaves the quarterback's hand, it should be coming to him. Hopefully, if he lands a job in the future, he will realize there are other receivers on the team.

Hey Joe: I grew up loving basketball and playing on a championship team. It gave me confidence for whatever came my way. What can we do to get our young kids more interested in sports, school and positive things?

Mike Henry, Maplewood

I imagine playing on a championship team was quite an experience. I've never been that fortunate, but I love the teamwork involved. I strive daily to promote the word "unity." Many decades back — before integration — sports were Black kids' motivator. Then came a group of college-trained kids who decided to tackle the system of racial injustice. They were joined by elementary and high school students, and together they did something positive.

As a result of their courage, every single establishment representative of Jim Crow-ism succumbed. Blacks found themselves enjoying jobs that were out of the question prior. And like Israel after being led out of Egypt, they went ape — eventually taking on the image of their captives. It's great to know that basketball and playing on a championship team gave you the confidence to overcome any obstacle.

As for the students, each day school administrators meet them, it should be with a smile, and they should be constantly reminded that it was young Blacks who changed the face of America in every facet. Maybe such flattery would provide the key to building their confidence, along with addressing their concerns. After all, each day they attend school, teachers are guaranteed a paycheck.

Week of January 12, 2006

Hey Joe: What do you make of the fact that two of the most popular Cardinals players, Reggie Sanders and Ray King – who, if I'm not mistaken, also happen to have been the club's only African-American players – are gone?
Larry "Doby" Gillis, Florissant

For many years now, since former Cardinal outfielder Curt Flood initiated the abolishment of the reserve clause, players have been shuffled from team to team. Regarding Tony La Russa's success as a World Series manager, I can only point to Oakland. It was because of this that he was brought to St. Louis, yet has failed to deliver in spite of Walt Jocketty's attempts to buy him a World Series.

In this respect, I am sympathetic towards the fans because they foot the bills while failing to realize they're the boss. Remember, back in 1947, it was mostly Black fans' support of Jackie Robinson (they jammed white baseball parks) that destroyed the Negro League. Fans are the employer and the team owner and players are the employees. In other words, once they grow tired of being used, they have the power to stop it.

At the time of the demise of the Negro League, it was Black America's third-largest enterprise; the other two were insurance businesses. However, due to Flood laying his career on the line to abolish the reserve clause — a document that gave white team owners the power to hold players indefinitely — free agency was born, propelling players from rags to riches.

Currently, every Major League roster has Blacks and Latinos, though before Robinson the Negro League was the only resource they had to play ball professionally. As a result, they are byproducts of the Negro League.

Their contributions to the game are unparalleled. Curt Flood not only demonstrated greatness as a player, but also as a humanitarian. This he did by spearheading the way for every player, regardless of nationality, to capitalize by earning millions. Until Black players stand in defense of the Negro League, I couldn't care less if they ever make a million.

As for Reggie Sanders and Ray King, they are prime examples of the Cardinals' biased past in relation to dealing with Blacks. Remember, it was the Cardinals who threatened to strike against Robinson if he was allowed to play. There is one thing I must say about King: He was right about voicing his opinion. It gave La Russa the opportunity he needed to cover his losing butt. I saw the beginning of his alibi when he jumped on the umpires in Houston, shortly before Pujols' game-winning home run. Other than be retained in St. Louis to become the game's winningest active manager, numerous Blacks and Latinos could accomplish what La Russa has done here — including Jose Oquendo, Ozzie Smith, Lou Brock and others.

```
Week of November 16, 2005
Hey Joe: I am curious about the treatment of African-
American people in your hometown during your professional
career.
Shermand Palmer, St. Louis
```

Brooklyn, in reference to everyone knowing one another, was forerunner to The Andy Griffith Show long before it became a TV hit. The town also had its share of Barney Fifes. There was no such thing as being read the Miranda Law. If a person was thought to have violated the law, that individual was going to jail, and — in most cases — that meant walking, because the town had no police car(s). One officer with several notches on his gun had no problem making arrests. So well known was he, he would send people to jail on their own and once they arrived there, he would tell them to tell the jailer that he said to lock them up. He never lost an offender.

This was the Brooklyn in which I grew up long before playing in the Negro League. Respect was the name of the game — the key words being "Mr." and "Mrs." Youngsters respected elders and vice versa, but this did not preclude violators. The town's only inkling concerning nationality was two of its drugstores. One was labeled "colored" and the other "white." People in the community had their choice. What they couldn't find in one, they got at the other. That's how business was conducted throughout the community.

However, Blacks received inferior treatment. Blacks lived in a different world. Employment stemmed from an assortment of businesses, which included grocery stores — owned by both Blacks and whites — nightclubs, barber shops, ice and coal sales, service stations and dry cleaners.

Although white mayors had presided over the town prior, during my growing up the community had a Black mayor. He was supervisor and school superintendent. During his tenure as superintendent, he converted Lovejoy Elementary into a high school. Prior to that, Brooklyn students had to travel to East St. Louis to attend Lincoln High. Brooklyn had two additional schools. My fondest memory of him was in 1953. Shortly after Ernie Banks joined the Chicago Cubs, the team visited St. Louis to play the Cardinals. Upon notifying the mayor, he sent his chauffeur-driven limousine to pick up Mr. Banks at the Chase Hotel. Along with Banks was Gene Baker. After they arrived at the school, classes were suspended in order for the students to congregate in the gym to meet both of them.

As time progressed, especially during the latter 1950s, jobs in the packing and steel industries began to close. A housing project was erected. Citizens began moving elsewhere and the tax base began to erode. Then came adult entertainment, followed by bad publicity, which hurt the town's name. Along with it, the 2,600 residents began to dwindle to the current population of 700.

```
Week of November 2, 2005
Hey Joe: What percentage of Major League ballplayers do
you think are gay? Back in the day, were you ever hesitant
to bend over and pick up the soap in the team shower?
Elroy "Toots" Dombrowski, Dupo, Illinois
```

Although we live in a society saturated with immoralities, I still believe in the word decency. Maybe the way I feel is: It isn't what you do but how you do it. Homosexuality, as defined in the American Heritage College Dictionary, is having a sexual orientation to persons of the same sex. Or a gay man or lesbian. But because I respect people as people, I try not to dig into their personal lives and on many occasions found myself defending people referred to as gays or lesbians against those expressing hate towards them.

Before the Civil Rights Movement, Blacks were Blacks and whites were whites. Such people of color were thrown into the same bag. The same applied to whites regarding "liberty and justice for all," which meant whites -- no matter what their sexual preference -- had access to everything available in America, while Blacks were denied most. By me being Black, I've felt the sting of hatred, as well as countless other degradations. Because of this, my heart has always gone out to those I feel are mistreated.

Then comes the Civil Rights Movement, which was designed to seek better treatment for Blacks. Subsequently, the majority gay and lesbian community sought to protest against being secretly isolated from society and moved to openly legalize their activities, as same-sex marriage partners. In this respect I say: To each his or her own -- but stand and fight independently. My dissatisfaction was that they used the Civil Rights Movement to enhance the possibility of this becoming a reality by promoting the idea that Blacks fought for their civil rights.

Blacks did not fight for sexual rights. They fought for the right of "liberty and justice for all." During the time I played ball, players were paired together in hotels and slept in the same bed. Had they entertained such fantasies, there was no need for showers or soap, etc. As for the percentage of gay men in the majors, the same as I have answered your question, I'm sure they would do likewise if asked.

```
Week of November 23, 2005

Hey Joe: Is it true Jackie Robinson proposed to your wife
before you were married to her?

Steven Grondalski, University City
```

Lu and I met in Birmingham, Alabama in 1958. At the time, Ed Steele

— her second cousin — was manager of Goose Tatum's Detroit Clowns, the team I played with. Formerly the Detroit Stars, the club had a long and glorious history in the Negro Leagues, playing against the league's most powerful franchises. Reece "Goose" Tatum, the original showman of the Harlem Globetrotters, was team owner.

My knowledge of Steele dates to 1950, when I played with the Memphis Red Sox and Steele played for the Birmingham Black Barons. On that Birmingham team was a young man named Willie Mays. Lu, as I was later to learn, attended many Black Barons games as a young high school girl.

Meanwhile, during Jackie Robinson's tenure with the Kansas City Monarchs, history was about to be written. But before becoming the first Black ballplayer in the Major Leagues, Robinson had already left a trail of history. At UCLA he starred in football, basketball, baseball and track. Later he became a lieutenant in the military. There one day, while riding a bus driven by a white civilian, he was ordered to take a seat in the rear. He refused — an incident that occurred because he was sitting beside his friend's wife, who was of a light complexion and thought to be white by the driver. For this disobedient act, he received a military court martial.

Robinson's refusal to take a back seat was his first step in spearheading what would later become known as the Civil Rights Movement. Therefore, Robinson predated both Ms. Rosa Parks and Dr. Martin Luther King Jr. by a decade. As the story goes, upon becoming a Dodger, Branch Rickey suggested that he marry his college sweetheart, Rachel. At the end of the 1947 season, Robinson and Roy Campanella — along with other Negro Leaguers — barnstormed in several southern cities, among them Birmingham. While there, Steele introduced Robinson and Campanella to Lu and several of her classmates.

In 1950, at Rickwood Field in Birmingham, the umpire became upset with my manager for protesting a call against one of my Memphis teammates. As a result, he beckoned for white policemen, who worked as security at the ballpark. Once at home plate, they demanded that my manager return to his third base coaching post. Because of his hesitancy, they commenced to beat him with billy clubs until blood streamed down his face, and afterward placed him under arrest. These officers were those of Bull Connor, the diehard racist commissioner whom Dr. King would face years later.

```
Week of November 30, 2005
Hey Joe: What are your thoughts on the salaries of
professional athletes?
Sean Breit, St. Louis
```

I wouldn't pay a ballplayer a million dollars if he strolled to the plate barehanded, stood there with his back to the pitcher, bent over with his cheeks spread and farted a ball out of the park. I say this particularly in reference to most Black baseball players, especially those who are unaware of how they got to where they are. I lay out a bit of history here, hopefully to open their eyes.

In reference to Blacks, the Negro Leagues was an employment agency. Team owners hired players, drivers and traveling secretaries that operated on the same level as the white baseball leagues. Most importantly, it was majority Black fans that made this organization work. Within the Black community, the Negro League was placed upon the same pedestal as any white team in a predominantly white community.

In spite of Jackie Robinson's greatness as a baseball player, had there not been a Negro League, his entry into professional baseball could have very well been delayed. After he joined the Dodgers' organization, however, the foundation of the once-powerful Negro Leagues began to collapse. Teams fell by the wayside. Players began to lose jobs. Traveling secretaries became smaller in number, and bus drivers who drove flexible buses — which were equivalent to Greyhounds — suffered job losses because the Greyhound lines did not employ Black drivers. Team owners were never financially rewarded for their enrichment of the white baseball leagues with Black baseball talent. There was a gigantic sacrifice on the part of all Blacks involved.

Recently, I spoke at Washington University at the invitation of Association of Black Students historian Antonio Rodriguez. Ill as I felt at the time, this remarkable young Black man refused to take "no" for an answer and even asked if I would accept $500 and spend the night prior in a hotel. I settled for $300 and no hotel. The $300 went to the people who made my visit possible. Prior to speaking there, I received an e-mail from a third-grade teacher in the St. Louis Public Schools. I was asked if I would speak to these young kids. "Regrettably," said the teacher, "the school district has no funds for these types of activities," which I thought to be despicable.

Before my appearance, I arranged for every student in the class to have two or three pictures of me. My parting words to those Black history-hungry youngsters were taken from Frederick Douglass: "Power concedes nothing without demand. It never has, it never will." In other words: Go after what you desire, no matter what complexion the opposition.

Week of November 9, 2005

Hey Joe: The past two World Series have featured American League teams that demolished their National League foes. To what do you attribute the AL's dominance - and, on the flip side, the NL's inferiority?

Jimmy, Houston, Texas

Although I am no avid baseball follower, I do enjoy watching it during postseason play. In recalling last year's series between Boston and St. Louis, the only difference between the two was Boston's combination of pitching and hitting. The same held true this year between Chicago and Houston.

Ever hear the saying, "Good pitching tops good hitting"? This was the case with St. Louis in successive years, first against Boston and then against Houston. Believe me, there are no inferior teams in either league. These guys are mostly millionaires, and on any given day, one team can beat the other. Remember the Florida Marlins' two World Series victories against American League teams?

During my earlier childhood, dynasties were the thing of the day. Teams such as the Yankees, Milwaukee Braves, etc. could remain powerful for years because of owners' control over the situation. Once free agency entered the picture, things changed. Owners were no longer able to retain players after a period of time. As a result, teams became more competitive because of big-pay involvement. But that did not always secure winners.

Case in point: the Yankees over the past two years.

The escalation of money to purchase players has proven fatal to the St. Louis Cardinals. For the past two years, they have run away with their division. In spite of having some of the best players in baseball — and this year a fifteen-game lead over the Houston Astros — and although it was thought that they would be in the World Series, they couldn't get past Houston after demolishing San Diego. But that's the size of the game. This is why I mentioned the Florida Marlins.

Week of October 26, 2005

Hey Joe: One of my frustrations with the classy strip joints in Sauget is that none of the strippers will finish me off, even for a C-note. I'm told that the ladies of Brooklyn might be more willing to go the distance, especially at massage parlors. Can you verify this? And what is the general opinion of Brooklyn's adult-entertainment presence among longtime residents such as yourself?

Hugh Jardon, Centreville

Route 3 is a meandering state highway. Beginning at the Kentucky border, it works its way along the Mississippi River through many counties and municipalities before arriving at local places like Dupo, East Carondelet, Centreville, Sauget and East St. Louis, as it heads through National City, Brooklyn, Venice, Madison and Granite City, etc. en route to its terminus at Alton some twenty-odd miles from Brooklyn. Brooklyn was surrounded by railroad tracks -- the most vivid being the track bearing embankments that surround it. Similar to a horseshoe, the tracks engulfed the community and portions of Venice at varying heights, until the town was dwarfed.

When the Mississippi River is mentioned, most people think of Mark Twain. I beg to differ. I think of it as the Atlantic Ocean, when Blacks were brought to America in chains. I think of National City, home of three of the country's largest meat packers. Here, cattle was brought from Kentucky and Missouri, etc. to be weighed and placed on the auction block to be sold to the highest bidder, like Blacks during bondage. Because the owners of these stockyards hired Blacks as cheap labor, the 1917 race riot in East St. Louis ignited. Across the Mississippi, Dred Scott fought for his freedom. In Brooklyn, the Methodist Church was a haven for runaway Blacks from Missouri to escape bondage. Lovejoy School bears the name of Elijah P. Lovejoy, abolitionist of Alton, Illinois.

Presidents Abe Lincoln and Franklin D. Roosevelt made great strides in helping Blacks. For years Blacks have been Republicans and now Democrats. Blacks, therefore, have been the source of their "P.O.L.I.T.I.C.S": People Oppressed, Livelihoodless, Isolated, Tormented, Insignificant and Castrated Subjects. Brooklyn, being America's first Black town, is owed a debt by both national parties. By distinguishing the word "politics," this should answer the adult-entertainment question.

```
Week of January 26, 2006
Hey Joe: Do you think rap music is inferior to '60s and
'70s R&B soul, both in terms of sociopolitical relevance
and musicianship?
Wilson, The Promised Land
```

Personally, I'm not too familiar with rapping, although it is not uncommon. During the '70s, I remember a group called the Last Poets. As far as I am concerned, they energized Black America at the time. I truly loved them. Maybe my ignorance concerning future rappers stems from not being able to understand exactly what is being said. And it can't be said that I haven't really tried hard. But there is one thing that can be said about their musical inclination, and that is their product is not inferior. Believe me, most rap artists are geniuses.

For the better part of my life, I grew up loving music, period. I was unable to distinguish between blues or any other sentimental songs. During the '50s and '60s, not only was I fascinated with Black performers' talent but also their stylish dress. Most revealing was the emergence of a white singer, Elvis Presley, who — after an abbreviated appearance on the Ed Sullivan Show — was put down by a sizable majority (white society) because of emulating Blacks. Later he became the pride and joy of white America.

However, many Black recording stars — because of dependence upon white recording studios — wound up their careers short of money.

The brilliance demonstrated by most Black rappers is their ability to see through a society waiting to put them down. Therefore, they've exhibited talent and formed their own studios. From their success, many became businessmen by peddling lines of clothing, etc. For example, St. Louis' Nelly is a businessman deluxe. He has yet to put down the inner city and, as a rapper, he has made his presence felt.

Over a period of years, I've seen several rappers interviewed by hosts, such as Jimmy Kimmel, Jay Leno and David Letterman. Not once have I heard one back off political statements that were made. It's about time that we all should do likewise. After all, I have often heard the words of a patriotic song, which includes lyrics such as "This land is your land, this land is my land."

Week of March 9, 2006

Hey Joe: Do you think Shani Davis was unsportsmanlike in the Olympics by not competing in the team speed-skating event and snubbing the media?

Norm dePlume, High Ridge

No matter how terrible slavery was, it overwhelmingly generated white support, though all Southern whites did not own plantations or so-called slaves, and some did not agree with the slavery system. From this group was born the phrase "nigger lover," which applied to any white voicing sentiments favorable to Blacks. Abe Lincoln was killed because of this reason and was later to become the most revered president in American history. The word "nigger," however, failed to desist.

I say this to shed light on the controversy surrounding Black speed-skater Shani Davis and Chad Hedrick, a white speed skater. According to a sensational story written by Michelle Kaufman of the Miami Herald, the dispute stemmed from Davis' decision to sit out of the team-pursuit event, which included Hedrick, in order to concentrate on winning his first individual race. This was viewed by many as a selfish, unpatriotic move designed to undermine Hedrick's quest to win five golds, and perhaps kept the Americans from another medal.

"It can get lonely being the only Black person in an entire sport, hearing snickers on the starting line, opening your website to find racist messages, always feeling just a little out of place," Kaufman wrote. Said Shani of his own Web site: "There are a lot of derogatory remarks in the comments, wishing me to break my leg and fall down, using the N word, a lot of ignorance out there."

He is right — beginning with the founding fathers when they contrived the Declaration of Independence and the Constitution, both seething of hatred. But I would advise Shani: Never be ashamed to speak the word "nigger." If so, you've acknowledged defeat.

The term meant to depict Blacks in the lowest form possible. Those who derived it didn't have the slightest inkling that they were referring to the greatest psychologists to ever set foot upon American soil. And their education didn't come via Harvard or Yale. It came from actual experience (the kind acquired at these schools and others is purely conjecture). Anyone desirous of earning an authentic Ph.D. in psychology should consult Blacks' assistance.

Blacks mastered the art of psychology by appeasing their oppressor. Saying "yes" when really meaning "no" and vice versa. This, along with a multitude of other strategies, entailed a loss of principle in order to survive. That's what is called psychology. In other words, it takes a wise man to play the role of a fool. With the assistance of whites (called "nigger lovers") who refused to be what other whites wanted them to be, wisdom has guided Blacks from bondage up to the time of Shani Davis — whether a so-called slave, colored, Negro, Black, African American or nigger.

I say right on, Shani. Speak your piece. Don't be suckered by that unpatriotic jazz. For every contribution whites have made to America, Blacks have been there, done that. And the beat goes on.

```
Week of November 2, 2006
Hey Joe: Have you seen the new Chevy commercial? Do you
```

think it's wrong for Chevy to use icons like Rosa Parks and Martin Luther King to sell pickup trucks? The spot also features images from the Vietnam War and 9/11.
John "Don't Call Me Cougar," Seymour, Indiana

> I've seen it several times. Since you mentioned it, though, it has really made me think. Prior to, however, I ignored it by seeing and by not seeing. Since then I've wondered how it is possible for a capitalistic society and a so-called Christian society to walk together hand-in-hand. The only answer I can arrive at is that both are corrupt. Take, for instance, this commercial. Just the other day a TV reporter remarked that more bodies from 9/11 had been found. Before this discovery, the bodies had been given up on and workers at the site were preparing to give them a concrete burial, like the one rumored about Jimmy Hoffa. Imagine the nightmare relatives were forced to relive turned into a commercial with intent to sell a damn truck!

> At 9/11's outbreak, Bush seized the opportunity to play his politics, standing by the demolished World Trade Center, making promises to avenge the foul play. Since that horrible occasion, much grief has followed. Protesters against his conflict in Iraq have been dubbed "unpatriotic" — the most vivid being Ms. Cindy Sheehan, mother of a fallen soldier, who voiced her feeling against the Iraq conflict.

> Sadly, the picture of Ms. Rosa Parks riding the bus and Dr. Martin Luther King speaking sparked the documentary Eyes on the Prize, a film that chronicled a people's fight for equality while facing dogs, cattle prods and fire hoses. For his role in the affair, King would be classified as a communist. He'd later speak out against the war in Vietnam and die. During the filming of Eyes on the Prize, buried bodies of civil rights workers Andrew Goodman, Michael Schwerner and James Chaney were found in Philadelphia, Mississippi. This, after taking a stand for this false belief that "this is our country" (a slogan developed a century after the American Revolution).

> Muhammad Ali, then the world heavyweight boxing champion, lost his crown for revolutionizing the country by not stepping up to be inducted into the military, because of his religious beliefs. The church in God's eyes is as one. In America it has been made into anything that serves one's

personal needs. For instance, Bush, the compassionate Christian, is supported by evangelicals, a group of churchgoers whose path leads back to bondage. The majority Black church continues to be silent in its neutral position, though claiming credit for the Civil Rights Movement. The church, period, is said to be the moral arm of any community.

Had politics not been thrown in with God's work, abortion wouldn't be an issue and neither would stem cell research. Then Michael J. Fox wouldn't have been made a scapegoat on these big-time TV ads regarding the stem-cell issue, a subject Ronald Reagan's son spoke out against. Maybe one day we will all learn that politics, TV commercials and the church make up a capitalistic society — all for one, and one for all, with truth being an unwanted item.

Week of November 22, 2006

Hey, Joe: I got married a month ago and both of my bosses attended my wedding. However, I haven't received a present from either one of them. I know people have a year to give a wedding gift, but I think it's strange. I work really hard and I even coach one of my bosses' kids in volleyball. Should I bring it up to them or try to ignore the problem?

J.D. - whereabouts unknown

Based upon how the question is asked, I really can't see where there is a problem. You state that you got married a month ago and that both of your bosses attended your wedding, though you haven't received a present from either. What I can't grasp is your connection between your bosses and you, which would cause them to send you a present. In other words, do you work for both and personally invited them to attend your wedding? If this is the case, I would've expected to have received a present too, due to the close association.

However, if not, there are quite a few loose ends. You indicate that you work really hard and even coach one of your boss's kids in volleyball, but you haven't given me anything specific concerning a close relationship. Anyway, if not personal, it is up to them to decide whether they want to give you a gift or not.

Should they decide not to, there is no room for anger. By working as hard as you do - both on the job and coaching the kids - you've proven your sincerity. The person you married, whether realizing it or not, was very fortunate to get someone like you. Therefore, you've fulfilled the saying that it is "better to give than to receive." Otherwise, your invitations were seemingly a way to receive presents. As a rule, it has long been said that on a job you don't mix business with pleasure.

```
Hey Joe: I drank too much at a party and cheated on my fi-
ancé. I swear, swear, swear I'll never ever do it again.
Should I tell him?
Anonymous
```

The best way to find the answer to this question is to reverse it. What if you were in the shoes of your fiancé' - a person that could very well become your spouse? Would you become upset under the same circumstances? How about trust from that point on? Would you be willing to undergo the trauma involved? Would you be able to forgive and forget? Then, if so, you need to be commended.

However, even in this case, everybody doesn't feel like you. In most cases, a flabby excuse such as "drinking too much induced you to cheat" is a no-no. What man wants a lady who sells out after having a few drinks? In all probability, only the guy that furnished the drinks - due to knowing he has a push over. Unless you are ready to suffer the consequences, I would think real hard before disclosing this secret. After all, it happened before you and your fiancé' considered marriage, and maybe you've learned something from the experience.

```
Week of November 29, 2006
Hey Joe: I know you live in Illinois, but the whole Amend-
ment 2 proposition about stem cells was a huge deal over
here in St. Louis -- and it narrowly passed. Would you
have voted for or against it and why?
M. Bree O'Nic
```

I don't vote for anything that I am in doubt about. I made up my mind years back to become thoroughly knowledgeable of the issues that confront me, before committing myself. Though this does not alter me from paying close attention to my surroundings, whether in Illinois, St. Louis or the nation, and you can better believe that I paid close attention to the recent elections, which among other things included the subject surrounding stem cells. However, any topic involving a life being tampered with doesn't sit too well with me.

Since St. Louis is so close to where I live, I couldn't help but focus on the political viciousness that was displayed via television, which featured Michael J. Fox, the actor, only in this case he wasn't acting. He was being truthful in his representation of stem cell initiative, a supposed cure for Parkinson's disease - a condition he and others are plagued with - which I believe he has a very good understanding about. Sadly, I don't. Hopefully, I will learn more about it in the future.

Personally, regarding him whom I've admired for so long as an actor, he - as a human being representing stem cell research - stood in his finest hour. His campaign for the potential cure wasn't limited to St. Louis but also for every other city and state throughout the nation, which included all people with diseases that the cure could possibly help. And, he did it with class without taking a backwards step, although faced with much criticism. His message was a lesson to most current politicians as to how the game is played…say what you mean, and mean what you say.

So elated was I about the losses of several Republican senators that I overlooked the victory of St. Louis' Amendment 2 proposition regarding stem cells, which was pushed to the back of my mind. Though, no matter how large or how small the margin, it is my belief that Michael J. Fox turned the tide in favor of the Democratic Party, though not because it's any better. In addition to Fox, the only other winners during the recent elections were the voters that ousted several Republican incumbent senators, who were up for re-election and supported George W. Bush. Both parties serve the Declaration of Independence and Constitution like most elected candidates claim they and their families are Christians.

However, in St. Louis the dog-heartedness in both parties was reflected in TV ads regarding the Missouri senatorial race between Claire McCaskill and Jim Talent, where all morals fell by the wayside. Anybody that watched these cutthroat commercials should have a pretty good idea about the true meaning of politics - an occupation so lucrative that those with aspirations to attain this goal will spend millions of dollars begging you and I for a job they want by making promise after promise, and after becoming successful at our expense, settle down among their constituents and enjoy the luxury of becoming millionaires through retirement and sellout campaign funds.

Remember Pharaoh, the Biblical promise-maker and liar. All those who followed the fool died. Remember Bush. These Republican senators that followed him perished, including the evangelical church. Hopefully future voters will recognize that they have the last say and can hire and fire anybody refusing to fulfill their promises by saying what they mean and meaning what they say.

Week of December 6, 2006

Hey, Joe: Whose tirade do you think was more offensive: Mel Gibson's against the Jews, or Michael Richards' against Blacks? Do you think these things were said out of anger or do you really think these guys are prejudiced?

Anonymous

Mel Gibson's thing against Jews can't be placed in the same bag with Michael Richards and Blacks. All three parties belong to the white majority; however, any expressed anger meant to hurt anyone is offensive. In all probability, this is what occurred in the Gibson affair. Anyway, the Jewish community can't be that upset about his remarks. It must be remembered that Freeman Gosden and Charles Correll - both of Jewish nationality - amassed a fortune by offensively mimicking Blacks as easy marks over a radio show called, "Amos and Andy" - not withstanding Al Jolson, who - in Black face - sang the song, "Mammy." Because Gibson and Jews are white, I suppose his outburst was similar to that of Blacks, especially when one Black calls another the word, "nigger." As a white person, this was Richards' mistake: he crossed racial lines.

However, no problem - absolutely NO problem - can be solved from a superficial standpoint. If a cure is to be found, it must be traced back to its origin. Richards' untimely denigrating of Blacks was different because Blacks are in the minority; but whatever the case, Blacks should not become upset over his insulting remarks, which stemmed from slavery. Ever heard of The Declaration of Independence and The Constitution??? Because of these documents, Blacks had no rights, which whites were bound to respect. Separation of Blacks and whites was law. As a result, love was destroyed. From this pattern, two nations were born due to prejudice - one supposedly superior, the other said to be inferior. Even in a world within a world of today, this is the legacy left by the Founding Fathers.

Although claiming to be a Christian nation, the system of slavery motivated hatred. Even in church, whites were taught to seek salvation through God but to hate Blacks, because they were said to be "children of Ham." The Black Church - when permitted - was monitored by whites, but not all whites adhered to this policy. The number of them was enumerable, though they were met with degradation. The most fascinating person during that era was John Newton, author of the song, "Amazing Grace," and also an evangelical Christian. Prior to his conversion, he was a captain in the slave trade and carried several human cargoes to the Americas. The words of his six-verse song encompass his confession beginning with, "Amazing Grace! (how sweet the sound) that sav'd a wretch like me! I once was lost, but now am found, was blind but now I see."

The nation should take a page out of Minister John Newton's book. Blacks and whites have been misled by deceiving leaders from jump street. Therefore, neither can afford the luxury of hating one another for past occurrences. The Bible has been grossly distorted. It is NOT a document of amendments like The Constitution; therefore, The Bible and Constitution can't mix. My final point surrounds Bob Motley. Motley, whom I happen to be in a book with, was one of the first Blacks to umpire in the Pacific Coast League. One day, he was faced by an angry white manager who gave him particular hell for calling a player of his out. The next day, Motley asked the manager why was he so mad at him for doing his job. The manager replied, "It's not you I'm mad at, it's Abraham Lincoln."

The Reverend Jesse Jackson and Reverend Al Sharpton cannot help Richards by urging his apology, but they can go after The Declaration of Independence and Constitution in revealing why America isn't a Christian nation. Hopefully (if so), other preachers will follow suit. The theme: complete equal revision or abolishment. God did it in Egypt. Those in America who claim to follow him should be able to do it too.

Week of December 13, 2006

Hey Joe: A friend wants to get back in touch with me after a few years, mostly because we grew up together and our parents are still friends. But to me, it's clear that we don't have anything in common anymore. Should I pursue this friendship for old time's sake or make excuses to not hang out with her?

Tender Lover, Joliet

It is my firm belief that true friendship is based upon sincerity - and of course having something in common - but absolutely NOT out of selfishness. Fortunately, I have experienced such friendship. It dates back to a very early age in my life between a buddy of mine named Eugene Crittenden blackness "Gene." Even today we call one another, if not everyday, then every other day. Currently, he is a resident of St. Louis, where he has resided since finishing college - and me, a resident of Brooklyn, the place our friendship developed. Oddly, I can't recall how it happened, though I do remember that of the multitude of things we did together, two stand out in my mind.

Gene had a full head of curly locks and a deep love for his grandmother, whom he called, "Granny." For some unknown reason, he was under the impression that she was responsible for his hair. Mine was always cut short. Many times we sat on the steps of a vacant house with me sitting between his legs on a step below as he played the part of a barber, using Popsicle sticks as his clippers. Obviously, during times prior, he thought my hair should be like his, because one day while working on it, he told me that he was going to get some of his granny's grease and put it on my head so my hair could be like his.

I can't recall us ever having a serious falling-out. Though we came close once. Gene's affection for me was similar to that of his granny. He thought I could do anything. One day, we ventured a few blocks from our homes, and believe me Brooklyn only consists of a few blocks, but the street we were on was Canal. Unfortunately, I got into a slight ruckus with a guy from this neighborhood with about the same height and weight as mine. Being the aggressor, I grabbed him. From this point on, I struggled to get myself free. Finally, while desperately trying to break loose, my elbow accidentally hit him in the jaw. Suddenly, he began crying and screaming about getting his brother for me. After this, I got tough. My reply to him was, "You gonna fool around until I get mad and hurt you!"

Anyway, it didn't stop there. I was foolish enough to hang around until he brought his brother, who was much shorter. As he neared me, I began to laugh while telling Gene, "I'm gonna kill 'im." About this time, he was upon me finger-pointing up in my face wanting to know why I bothered his brother, before he jumped into the air and slapped the taste out of my mouth. Before releasing me, the whipping he gave me was so severe that I begged him to kill me. On our way back home, Gene was in front of me walking backwards, asking repetitiously if I was "gonna get him." "Hell no!" I replied, "Didn't you just see me get got!!!" Because of my answer we took separate routes home, but before nightfall we were back in each other's good grace. Eventually, during later years we undertook separate lifestyles.

The moral to the story is this: Our friendship didn't evolve from our parents' friendship. It was how we perceived each other. Since those days, our parents have long ago passed, but we still reminisce about the good times. I'm sure you and your buddy experienced many of these. During your phone conversations with the individual, if any, bring those days back to life while explaining how yours have changed. After a few times of this, if it gets boring, the person will slowly bow out.

```
Week of December 20, 2006
Hey Joe: What do I do when someone gives me a present and
I didn't get anything for them? It's so awkward.
```

Send them a nice 'Thank You' card in return. Then, the first opportunity you get to return the favor, respond. It's not that awkward. It's nice to be thought of. Then, too, you're not a mind reader. Each kind deed deserves another. Everybody loves kind treatment.

Hey Joe: Every year, I print out a two-page letter to put within each Christmas card. The letter updates everyone on each member of my family: the kids, the dog, me and my husband. People call them "brag letters" but I think they are time savers -- you don't have to spend time to make the cards all, you know, personal. Do you think it's bragging or a good idea?

I don't know whether it's a good idea or not, but one thing I do know is that it's different. If people that you send them to call them "brag letters," don't follow up the next time Those who indicate it's a good idea, stick with it.

Hey Joe: What do you want for Christmas?

If I had the power to wave a magic wand and turn all the sadness into beauty, this would be my greatest want.

Hey Joe: You know when you go into a coffee shop and they've got those tip cups up there by the register? Don't you think it's kind of rude that they imply that you should tip something? I mean, making coffee and handing it over the counter is their job for Christ sakes! You don't tip doctors for removing your appendix, so why should these people get tipped on top of their hourly wage?

I've never experienced such service and if so, I never paid it any attention. All my tips have been given to the person that served me or left for them on the table, before being checked out at the counter. Though I have patronized businesses that placed some sort of container near the register for the purpose of charitable donations, but this was made clear before hand. Anyway, I'm not an avid coffee drinker; therefore, I can take it or leave it. Most times, I'm leaving it.

Apparently, the type of place you speak of don't make thing too clear regarding the cup near the register, because you say they imply that you should tip something. Since I'm not familiar with the shops' policy, it would be hard for me to make a snap decision, but it's your prerogative to speak your mind and you did. The only suggestion that I have to offer is if you can't stand the atmosphere, change climate.

`Week of December 27, 2006`

`Hey Joe: Did you see that special on Creflo Dollar Saturday, December 16th @ 6pm called "Does God Want Us to Be Poor" on Channel 30? If you saw it, what did u think about it?`

`Mike in Granite City, IL`

In viewing the program, I watched it from a Black perspective - the reason being the question asked, Creflo Dollar, a Black multi-millionaire preacher, and a white interviewer. The crux of it dealt with prosperity. It didn't take long for me to figure out that the question "Does God Want Us to Be Poor?" stemmed from Dollar, who regards himself as "doctor," which gave him the needed leverage to attribute his multi-million dollar status to prosperity. The word "us" in the question however aroused my interest. The word "prosperity" reminded me of an old time politician speech, which goes like this: "And if I am elected President, there will be biscuit trees on every corner and syrup flowing down the gutters, so step up, grab yourself a biscuit and sop your way to prosperity."

Though, in reference to the program, I listened attentively as the interviewer posed question after question to Dollar relative to his prosperity. Not once did I hear him relate to anything even remotely close to being sacred regarding it, in spite of every Sunday the church being the most segregated institution in America. The truth is God had nothing to do with the situation, but His name has been constantly used in vein as a way for some, who profess Him to rise from rags to riches. I'm sure that Creflo Dollar began his meteoric rise to fame by feeding off poor Blacks before preaching to mixed congregations and joining white televangelists, which I've seen via television several times.

Seemingly the program about Dollar was a way of showing the nation how one Black can get ahead by outsmarting another. In other words, pull yourself up by your own bootstraps with Black parishioners. The sad thing about it is there are other Black preachers made of the same cut. Of these, T.D. Jakes and Frederick K. Price are the most notables. They - like Dollar - are of great concern to me, especially in the field of ministry. Together, they are three of the Bible's biggest money-making turncoats, who abandoned God for the want of money. Obviously, these guys aren't hip to Nat Turner, Adam Clayton Powell or Dr. Martin Luther King, Jr. - all preachers.

Turner, during the 1800s, led a revolt against slavery and was killed. Powell, during the Separate But Equal era, coined the phrase "Keep the Faith, baby" and King, during the Civil Rights Era, led marches that broke down mostly all public accommodations that previously had barred Blacks. In between Turner and King, most Black preachers were programmed to console Black churchgoers with the phrase "Turn the other cheek." Branch Rickey, after hiring Jackie Robinson for the job of playing baseball with the Brooklyn Dodgers, asked him to use the philosophy of "turn the other cheek" – but only for two years. Robinson's entry - backed by overwhelming Black support - eventually destroyed the once powerful Negro Leagues.

Behind Dr. King's advent, scholastic degrees became the order of the day for obtaining "good-paying" jobs. Black parishioners have provided jobs for Black preachers for decades. Though, there is a saying that "The wages of sin is death," but most Black preachers believe that "the wages of TRUTH is death." It is said that if you want to trick Blacks, put it in writing. The Bible gives credence to this saying. With all these degrees floating around, there should be no problem in Bible interpretation, or - in paraphrasing the words of Elliot Davis, St. Louis' well-known television reporter - "You Asked For It!!!"

```
Week of January 11, 2007
Hey, Joe: What, if anything are the St. Louis papers
saying about the exhibition game scheduled for March 31,
2007? The financial proceeds are to go to the National
Memphis Civil Rights Museum and other charitable Civil
```

Rights organizations.

Juzanne - Memphis, TN

Before Jackie Robinson's name became a household word in the world of White baseball, the Negro Leagues lay in obscurity, outlawed because of its Blackness. Team owners, players and bus drivers alike - undaunted by the daily ritual of racism - trudged on while securing a solid foundation for this great organization, which was guided by men such as Rube Foster, C.I. Taylor and the like, who molded together this powerful entity. Later, it would be the foundation that awaited Robinson, star athlete at Pasadena Junior College, UCLA and a former military officer, who had to take a step backwards because the white baseball leagues had no place for him in spite of his athletic prowess. Had there been no Negro Leagues, his presence on the national scene could have very well been prolonged.

Recently, I read a story published in the Memphis Tennessee Commercial Appeal Newspaper pertaining to an upcoming charitable baseball game between the St. Louis Cardinals and Cleveland Indians to be played March 31, 2007 at Memphis' Auto Zone Park, which will be televised over ESPN - an event that will possibly take place again the following year. Stated in the story also, was that a luncheon and presentation of Major League Baseball's new Beacon Awards is planned along with player visits to the Civil Rights Museum and viewing of a short documentary by Spike Lee. Listed as charitable recipients are the Jackie Robinson Foundation, the National Civil Rights Museum, several local charities, the NAACP Legal Defense Fund and the Negro League Baseball Museum.

As a footnote introduction, a space at the top of the story reads "Inaugural Civil Rights Game to Honor Past, Re-link Black Fans, Athletes to National Past Time Again." Most disturbing to me about this story was that the credit for such idea was given to Dave Chase, General Manager of the Memphis Redbirds. After reading the story, so angered did I become that I tried to contact David Williams, the writer of the story, to correct this statement about Dave Chase. I also contacted personnel at the Civil Rights Museum. Neither returned calls or responded to email.

Since I have so much to say regarding this subject, and so little space to voice it, I would like the nation to know that the idea about such games was that of Joe Henry and NOT Dave Chase. The first step in this direction was brought about by the Riverfront Times (RFT), after being rejected by the Belleville-News Democrat (Illinois) and St. Louis Post-Dispatch, because of certain differences following Bud Selig's lie to the nation regarding pensions to former Negro League players, who he said were in need and had to have played parts of at least 4 years. Rather than stand behind his word, Selig retracted his statement and wound up cutting the life of the Negro League short by announcing that after the Dodgers signed Robinson, segregation in white baseball was ended.

However, because of the RFT my story is documented throughout the nation, which includes websites, etc. – the most recent being www.gatewayredbirds.com Among other things, it speaks of the letter I wrote about three years ago to Selig and Jim Martin, Executive Director of Baseball Assistance Team (BAT), in reference to staging 2 or 3 games to include pensions for every former Negro-Leaguer that was denied, including myself, though definitely eligible. I took this stand by denying myself $30-$40,000. Hopefully, the NAACP and Civil Rights Museum won't sell out their history in exchange for a few pennies. Make George Bush's "No child left behind" become a reality by not leaving "A former Negro Leaguer behind."

[Editor's Note: The four questions and answers immediately following have been printed independently and were NOT printed in The Riverfront Times.]

Hey, Joe: When's the best time to tell a child they're adopted? Our daughter is now in high school and we don't know how to bring up the subject.
Anonymous

My suggestion would be immediately after adoption. I've never adopted a child, although my wife and I raised our grandson, Sean. We got him as a baby, and always reminded him about his mother, our daughter, so he would never forget her. He was raised in our home. Our purpose for getting him was to grant her the opportunity to finish high school and college, due to having him at a very young age. After finishing school and becoming employed, she chose a career to proceed on her own after opting to leave him with us. From this perspective, they were always close, although my wife and I stayed afraid for years that he would someday choose to live with her. To deny a child knowledge of his parents, in the long run, might one day prove very hurtful, such as in your case.

Hey, Joe: Why don't more Black guys like hockey?
NHL LoVeR, Calgary

For the same reason baseball was abandoned - which prior, they caught nothing but "hockey," if you catch my excrement drift, when first trying to break the color line. Though after basketball and football became available, they gravitated toward these fields. Additionally, they made big paydays in getting to the top, rather than undergoing farm systems, while earning less money and spending more time, which was achieved by jumping from the ranks of high schools or colleges.

Hey, Joe: If someone offered you $50,000 to do a commercial for something unattractive, like erectile dysfunction (ED), would you do it?
Dick Dastardly (on tour somewhere over seas)

To be quite honest, "No." I'm not Bob Dole, the former presidential candidate. I've been told several times by a close friend that the greediest man alive is the one that makes his first million dollars. Dole, by advertising Viagra, acknowledges this by letting the world know that he has a dead sex organ, and it has nothing to do with the war - sorta like most of those old antiquated geezers in Congress who wouldn't pass up the opportunity of jumping on Mark McGuire, Barry Bonds and others that supposedly used steroids. Not to say that I won't jump in line for some free (of charge), but probably would get run over by Bud Selig, who would be hustling to get some too.

However, unlike Dole, I've never seen a ballplayer advertising steroids. I wonder if steroids served the same purpose as Viagra, would Congressmen - those who are so adamant about going after athletes - feel the same way.

It must be noted that steroids have long ago made its way through every athletic system, including schools. It's a proven fact that all of these drug users have turned a deaf ear to Nancy Reagan's philosophy of "Just Say No." If there is a way to curtail the use of these so-called "performance-enhancing" drugs, it must begin with cracking down on manufacturers. Or, would big business stop its financial contributions to politicians' campaigns??? By putting a stop to this drug business, maybe the millionaire image will cease and also the drugs. Then, the people's social problems will be readily addressed.

Hey Joe: Is it racist or just descriptive to start a story like this: "So there was this Black guy..."? if the race isn't that relevant to the story?

Curios One, Deep South

Being racist is predicated on hatred of a person because of nationality without cause. Sorry, but we were brought up in a society that initiated such between Blacks and Whites, otherwise, we would be colorblind.

Week of January 25, 2007

Hey Joe: What do you think of Bush's so-called troop "surge" plan for Iraq?

The Colonel, Shreveport, LA

Before observing George Bush's psychology via television, etc., I had my doubts about the movie, "Three Faces of Eve," a story based upon the life of a person with multiple personalities. But after studying him closely, now I am convinced. Presently, he represents the true meaning of the phrase "in denial" regarding the lie he told about WMD, which triggered the Iraq conflict. Since the war's beginning, better than 3,000 soldiers have been killed - and no telling how many maimed.

Only God knows the destruction of how many innocent people abroad in addition to families at home that have undergone such trauma, because of injuries to service-connected relatives. Yet he appears before television cameras, carefully picking his spots like military bases, where things for him are more favorable to emphasize that he is protecting America. Though those who disagree with his philosophy, like Cindy Sheehan, he deems unpatriotic - a psychological ploy used before the nation to belittle their character, which most Democrats - when in defense of their political jobs - punked out.

Based upon how he was elected president, though millions refused to buy into it, his election might be revisiting us. A self-proclaimed, compassionate conservative - of which there is no such thing - and embraced by the evangelical faith, he was given the presidency by so-called "justices" who used a law of the 1700s and resurrected in the year 2000 to beat Al Gore, who he was soundly trounced by with the popular vote. This was achieved because the Electoral College, which decides votes by states. At the time of its existence, Blacks were excluded from "We the People". Therefore, because of this law, the votes of Blacks were denied, after living a nightmare of fear in fighting for the right to vote. In all probability, millions of white voters - because of such a law - experienced the same.

Bush - in his anxiety to establish a Democratic government in Iraq - failed the opportunity at home to exemplify the true meanings of "Democracy" and "Christianity." Had he wanted to cement his legacy, devoid of politics and selfishness, he could have achieved it by stepping up and announcing to the nation that the way he won the presidency was far from Democratic. Thus, declaring that Gore was the winner by majority rule. Had this occurred, he would have defied an outmoded law and avoided placing his hand on The Bible, while being sworn in to uphold an anti-Christ Constitution. Had this been followed, he would have become the most powerful man in America and loved by Blacks and whites.

Now, he seeks a legacy at the expense of the American people. His poll ranking - in every respect - is below par all because of lying, blaming others for his shortcomings and acting out the part of a spoiled brat – whatever junior wants, junior gets. His presidency has exposed the corruptness of politics. Congress is in a confused state of decision-making because of allowing this to happen by not taking a stand regarding his lie, and it can't be called "a little white lie." At present, despite all the bickering, the lie is hardly mentioned. Now he claims to have a new strategy to correct what he created. Bush should know that genuine leadership never puts followers or country in harm's way by entertaining illusions, which he is now doing with his new idea of strategy called "Troop Surge."

Transform "surge" into "insurgence" and then you have "Troop Insurgence," which our soldiers will be viewed as in Iraq. Fess up to your lie George! Don't be like George Washington who said he never told a lie. Show the country your patriotism by excusing yourself as president. Allow some decent human being a chance without hang-ups like "Mission Accomplished" - someone who the people abroad can trust, so there can be a peaceful solution derived in order for differences to be resolved.

Week of January 25, 2007

Hey Joe: What do you think of Barack Obama? Do you think he has a chance for the presidential nomination, or will people not support him because he's Black?

Young Black Republicans - Washington, DC

As for the part of your question regarding Obama's "blackness," no matter how hard Blacks have tried to forget it, America will not allow it to happen. This goes for Blacks like Oprah Winfrey, Condoleezza Rice or others who - if trying to avoid being Black - are quickly reminded by not only more affluent whites but also by those on welfare. Ask O.J. Simpson. Rush Limbaugh, the conservative talk radio host, recently began spreading his poison by alerting his listening audience to the tune of Obama's middle name being Hussein.

The manner in which this was said, the political hype was on. TV stations began playing up the idea about Hilary Clinton and Barack Obama as a white woman and Black man vying for the Democratic Presidential nomination. However, what hasn't been said is that Sojourner Truth, a Black female abolitionist and feminist who escaped enforced slavery, fought for women's' rights after Blacks were released. Afterwards, I know of no white male group that has further supported the idea. At the time of this occurrence, the Democratic Party was referred to as the "party of the solid South." Since then, the Black man and white woman have been the most scrutinized individuals in the land, which both have been hurt severely.

Now, since all the control and myths have been destroyed, two people with political savvy have the popular potential to face each other in a Democratic primary showdown. But wait, politics is a vicious game. Hilary is being blamed for voting to give Bush the power of going to war or not. So what?!?? It was left up to his discretion. She can't be blamed for that. The intelligence report he received regarding the situation was second hand. He should have read every single word of it, before making a decision and if there was anything he disliked, it should have been trashed. Otherwise, he took somebody else's word. Each time I release an article to the publisher and something is wrong on my part, it is my fault, and nobody else can be blamed. Hilary is a magnificent woman. In my book, her greatest triumph is when she refused to allow anyone to persuade her into destroying her husband during the time he was at his lowest ebb.

Of Barack, he has proven to be everything that wasn't supposed to be accorded a Black man. All of a sudden, though, it is said that he is inexperienced. Look back over the number of presidents who served the country and find how many of those were inexperienced about the condition of Blacks - then, people will begin to realize all this political jargon like "conservative," "liberal," "moderate," "middle-of-the-roader," "far right (and left)," etc. Make these politicians accountable for such terms by explaining what they mean. Everytime I see Obama, a child of Black and white parents, I think about what some of these hypocritical country people say, like "I don't mind a Black man and White woman being together, but what about the children?" Obama is in a unique position to step back and let Hilary run, and could very well say, "I believe I will gain a bit more experience to make the way clear for her." He doesn't have to be president to exercise his moral values. He has already placed his hand on The Bible to be sworn in to uphold The Constitution, which has (and continues to) destroyed his people. Then, he can fight for the abolishment of such unjust laws, while as a senator. If he should lose his seat in trying to succeed himself, then he knows how the voters in Illinois and the country feel towards him. Though, if not successful, he would have accomplished so much in such a little time. The Clinton's are deserving of this, excluding what President Clinton did for Blacks, but for the compassion the family gave to the world.

Week of February 1, 2007

Hey, Joe: Regarding your recent column on Black preachers, there are two statements that I don't fully understand, but I am extremely curious to learn exactly what you meant (I always find your viewpoints interesting). If you don't mind, could you please answer these questions, regarding:

"I listened to the program attentively as the interviewer posed question after question to Dollar regarding his prosperity. Not once did I hear him relate to anything even remotely sacred regarding it, despite that the church is the most segregated institution in America."

(1) How does segregation relate to dollar's remarks about prosperity; and (2) do you really believe the institution of church is most segregated? (I find more acceptance there than anywhere). Also, regarding: "With all these degrees floating around, there should be no problem in Bible interpretation..."

By this statement do you mean something like "why do we need preachers?" I hope you don't mind these questions. I enjoy the way you think but sometimes you are hard to follow! P.S. Thanks so much for this week's column on the Memphis game. Didn't know at all about it, but now I want to try to attend!

Kathy Wentzel - St. Louis, MO

> The manner in which your question is asked is a true mark of excellence; it was so eloquently done. It reminds me of a passenger, who once was riding in a car driven by its owner. En route to their destination, the owner exceeded the speed limit at a very dangerous pace. The passenger, feeling quite uneasy over it, called the owner's attention saying, "Either drive the speed limit or let me out." The bottom line being if the driver wanted to be a fool, that was perfectly all right, but not at his (the passenger's) expense.
>
> No, I'm not suggesting that we don't need preachers. I'm only suggesting that we hold them accountable for preaching The Bible correctly, that is if

they understand it. I love how you asked me to clarify the things that I've said which you didn't understand. That's exactly what parishioners should do to preachers. In reference to Black preachers, especially the "biggies" like Dr. Creflo Dollar, T.D. Jakes, Frederick K. Price and also those of a lesser degree. I want them to understand the history of the Black church. It has been - in the words sung by Aretha Franklin - "like a bridge over troubled waters." It provided Blacks hope within a hopeless world of no recourse. Like the old Negro hymn "Steal Away," it provided them with a place where they could steal away and take their burdens to The Lord.

The source of the problem occurred at a time most Black parishioners were unable to read, and most preachers, due to incompetence, were called "jacklegs" - most never learning the basics of The Bible, which the crux of it can be found in the Book of Exodus. Then came Rev. Vernon Johns, Rosa Parks and Martin Luther King, who challenged and conquered the South's notorious laws. Eventually King would become known as "doctor," a title befitting him. His legacy speaks for itself. His dream amplified his ambition. His doctorate served to heal a racially split society, including the church.

Dollar, who exalts himself as "doctor" during the show titled "Does God Want Us to Be Poor?" exhibited a different personality. His ambition reflected the want of money; he even encouraged his followers to pursue it. The Book of Luke Chapter 19 Verses 1-8 presents a clearer picture into the subject. Zacchae'us, a rich man and a tax collector, who hadn't received Christ, sought him. Before repenting, the people called him a sinner. Dollar, also a rich man, is completely the opposite. He claims that God called him to preach, yet misleads his followers by using God's name to sell them his books and tapes, etc., which are tax exempt. But by referring to them as "gifts" and/or "donations," they are classified as "non-profitable".

In reference to his cohorts, Price and Jakes, they are guilty of the same. Price - at one time forgetting that he preached to a mixed audience - attacked Christianity by pointing at racial differences within the white church. For this, he was ostracized. In order to Atone for his "sins," he jumped on Min. Louis Farrakhan, The Holy Qu'ran and the Black Muslims. Though, had America been a Christian nation, there wouldn't had been a need for the Black Muslims, Abraham Lincoln, The Civil War and Dr. King.

As for Jakes, his emotionally packed sermons - without substance - serve to mesmerize his audiences. However, of the three, none follow the lead of Dr. King. Their way has proven to be for self-gain. Maybe they should check out the Book of Jeremiah, especially Chapter 22 Verse 22 in particular.

Week of February 8, 2007

Hey, Joe: I was so excited to see not one, but two African-American coaches make it to the super bowl. Do you feel the same way, and once again does this show how great we can be?

Mike - Granite City

History has a way of leveling the playing field. For 41 years, it was unheard of for a Black coach - let alone two - to be coaching in a Super Bowl game. However, back then there was no Black History Month. Coincidentally, Lovie Smith and Tony Dungy pulled off their feat at such time. During the 30s, all-Black Sumner High School in St. Louis coined a motto at one of its graduating classes that said, "A race without a history is soon forgotten." Years later, two of the school's most notable personalities - Dick Gregory and Grace Bumbry - left their marks on the sands of time. Gregory, an athlete turned comedian, has used his skills for years fighting for Black equality. Bumbry has exhibited one of the greatest operatic voices ever akin to that of Leontyne Price.

The February Black History Month has consistently accentuated the positive and eliminated the negative regarding the genius of Blacks while under adverse circumstances. Presently, I am no longer a big fan of the Black History Month as I once was, because of feeling that the novelty has worn thin about those displayed and that the genius that elevated them to such level should be revealed in its entirety. In other words, the whole story should be placed in school curriculums. If there is opposition, challenge it. Think of the words of Frederick Douglass, a Black abolitionist and journalist, who wrote, "Power concedes nothing without demand. It never has, it never will."

Smith and Dungy bring to mind the firing of former NFL commentator, Jimmy "The Greek," who made a mistake by suggesting that white quarterbacks would one day become a thing of the past, because Blacks during slavery were bred with quality mates - which is hog wash. I dug Jimmy, and he shouldn't have been fired. He added much flare to the game. His comment regarding Blacks was no more than a fairy tale that he had grown up with, which he was taught - myths that Blacks have undergone for centuries. Football quarterbacks are said to be the brains.

Truth is, history judges people. It has judged Blacks and found that the myths spread about them to be lies. Take Gregory for instance. Had he chosen to remain as a funny man, he would have been viewed as amiable, but because of his involvement for Black equality, he was said to be an activist, militant or radical - terms suggesting the opposite of nice. Bumbry and Price - despite all their talent - better not have walked freely into the metropolitan opera house with their Black faces, unless it had been sanctioned by some white person. This has been the life of Blacks in America, controlled by others. In spite of it all, they have taken the lemons given them and made lemonade.

Historically, as for Smith and Dungy, I see them as a part of the last hired, first fired syndrome - which has been the trend for Blacks seeking employment. Had their feats been accomplished before the 30s, it would have been classified as a credit to their race, because it was thought that Blacks were more physically astute than mentally. In reference to saying a "credit to their race," Jesse Owens and Joe Lewis were chose politically to defuse the notion Adolf Hitler had about an Aryan nation. These victories alone were a credit to America. If there is any doubt about how great Blacks are: only geniuses could make it through bondage. The month of February is only a snapshot of Blacks' history.

Week of February 22, 2007

Hey, Joe: A recent post on an online message board delivered a bitch-slap to The Riverfront Times, questioning whether your column (as well as a similar column, "Ask a Mexican," which runs on the RFT's Web site) appears "for

```
any reason other than sheer racism."  The poster also
asked, "Does anyone -- anywhere -- find [the columns]
funny?"  Please discuss!
Sincerely yours,
Heywood Jablowme - St. Louis
```

> Thanks for being so complimentary. I find that you are quite smart. Thanks also for teaching me about the word "racism" or in fact "racist." It reminds me of the saying, "He who gives the mostest, takes the leastest" or "One has to be one to know one." I'm not familiar with the column "Ask A Mexican," but I do know that we are both in America's minority and didn't put ourselves there. Obviously, you don't know your history. It is the country's best educator - not Harvard, Yale nor any other supposedly elite university or college. It can't be argued against by any psychologists or any other so-called "professional" mind-probers. Knowledge is not confined to any certain group or individual. It is there for those who seek it. Apparently, you never have.
>
> Take some time to delve into it, beginning with the Declaration of Independence and Constitution and you just might find how you got that false sense of superiority. Otherwise, without these documents to support your cause - in this day and time - you might be considered a "functional illiterate" or better yet a "dysfunctional literate." This is what your brief history concerning the online message board reveals to me about you. Your ignorance is exhibited in the manner in which you promote your idea by begging for help elsewhere regarding "sheer racism" and what the poster asked, because you don't have the courage to stand up and speak for yourself. Ya dig?!?? Do you find this funny???

Seemingly, the way you have expressed yourself (shows) you're guilt-filled over your own history - just the opposite of millions of open-minded people who understand they didn't make the rules. Or is it that you don't have a mind to open? It is your kind that fits the category of "I would rather keep my mouth closed and be thought a fool than to open it and to remove all doubt." The "bitch-slap" that you spoke of should be directed at your freaky character. The RFT exposed it, which is indicative of the combination of your first and last name - whether real or fictional

- my answer to "Hey, would you blow me" is "U do me...I owe U 1"!!! The section for letters stand ready for your reply. See how open-minded the RFT is???

```
Week of March 15, 2007

Hey, Joe: Did you read the story about the village of Val-
ley Park recently published in the RFT (3.1.07)? If so,
what did you think about it?
```
Anonymous

I think that Kristen Hinman is a super writer. I couldn't help but read the story no sooner than my eyes fell upon the mostly green colored front cover of the paper. Emblazoned on this part in white lettering was: "City Limit - Valley Park Pop 6,518." In parenthesis was "No Wetbacks," but this was no slur at the Mexican community. It reflected the ignorance of the town's mayor, who has worked diligently to get an ordinance passed exclusive of Mexicans in his town, whom he characterizes as "illegal immigrants."

But this isn't what words on the Statue of Liberty imply; they say, "Bring me your poor, bring me the downtrodden, etc." By the mayor's actions, he certainly reveals that he is short on his history. Prior to the Statue of Liberty, the original illegal immigrants were Blacks and Europeans; therefore, he is a descendent of "illegal immigrants." Though at the time, Native Americans inhabited the land. From this point on, once they were decimated, things began to change into a one-class system. Blacks became a pariah. Jeffery Whitteaker, Valley Park's mayor and a self-proclaimed Democrat - by doing what he has done - reveals the Democratic Party's primitive nature, when it was known as "the party of the South" because of embracing slavery. Missouri was a party to this system.

Strangely, in St. Louis just recently, the anniversary of Dred Scott's court case decision was held. Then, he fought for his rights as a free Black man. Unfortunately, the court saw differently. It said because of him being Black he was no American citizen. If this be the case, he was violated twice - once as an illegal immigrant and then as a non-citizen.

The illegal immigrant issue that plagues Valley Park has another twist. This is - at one time in the community - an interracial couple suffered so much harassment that they chose to move. If Whitteaker doesn't 't change his position, he's as hypocritical as the words on New York's Statue of Liberty and as perverted as the St. Louis Arch - the kind that pimps off America by adhering to racial poison and claiming to be patriotic when the country needs love moreso now than ever before in its history.

Hinman's story has the potential of becoming a national showcase. It has the earmarks and should be read by everybody. By using Whitteaker as her target, she uncovers the good, bad and indifferent. It reflects life in America for certain people that date back through centuries. About that interracial couple's harassment, I can't imagine how many times they were addressed as "nigger" and "nigger lover." I can understand how Mexicans feel about the term "wetback," but like in Hinman's story, she points out the good, courageous people that spoke out against such policies. We know who the bad is, so the indifferent has to be the church, similar to those in St. Louis. Of the seemingly million scattered about the city - although I hope I'm wrong - the only reverence that I know of that implements God's will are Ronald L. Bobo and Larry Rice. Recently, I saw over the news where the president of the Urban League and a few Black preachers had launched a campaign to negate use of the "N" word. Instead, I prefer to be called "nigger." Let it ALL hang out. Everytime it is used, it advertises the Declaration of Independence and Constitution. Launch a campaign against these. If these churches don't begin speaking out against social ills, they're going to force God to apologize to Sodom and Gomorrah.

Week of March 22, 2007

Hey Joe: Have you read Jeremiah 23? I just read your article on Creflo Dollar a.k.a. Cashflow Dollar-penny. I agree with you, but read all of Jeremiah 23 and get back with me. I have more ... to share with you.

Urijah E. Israel - St. Louis, MO

Jeremiah 23 - because of God's outspokenness against preachers during ancient history - sheds light on preachers during American history, especially in verses 16 and 31. During ancient history after slavery, The Bible states in Exodus 20:1-7, "And God spake all these words, saying: I am the Lord thy God, which have brought thee out of the land of Egypt, out of the house of bondage. Thou shalt have no other Gods before me. Thou shall not make unto thee any graven image, or any likeness of anything that is in Heaven above or that is in the earth beneath, or that is in the water under the earth: Thou shall not bow down thou self to them: for I the Lord thy God am a jealous God, visiting the iniquity of the fathers upon the children unto the third and fourth generation of them that hate me. And showing mercy unto thousands of them that love me, and keep my commandments. Thou shalt not take the name of the Lord thy God in vain; for the Lord will not hold them guiltless that taketh His name in vain."

Following His creation of The 10 Commandments, He dispatched Jesus, His son, to earth to walk the land among the people teaching and preaching the word to them so they could better understand the meaning, until his death. Christ's rallying cry while on earth was, "If you believe in me, you will have everlasting life." Better than 2,000 years later, slavery was initiated in America. Unfortunately, once the teaching of The Bible commenced, its conveyance consisted of half-truths, which according to the American Heritage College Dictionary, is "a statement, esp. one intended to deceive that omits some facts."

Fact is: the same Bible that contains the stories told by Moses, Jeremiah and so many others during ancient history contains the same scriptures used in American history. However, once Pharaoh was removed, the Book of Exodus relates to God's direct contact with Moses, as he encountered when dealing with the Israelites. The same Jesus experienced later. The Israelites witnessed these people and their wonders. Once The Bible was brought to America, there were no witnesses to the actual occurrences that took place during that time, other than what The Bible recorded. It then became the preachers' living witness.

Though, rather than accept it as knowing God was real, it has been re-played daily as happened when Jesus walked the land asking, "If you believe in me, you will have everlasting life." By doing so most preachers have lead parishioners astray. Throughout The Bible it tells of false prophets who never tackled this subject surrounding them and their actions, as if they were Gods. No greater lesson can be learned about salvation than the story of John Newton, a white male once a captain in the slave trade, who denounced it in his change for the love of God. The words of his song, "Amazing Grace," sums up The Bible in its entirety.

In his own words, he confesses his sinfulness and lays blame on nobody but himself. From this point on, he follows the dictates of God rather than inventing a God and interpreting His meaning - something that preachers aren't capable of doing. Anyway, slavery in America violated God's three basic laws: there shall be no other Gods before me, love and obedience. Somebody has been disobedient.

```
Week of April 5, 2007
Hey Joe: According to the Institute for Diversity and Ethics in Sport at the University of Central Florida, Major League Baseball's Black population is now 8.5 percent, the lowest in 26 years and about half of what it was a decade earlier. Why the precipitous drop and do you think it will continue?
"Jimbo" - San Francisco
```

Based upon Blacks' contribution to MLB without adequate recompense - unless it can find a way to Atone for its past practice - I think baseball is a thing of the pass in the Black community, both among fans and players. Not even Black preachers can sway the minds of Blacks in returning to the game. However, during times prior, when Blacks underwent injustices at the hands of the dominant society, Black preachers - especially the weak-kneed - were called upon by it to quelch the disturbance, which they immediately responded with words of wisdom like "Let God handle it," but more astute Blacks have different ideas today.

There are those old enough who remember what happened to Jackie Robinson and passed it down to their offsprings. They relate to the great Negro League teams that underwent the same treatment. I can understand the protest of white players against Blacks infringing on their jobs. Had not the law forbade Blacks and whites from playing together on the same fields, the Negro League would have ceased at that point, rather than began to crumble in 1947. Though, the so-called Major League would have been "major" because the rosters would probably have been like those currently in basketball and football. However, the appearance of Robinson playing on the same fields with whites sounded the death knell for the Negro Leagues.

The amazing thing about this organization is that it had no prejudices. Promotion of the games was shared by both Blacks and whites. In addition, there were white owners of the Kansas City Monarchs, later followed by the white owners of the Indianapolis Clowns at a time that law prohibited it. The Monarchs ushered in night baseball by traveling with portable lights in the early 1930s; and Willie Wells, Black infielder deluxe, brought about the protective head helmets by wearing a miner's helmet when at bat. I am truly convinced that Robinson's early death resulted from chronic stress.

Although those great Negro League teams prior to Robinson weren't permitted to transform the so-called Major League teams into Major League caliber by incorporating players during their heyday, we - who are old enough - saw it materialize following Robinson's entry. Those teams then, though slowly dying, still had talented players: Black Americans and those of color who spoke in different tongues who transformed the game called Major League into "major" by challenging every single record set beforehand. Then came Curt Flood, a by-product of the Negro League, who broke the strangle hold that White team owners held over both Black and white players.

But there is a deeper side of this story within this writing. In spite of all the contributions given by the Negro League in developing the so-called Major League into being "major," some of its living members have been denied baseball pensions by Bud Selig, MLB Commissioner. On Saturday, March 31, 2007, a game was played billed as "The Inaugural Civil Rights Game." Beneficiaries from that game were the National Civil Rights Museum, NAACP Legal Defense Fund and the Negro League Baseball Museum. If I remember Thurgood Marshall correctly, he fought to break down segregation in education. These organizations should check their education. "The Inaugural Civil Rights Game" occurred when Jackie Robinson stepped out onto the field wearing a Dodger uniform. Had there been no

Negro Leagues, there would be no Negro League Baseball Museum, and Branch Rickey and Jackie Robinson's collaboration was the beginning of the Civil Rights Movement. Buck O'Neil's final plea was for all former Negro Leaguers to receive pensions. If anybody has allowed Commissioner Selig to cut Negro League history short by denying former players pensions, shame......shame......shame on you!!!

Week of April 12, 2007

Hey Joe: My dad was a Brooklyn Dodger fan, and I became a Dodger fan as well, so I can't remember not knowing about Jackie Robinson. What can Baseball and America do to help educate kids today about what Jackie did for America on and off the field? I'll just keep wearing my Brooklyn Dodger road jersey and hope people ask me about number 42.

Thanks,

Paddy - St. Louis, MO

Shamefully, in a nation supposedly "civilized," the heroics of Paul Robeson never reached the peak of exposure accorded Jackie Robinson, although both fought their racial battles alone. Robeson, a Phi Beta Kappa at Rutgers and later a law degree student at Columbia, was a multi-talented individual in a variety of ways. Robinson's brilliance was much more publicized regarding his exploits at UCLA, but in the sense of the word "education," it has to be defined as one perceives it. Too many perceive it as (one) having attended some college or university, which is far from truth. I perceive it as knowing who you are and from whence you came, similar to Robeson and Robinson. Robeson, while his varied talents and outspoken defense of Civil Rights brought him many admirers, it also made him enemies among conservatives trying to maintain the status quo. Robinson was the modern-day patriarch to the Civil Rights Movement - thus predating Rosa Parks and Dr. Martin Luther King, Jr.

Robinson, while at UCLA, doing what came natural in athletics - the same as Robeson at Rutgers - was spotted by Jimmy Dykes, the then Chicago White Sox manager. Dykes - it has sense been recorded - called the White Sox top brass to report that he saw a "colored boy" playing baseball that he would be too glad to pay $50,000 to play for the White Sox. Though, nothing more was heard of this, the team was formerly the Chicago Black Sox, who - at the time - was a member of a league supposed to be "major." The team was managed by Cap Anson, who - after seeing a Black player with the Toledo Mudhens - hollered, "Get that nigga off the field!!!"

Following Robinson's college days, he was inducted into the military, where he served as a lieutenant. One day while riding a post bus, he was ordered by the white civilian driver to take a seat in the rear, which he refused to do. This incident occurred because the driver was under the impression that a highly light skinned lady that Robinson sat by - who was his friend's wife - was white. For this, he was court-martialed. Several years after his discharge, he - along with other Black players - tried out for so-called "Major League" teams but was rejected.

When joining the Brooklyn Dodgers in 1947, his non-violent approach to subdue adversaries by turning the other cheek set the stage for the Civil Rights Movement. A decade later, it was led by Dr. King. By then, Robinson's leadership in the National League had broken the barrier of hotels that rejected Black players throughout the 16-team circuit. It was his class that educated young Blacks and whites that followed him. Baseball has lost its appeal in Black America. I'm quite sure that it is the educational system in America that needs a rude awakening. The recent action of METRO High School students in St. Louis points in that direction. Initially, they occupied the mayor's office in protest against their school losing accreditation - later traveling to the capitol at Jefferson City to complain to lawmakers about a state takeover.

Since most students were Black – and Missouri being a former slave state – their idea would have been unprecedented if they had demanded a test in their school concerning Black History in America. I'm not a betting man, but I would have bet that both Black and white students would have failed the test, as well as most Black and white teachers, in spite of their "degrees." If this same test was applied throughout the country in the best high schools and colleges - Black and white - ALL would lose accreditation. Then, the playing field would be leveled. The educational system then could start over again the right way. Until this occurs, there aren't too many "educators."

Week of April 18, 2007

Hey Joe: I think it's very hypocritical of how the local fans and even some media sources are viewing Tony LaRussa's arrest in Florida for DUI. In this country, if you are white and/or have big money (or prestige), you can get away with a slap on the wrist. A couple of years ago, the cardinals' organization fired hitting coach, Mitchell Page, citing that he had 'alcohol problems'. How ironic?! And just last week, two St. Clair County judges were slapped on the wrist for driving drunk and for causing an accident that nearly killed a man. How hypocritical! What are your thoughts on this, sir? Thank you.

Respectfully,

Ray Hughes (FAM Edutainment)

First and foremost, it must be remembered that long before the Civil Rights Movement, the nation's lawmakers were white. After the movement, Blacks with money, such as O.J. Simpson and Leonard Little (football players), were able to escape severe punishment for offenses against the law. Simpson's involving a trial by jury for the alleged murder of his wife, Nicole, of which he was acquitted - but later found guilty in a Civil Court (pertaining to money) - something the plaintiffs yet seek. Little's charge, which involved a car death of a white female, was ruled accidental, but many people are still dissatisfied about his outcome. If neither had money and high profiled lawyers, they would have wound up like the title of the song "Bye, Bye, Blackbirds." Therefore, your overall feeling about whites in such situations, history will attest to that.

However, in reference to LaRussa, you can bet your bottom dollar that he will be vindicated, but not in the minds of many baseball fans. There is no doubt that Cardinal fans are the most loyal in baseball. Though, during the course of this season at home and on the road, Tony will be reminded over and over again about his highly publicized wine-drinking incident. It wouldn't surprise me if somebody nicknamed him "Wine," especially if some of his baseball strategy backfired. But being called "Wine" shouldn't be taken as a slap in the face. I remember a guy in my hometown who was called "Wine." He was the best person anybody would want to meet; he just liked drinking wine. Recently, after the Cards were swept by the Mets, I heard a few members of the press talk about LaRussa as if he had a tail. This happened many times last year when the team was seemingly down and out. Hypocrisy, among other things according to the American Heritage College Dictionary, means "the practice of professing beliefs, feelings or virtues that one does not hold or possess, falseness" - a definition that fits many of the Cards' radio and TV personalities. In other words, when the team is hot, it's unbeatable...when down, its ostracized. This type of judgment could affect their fans, but they are too loyal to concede.

Much has been said about Black fans and players returning to MLB, but I've never read a story so succinctly put about this matter than I did by Otis L. Sanford, columnist for The Memphis Commercial Appeal, which was published Sunday, April 1, 2007 following Saturday's so-called "Civil Rights" game, which involved the Cards. In following the story's caption entitled, "Trying to Reclaim that Thrill from the Greatest Game," he outlines his position concerning things about the game that once were important to him. In speaking of the Cards' guide book, he says, "I come across the only American born Black player listed in the guide, outfielder Preston Wilson, who joined the Cardinals last August, just in time for the title run." In a lower passage, he states, "There are six pages devoted to profiles of the team's front office executives and I discover, to no surprise, they're all male and all White. And this team was picked to participate in Saturday's first ever Civil Rights game?"

Although I am a former Negro-Leaguer, this same game has caused me to lose respect for the national Civil Rights organization, the NAACP Defense Fund and the Negro League Baseball Museum for accepting money from it, while remaining silent about Bud Selig, who earned $14.5 million last year - cutting the Negro League history short by refusing to give some of its members pensions. About the Cards' management, it has a history of short-changing Blacks, such as denying Black women attendance at games on "Ladies' Day," and so many other things that I can name. Even now, by bilking its loyal fans out of their money, management shows that it cares less about their well- being. As for LaRussa, I don't have to worry anymore about why he cut several Black players, whether drunk or sober, that's his nature. He, as a lawyer - the same as the St. Clair County judges - has proven NOT to be Gods!!!

Week of April 25, 2007

Hey, Joe: Both Reverend Al Sharpton and Al Roker say Don Imus must go. Do you think Imus' labeling of the Rutgers women's basketball team as "nappy-headed hoes" is a comic observation meant to be brushed off, a firing offense, or a commentary on hair care?

Al - Loma Vista Memorial Park, Fullerton, California

I love Don Imus. He represents the flip-side of "America the beautiful" - you know...the part about slave quarters, where Blacks were stripped of their names and women called "nappy headed hoes" by slave masters, who raped them at will after they were kidnapped from their African homeland and then forced to serve them. Now, I've heard a zillion stories relating to how Blacks got to America - the best being their own people sold them. Had the people who purchased them been civilized, conscience would have dictated them differently. Now based upon the criticism Imus has received, since his infamous remarks, if I was him I would petition the government, claiming that I'm being slandered, which violates my Freedom of Speech found in The Constitution under the Bill of Rights. In fact, I would do the same about Freedom of Press, which is found under the same law. Then, he wouldn't have to vow that the phrase he used was originated by rappers in the Black community. This part of America is only an extension of the slave quarters. By the time it became available, evil forces had characterized Blacks as animals. Remember the phrase "Association brings on assimilation." The ill-fated Constitution covers all these destructive laws.

Biblically, it included Freedom of Religion, which is man's law. God gave man free will to choose his own fate, after He (God) set the standards. Anything contrary is a violation. The Bible - in Leviticus - states one law - "one for the home born, same for the stranger." Ironically, both Blacks and whites are strangers. Before their arrival, Native Americans inherited the land. Anyway, America chose Christianity as her religion. Her offspring unfortunately included people like Imus. Obviously in this respect, they forgot (or distorted the fact) that God was Father of the Universe. Instead, America came up with a group of presidents, called her Founding Fathers - two of which strayed from certain policies. John Adams signed a treaty with Tripoli stating that America wasn't a Christian nation. I concur. Money is more contagious than Christianity. Financial actions of the churches is evidence. Monrovia, a community around Liberia, was named after James Monroe. Would-be slaves were detoured there to avoid bondage.

According to the Pledge of Allegiance, America has operated under the banner of "one nation under God, indivisible with liberty and justice for all." Truthfully, paraphrased it would read, "One nation under God, divided with liberty and justice for all Whites." With this said, God's name has been used in vain. He said He would separate the wheat from the tare. Somebody stepped into His shoes, thus violating His commandment about "There shall be no other Gods before [Him]." As for the National Anthem, its closing line "O'er the land of the free and the home of the brave" gives a better description. The free are those who - after running away from their homelands to escape oppression - orchestrated the building of their own Promised Land in America - something Moses was denied during ancient history, because of not following God's command. The brave were people like John Adams, James Monroe, Abraham Lincoln and most of all John Newton.

Lincoln's bravery stemmed from his courage to free Blacks from bondage. Later, this led to the 13th, 14th and 15th Amendments to The Constitution that governed change. By then the damage to Blacks had been done. Newton, a captain in the slave trade and author of "Amazing Grace," demonstrated the meaning of change by converting himself to God and becoming an evangelical minister. In doing so, he denounced slavery. In the case of Imus, every person that went contrary denounced his remarks. Whether business people or otherwise, these were those of good will. They refused to be overcome by evil. Those who didn't exercised their Constitutional right. Maybe Imus should check what slave masters did to Black women in the slave quarters centuries ago before pointing fingers at Black rappers, who realize they have been wrong - not to withstand what the Constitution did to both Black and white women. I'm sure Jesse Jackson has apologized many times for his negative remark about Jews, although they are in the majority. Seemingly members of that group have caused them the most problems - the same as the Black reporter, who leaked Jackson's remark to the media, a prime example of Malcolm X's version of "house nigga/field nigga." Had Blacks received equal protection under the law, there would have been no need for Al Sharpton nor Jesse Jackson. Recently in St. Louis, a convention was held for NRA members. A prominently named Black preacher opposed it. He was told by one of its sponsors that The Constitution upheld that. About the same time, Pat Robinson's 700 Club was advertising a planned 400-year-old anniversary entitled, "Reclaiming the Covenant." Although Imus lost his national radio advertisements, people of good will decided his fate. To top it off, the Rutgers women's' basketball team forgave him. Now that's what you call class. Supporters of Imus should change their alibis; they are TOO weak to hold water.

Week of May 2, 2007

Hey Joe: Did you happen to catch the Cards/Cubs series last weekend? If so, what do you think of the two controversial calls made? Thanks.

K.A. - St. Louis, MO

There's nothing better than understanding, and that's exactly what I need following decisions made recently by umpires on two separate occasions in a game between the Cards and Cubs. The first decision concerned a triple play the Cards pulled, which was later reversed by the umpires. The call stemmed from a batter at the plate with two men on base and nobody out. Obviously the batter - in an attempt to bunt to advance the runners - popped the ball in the air above his (and the catcher's) head. The catcher, while in pursuit of it, seemingly used the batter's back as a springboard to catch the ball in mid air, which failed. Meantime, the runners were stalled nearby their respective bases, while pondering the outcome. Immediately, the catcher - after retrieving the ball - tagged the batter, threw to third, and then the ball was relayed onto second, thus completing the triple play. The umpires - after a lengthy discussion over the play - ruled interference against the batter and returned the runners back to their original bases.

Now the above account was what I gathered from the radio broadcast, because I didn't see the game - later only to see excerpts of it without too much explanation. By being familiar with the Infield Fly Rule, which was designed to stop infielders from purposely dropping balls to double up runners, my explanation of the play, whether right or wrong, was meant to give the reader a better perspective of what happened. But the real bummer occurred in the Cubs' bottom half of the 9th. Then - with two out - a man on first, with the batter having a 3-2 count, broke for second. By this time, the pitcher had delivered the ball to the plate, which was called ball four. The catcher - upon receiving it - threw to the shortstop covering second base, who tagged the over sliding runner, who then was called out. According to the radio announcer's indication, it was a Hit-And-Run.

Now something went wrong on that play. As long as I played ball, that was the first time I'd ever heard of such, or maybe the rule has changed...or maybe there was never a rule, and the umpires were caught off guard - thus making up a call. Whichever way, there were some dummies involved - either the runner, coaches, manager or the umpires. In this respect, imagine Gary Coleman of "Diff'rent Strokes" sliding across second base and being called out on this same play with his TV brother being the umpire that made the call. Can't you just envision him looking up with face contorted saying, "Whutcha talkin' bout, Willis?"??? Better yet, this play reminds me of one of my original gimmicks. Before going to bat at one of my times, while clowning with the Indianapolis Clowns, I would conceal a base in the large, baggy pants that I wore. With assistance from the umpire, I would get a walk. Once I was on first, I wandered off, got picked off and found myself in a rundown between first and second. Knowing that I was unable to escape, I would snatch out the base, put it on the ground and step on it. The umpire would call me safe.

Whether Hit-And-Run or intent to steal, the runner should have taken a comfortable lead and froze. He was about to be put in scoring position anyway. As for him stealing, why steal something you're about to be awarded? This is like the crack-smoker, who said he didn't know how serious his problem was until he began stealing his own furniture. My contention is that after the ump called ball four, following the runner taking off for second, he should have hollered, "Time out!" and stopped all other activity. Somebody tell me I'm wrong. It won't hurt my feelings. At least I would have learned something new, or alternatively tell me what was the name of that play.

Week of May 9, 2007

Hey Joe: I just read your response to the question about Don Imus. In response, I wanted to ask you, respectfully and hopefully as a means of initiating a real dialogue on this issue, if you ever listened to his program? Honestly, did you?

> I was a fan of Don Imus for decades. Through his program I was introduced to the music of the Blind Boys of Mississippi, who Imus plugged and had on his show, exposing them to millions and dramatically increasing their album sales. I heard the magnificent preaching of the late Bishop G. E. Patterson: Imus used excerpts of his sermons as "bumper music," and they were so good I found his services on cable and listened to more. The Bishop and Imus became friends, and when he died, the Bishop's widow was on Imus' program, and spoke at length about his ministry and career. I always looked forward to Martin Luther King, Jr., Day, when Imus would insist on playing the entire "I Have A Dream" speech, not just a sentence or two like the other networks or shows, and devoted that day and most of the week to meaningful discussions of race and society with Black leaders. I learned about the leader of a new generation of African-American politicians, Harold Ford, Jr., who was on Imus' show more times than I could count, and who was promoted extensively during his senatorial campaign over the white republican opponent. There are literally hundreds of more examples like these.

Hey Joe: I am a 54-year-old white goober, living in Oklahoma. I got more exposure to decency in race relations from Imus than anything I've ever seen or heard. That's the sad irony of his comments, and the tragedy of his firing. African-Americans who never listened to Imus have no idea of the friend they have lost, all due to a thoughtless use of words magnified and repeated until enough damage was done. Imus' words racist? The last time I heard "nappy-headed" was on a Stevie Wonder album, and Imus was known to refer to his wife as "the green ho" repeatedly. Saturday Night Live uses "ho" to refer to Britney Spears: does she deserve that appellation? I agree that the Rutgers players do not, that the comment was thoughtless and he should have apologized. He did. But because of the over-reaction, and what I see as selective enforcement of censorship after the fact, we've lost a thoughtful voice in the morning who taught me a great deal.

I hope you will read this in the spirit in which it is intended. I am much more sad than combative, and I have come to cringe at the way the word "racist" is used as a bludgeon to assault people who voice opinions or advance ideas that are different. It is sadly causing society to simply avoid discussing any of these topics altogether. That's safe, but it's hardly conducive to progress. Thanks for abiding my rant.

Gary Giessmann - Oklahoma

> No, I'd never heard of him before. Though after reading your email, if I ever needed a friend, I wished it would be you. Other than Bishop G.E. Patterson and Harold Ford, Jr., I was well award of The Blind Boys, Dr. King and Stevie Wonder. Like The Blind Boys, my mother and father - before migrating to Illinois - were from Mississippi. Coincidentally, Emmett Till - before being killed in Mississippi - hailed from the state of Illinois. During time of this occurrence, the Civil Rights Movement was just getting off the ground. King - in years to come - would deliver his famous "I Have A Dream" speech in Washington, DC.

> Now, I wouldn't doubt that you've heard the phrase "nappy-headed" in one of Stevie Wonder's songs. It's as common as apple pie within the Black community. But originally, it surfaced during bondage long prior. At the time, the derogatory title affected Blacks so badly that they became ashamed of their hair. Black males began conking their hair with a solution consisting of sweet potatoes and lye to make it straight like whites - later to come up with a solution called "processing," which did the same. Nat "King" Cole - among other Black males - kept his hair intact with this

remedy. Because of Black females' hair, Madame C.J. Walker and Annie Malone, Black females with local ties, became famous for originating hair cosmetics. Madame Walker, who invented the straightening comb, became the first female millionaire. A close check of history might disclose that the idea carried over into white businesses, such as Pantene. Had Blacks been familiar with The Bible, they would have known what Christ said - his hair was like lamb's wool, his eyes, red like balls of fire and his feet, like burnt brass.

If I read you right, you say that Imus repeatedly called his wife "the green ho." If so, I can understand him better. As a result, it became a habit with him, and he became calloused to saying it. Unfortunately, he called the Rutgers' lady basketball team "nappy-headed ho's" which got him in trouble. In reference to Saturday Night Live and Brittany Spears, that "ho" referral to any lady is disrespectful, but such is a luxury granted the ol' boys network via The U.S. Constitution.

Stevie Wonder has a history of standing up for Blacks' equality. His singing of "Happy Birthday" on behalf of Dr. King was phenomenal. I'd certainly like to know what was Bishop Patterson's take on such an issue. Hopefully, his was different from most Black preachers', who are addressed as "Black leaders." Stevie Wonder and The Blind Boys are more sensitive to what's going on both spiritually and socially than they are. They have more imagination and creativity. The best teacher in the world about racism is history, and The Constitution contains it all. Harold Ford, Jr., who I saw on Tavis Smiley's program on PBS, feels the same way you do about Don Imus. Had he been successful in his senatorial run, he would have had to place his hand on The Bible and swear to uphold The Constitution - the same as when winning his congressional seats. Your email has proven to me that Imus has a good heart. There is still a possibility that he could become famous in a positive way.

```
Week of May 16, 2007

Hey Joe: It was a kick reading about your reminiscence of
Pat Scantlebury. You see, Pat was my dad. There aren't many
people around that still remember him as a ball player.
```

It's great to see that his memory still lives with those
he both competed with, and against. Take care.

Brian P. Scantlebury

Your email was well received. I'm sure your dad made many guys dance around in the batter's box like he did me, because he was all business. It's a strange thing, but batters never forget good pitchers, and good pitchers never forget how bad they made batters look. Coincidentally, shortly after that column was published regarding your dad and me, I received pictures of the 1948 East and West All-Star teams (which included your dad, who made the East team) from Reggie Howard, a Negro League historian and close friend of mine. With this group of players from both teams, he was in some pretty good company.

Sadly, at the time of these pictures, I was completely oblivious to the Negro Leagues and the great talent within it. My first real knowledge of the Negro Leagues occurred when Jackie Robinson took the field with the Dodgers in 1947, followed by Larry Doby, Cleveland Indians, during the same year. The comedy about this was the year prior. Robinson was supposed to have been sent to Montreal for further seasoning. The only adjustment he needed was to be mentally acclimated to the racial environment surrounding him. Doby stepped off the Newark Eagles' bus and put on a Cleveland Indians' uniform.

Although I didn't join the Memphis Red Sox until 1950, Willard Brown and Hank Thompson went to the St. Louis Browns straight from the Monarchs in 1947. Both were released during the season. Brown returned to the Monarchs, Thompson went to the New York Giants, where he starred the next eight years. The Browns was the worst team in baseball. Several years before 1947, they had a one-armed outfielder, whose name was Pete Gray. After Bill Veeck became owner in the early 50s, he hired Ed Goedel, a midget. Willard Brown became a member of the 1948 West All-Star team.

In 1950, only 10 teams were left in the league. Before the season's ending, two or three more teams would drop operations, but the league was over at this point. In observing many of the players included on the East and West teams, I would play with or against many of them. Of the teams listed, I would never play against the Homestead Grays. The teams I played against gave me an idea as to how powerful the Negro Leagues were before I became aware of it. From my observation - including the team I played for - at least eight players on each team left could have done the same thing that Larry Doby did (and later Ernie Banks) by stepping off their team bus and joining any team in the "big leagues." Although your dad - along with Frank Robinson - didn't go to the Cincinnati Reds until 1956, had there been any fairness practiced before Robinson joined the Dodgers, he would have had many guys jumping around in the batter's box trying to hit him.

Other than Willie Mays, Ernie Banks and a few other players that I played with and against, many went down the drain in some of those Major League farm systems. I can understand Blacks' abandonment of baseball after the door to basketball and football opened, because both offered some kind of financial incentive - rather than getting lost in a baseball farm system without a guarantee.

```
Week of May 23, 2007
Hey Joe: I heard that Professor Griff from the world-
renowned rap group Public Enemy will guest lecture in St.
Louis at the end of the month on messages in music, sports
and entertainment and how they affect peoples' minds.
Have you ever heard of Public Enemy or heard any of their
music??? If so, what do you think about what they have to
say?
My gratitude,
Ramón (P.E. fan 4ever!!!) - Long Island, N.Y.
```

I've known about Public Enemy for years. Although - like many other rappers - I've been unable to follow the lyrics of the message they convey, and then too, once something is said in a degrading manner about women, I'm turned off. I failed to realize at the time that I was throwing all rappers in the same bag. Not until I learned from young kids, who quoted the lyrics of some songs verbatim, that many messages were directed at the very society in which numerous rappers grew up in with the door of corporate America closed to them.

The rise of successful rappers - especially in their disrespect of women - followed a pattern similar to Richard Pryor, Eddie Murphy and Chris Rock - all notorious in their language usage. Pryor, as a comedian, used unbelievably foul language before his audiences. Murphy, on Saturday Night Live, played the role of Buckwheat, a little Black kid along with White kids in a show called The Little Rascals also known as our gang. His platted hair stood straight up on his head. Rock - like Pryor as a comedian - also uses foul language. Had these guys performed before mostly Black audiences, they would have never wound up as TV or movie producers. It was the White crossover that made them enjoy the kind of success they attained.

Had Black rappers counted solely on the Black community to escalate their astronomical sales of tapes and CDs, etc., it wouldn't have happened. Whether one believes it or not, there is much dignity within Black America. However, when a group of people are negatively stigmatized - as have been Blacks (and still are) - where money is key to their woes, dignity flies out the windows. Case in point, the sale of crack cocaine. The never-mentioned part of this story is that if Black kids had to get this drug in the country, it would be drug-free of this substance. The supplier is seldom mentioned, yet prisons are lined with Blacks. I'm sure had there been decent jobs available, many of the cellblocks would be empty. Nobody wants to face death or jail each time a piece of crack is sold. I learned this long before crack became a moneymaker.

My experience commenced with the sale of a bushel of wood called kindling, which sold for 10 cents. The purpose of needing it was to start fires in the cooking stove and also heater. Early one Saturday morning, Mrs. Daisy, an elderly woman who lived nearby, sent word to me about bringing her a bushel of kindling. I went up and down every alley in town looking for wood, only to find that they were cleaner than the Board of Health. Later that night, I scouted a house surrounded by a picket fence. It happened to be my Savior. The next morning, it had several missing pickets, but I had my dime.

I'm sure that Professor Griff - if asked about his named topics along with those mentioned above - will shoot straight with his audience and not politic with truth, like some of these sorry Republican candidates, who vie for the presidential nomination. Many successful rappers have proven to be brilliant businessmen. If they are committed to cleaning up their act regarding women, the same should apply with these money-grabbing politicians in reference to the American public.

Week of May 30, 2007

Hey Joe: I am a recent graduate from Texas Southern, and I've received my degree in Criminal Justice. I would like to pursue my graduate studies and enter law school, and maybe even run for president one day. What do you think about Bush and these presidential candidates???

Bianca M. Edwards - Houston, Texas

If anybody wants to know how Christian America really is, check its political history. John Newton, former slave trade captain, evangelical minister and author of the song "Amazing Grace," set the standard for Christianity in the late 1700s. Though his song carries on, history of this angelic man has been kicked by the wayside. Had his ideals been practiced, the way of Dr. King - America's bright and shining star - would have been made easier or there might have been no need for him. As it was, despite the difficulty he encountered trying to open the eyes of people regarding Christianity, his concerns regarding the Vietnam War was the mean of his demise.

Currently, with all the selfish motives of presidential candidates - both Democratic and Republican - one should wonder is there no honor in speaking truth. The only bright spots evident among this group of opportunists are Hillary Clinton and Barack Obama, whose interests have been enhanced by the American public. According to history, never has such an event been witnessed. Since advent of the Founding Fathers, presidential occasions have been dominated by white males. White females were assigned to "womanly chores" and Blacks were subservient. These laws were written into The Constitution. Although there have been amendments to it, Congress presently operates from the original.

I think that over the past four years, the American public has caught up with the fact that these people running for the presidency are no more than a bunch of game-players, who are cashing in politically at the expense of innocent lives - beginning with 9/11. Rather than devote every ounce of

energy to comfort the families of victims, seemingly this sad occasion was welcomed for the purpose of fulfilling other aims - this being the conflict in Iraq. In this respect, Bush could possibly be the best thing that ever happened to America regarding lying. With every passing day, we witness how destructive it has been and still is. The irony about the whole situation is he is a man that professes to be a compassionate Christian.

By now, it should be clear that in order to win the presidency one has to almost be a pathological liar. The presidency can't be won by telling the truth. At one time, it might have been possible, but things are too complex now. Candidates will lie about anything to gain votes or to find favor from special interest groups, who ultimately own them. To top it off are these so-called "debates," which are conducted by the big time TV industry and are no more than popularity contests, where questions such as "What would you have done?" are asked.

The voice of the people spoke recently, when several Republican incumbents- followers of Bush and the religious right - were knocked from their thrones. Even behind this reality, Democratic presidential contenders have played it safe by not stepping up to the plate and saying that Bush lied about WMD, although his "ace boon coon" Tony Blair has been pushed out of office by his people, who viewed him as Bush's puppet. Since Bush has made a habit of calling his Democratic opponents "unpatriotic" because they disagree with him, obviously they feel that there is no honor in losing. But when a person stands up for Righteousness, that is a patriotic person. One person is a majority. The country is begging for change. Hillary Clinton and Barack Obama are prime examples, along with the crookedness of politics that surfaced within the Bush Administration. Now, we should know that these candidates that claim Christian backgrounds are no more than players.

```
Week of June 6, 2007
Hey Joe: I grew up in a small town where the elders nur-
tured us young-uns. We knew nothing of the violence that
our neighbors in surrounding municipalities experienced
as children. The only thing that we feared at night were
```

mosquitoes. Although I have lived in Houston, Texas, for nearly thirty years, my heart has never left the small town that I grew up in, Brooklyn.

Recently our mother passed and my siblings and I faced the task of bringing her home to be laid to rest. It was on this journey that I was made aware of the fact that Brooklyn was "The Oldest Black Incorporated Town In America." I began researching the history and was amazed at what I discovered about Brooklyn. We have constructed a web site www.brooklynillinoisourstory.com to display the documents and history related to our small town.

My question to you is, "How can we get our elected officials involved in our efforts to revitalize Brooklyn, Illinois, with new businesses and to receive the Historical Designation that is due for the town as well as the two churches (Quinn Chapel A.M.E. and Antioch Baptist) that were used in the Underground Railroad that Priscilla Baltimore, Reverend William Paul Quinn and Ezekiel Pines established with Brooklyn being the first station on the journey through Alton, Jacksonville, LaSalle, on up through to Canada? Everyone seems to have forgotten Brooklyn and the role that her founding families played in the anti-slavery movement.

Sincerely,

Cathy Thompson (Irene Dale's daughter) - Houston, TX

Based upon the number of massage parlors in the community, it is understandable why it was labeled "Sin City" several years back, but those who labeled it as such was unfamiliar with its history. Granted, prior to the strip joints' arrival, the town had undergone several lean years, which basically explains how this materialized. The outcome was cleverly manipulated with a promise of jobs that caught an unsuspecting mayor off guard. Though poverty stricken at the time, Brooklyn is historically rich. In fact, its history denotes that it is the only original all-American town in the country. With a population of 2,600 - as compared to 700 currently - townspeople were naturally colorblind.

Though predominately a Black community, at one time there was a white mayor. Blacks and whites lived as one and picked their mates by choice without it being mandated by law. Similar to a fortress, the village was surrounded by railroad tracks, many atop encircling embankments, seemingly to separate itself from adjoining townships that adhered to racial separation. The most significant thing about it was being surrounded by history. A headstone at a grave site on its outskirts display an 1840 date, twenty-five years before Abraham Lincoln's Emancipation Proclamation.

One hundred miles East of the township in Springfield, Illinois, Lincoln began his rise to the presidency. Less than one block North of Brooklyn's boundary in Venice, a high school called Lincoln of Venice was named after him. Brooklyn's adopted name "Lovejoy" was named after Elijah P. Lovejoy, the abolitionist who was murdered by mob action in Alton, a community twenty-two miles North of the town, for his belief in Freedom of the Press. Named after him also is the school and postal office. West of the town and across the Mississippi River in St. Louis, Missouri, Dred Scott - a supposedly free Black - fought for his freedom, which was denied, because it was alleged that he wasn't a U.S. citizen.

In East St. Louis, two miles South of town, was the scene of the 1917 Race Riot. During my upbringing, Blacks politically - in East St. Louis - could be no more than precinct committeemen. At the time, Brooklyn's mayor, William Terry, was as powerful as Richard Daley, mayor of Chicago and Alvin Fields, former mayor of East St. Louis. Terry was orchestrator of Lovejoy Elementary School becoming a high school. By doing so, Black kids - prior students of the elementary school - were stopped from walking or hitch hiking to get to Lincoln of East St. Louis - subsequently, Jackie Joyner-Kersee's alma mater. The little hamlet of National City connected with East St. Louis to the North. Because of the packinghouses in that locale, this gave rise to the title "National Stockyards."

In Brooklyn, Terry - who was Black - ruled with an iron hand. He was mayor, supervisor and school superintendent - often calling the town his. During his long tenure, he gave no quarter nor took no step to the rear. Of a town where every street block was replete with homes of a variety - some good, bad, ramshackle, shotgun or what not - townspeople strived

The Prince schools a young Sean (author) on something.
Bubble thoughts courtesy of Aunt Joyce. Quick! Get the Poloroid!

independently. Every inch of land was utilized prudently - the open land used for community gardens. Even houses were placed opposite to the railroads, where trains ran. Of the seven major East/West streets, five of the Founding Fathers - namely Madison, Jefferson, Washington, Adams and Monroe - have been advertised for 100 years. The police force has never been restricted to arresting only certain citizens. One of the town's three schools sported a two-story brick building with a date of 1890. Quinn Chapel A.M.E. Church was connected to Harriet Tubman's Underground Railroad. One of many Black entrepreneurs was the Dale Family, but first and foremost the town is the oldest Black town in America.

So, step up Yvetter Younge and James Claiborne, state representative and state senator respectively, grab Jerry Costello by the hand and get this town officially declared as such nationally. For many, many, many years St. Clair County Democrats have used this town's votes, until they're almost "used up." If you can't get it done, maybe the Republican Party can. The Founding Fathers belonged to both national parties. People left this town because of major businesses closing, along with bad promises. If this history isn't sufficient enough to get it officially declared, then you tell us.

Week of June 13, 2007

Hey Joe: Just what do you think of this Barry Bonds/Hank Aaron scenario???

Wendell - Madison, IL

I think Barry Bond — before this season is over and barring injuries and sickness — will be the greatest hitter to ever pick up a piece of lumber and stroll to the plate. But because of his brashness, many have turned thumbs down on him, which he cares less about. However, due to this alleged steroid thing, matters have grown increasingly worse. Lately, I've heard talk that Hank Aaron has decided not to attend the game that proliferates the breaking of his 755 homerun record, which seems to be a matter of concern. If this be the case, whether Aaron likes it or not, it is going to happen.

Hopefully, he hasn't developed animosity towards Bonds because of him closing in on his record. If so, let it be!!! If he is duped into believing like many of Bonds' disgruntled fans regarding his personality and alleged steroid use, then he has fallen victim of the "divide and conquer" game, which is a philosophy that has been used for centuries to keep Blacks from galvanizing. Aaron must remember that during his playing days – no matter how congenial he was – once he neared Babe Ruth's record, hate mail came from everywhere, and he became the bad boy. Anyway, had not Willie Mays been drafted into the military for two years, he would have broken Ruth's record first, and Aaron would have been chasing his record. I'm sure that Mays will be sitting in the ballpark to congratulate Bonds when it happens. There are some things I think over deeply and allow them to disturb me. Such was the case last Sunday night, while watching Sports Plus on Channel 5, St. Louis' local TV station, hosted by Rene Knott and Frank Cusumano. During Cusumano's interview with Tony Hawk, a White skateboard champion, I heard him refer to Hawk as the "Babe Ruth of the skateboards." It let me know that the name of Babe Ruth would never disappear from white history. It also brought to my attention a recent TV court case heard by Judge Greg Mathis, featuring a white plaintiff and defendant. The plaintiff stated that their reason for being in court was because the defendant was racist. Admitting that it was so, the defendant said, "Being racist is wrong, but being Black is worse."

Even during the time when the Negro Leagues was oblivious, Josh Gibson, a prolific homerun hitter, was called the "Black Babe Ruth." Then came Jackie Robinson and the rest is history. In 1997, as a financial token for the destruction of the league, a few players who played before and after Robinson were given lifetime pensions. This was MLB Commissioner Bud Selig's way of winning over the public by exhibiting how benevolent the league was to the breaking up of the Negro League. In 2004, he announced to the public that more monies were available for pensions to be paid to needy former Negro Leaguers, who played parts of at least four seasons. Subsequently, this was a lie. Many of the 20 handpicked players were anything but "needy," and it was said that they met the requirement of having played four consecutive years. With this completed, several former players – including myself – were eliminated and rejected. I fought this injustice by taking on MLB – even wrote Selig a letter about staging a charity game with the proceeds going to the players as pensions. Earlier this year, my idea

Prince Joe sharing a light moment with his wife, "Lu" and former Memphis Red Sox teammate, Ollie Brantley (above)

Prince Joe has always been a family-oriented person. (Above) Pictured with his wife "Lu", seated like a king and queen at their throne.

(Right) Pictured with his wife, "Lu", and a newborn T'Asia, one of 20 + grandchildren.

was stolen. A game was played between the Cards and Indians as a Civil Rights game. Benefiting from it was the nation civil rights organization, the NAACP Defense Fund and the Negro League Baseball Museum, along with two other Black people. Don't sell out Aaron...this is all related to the Negro Leagues and two former players, you and Mays, and a by-product of it in Barry Bonds.

Week of June 20, 2007

```
My name is Bliss Boussant from L.A., Cali...Joe how do
you feel about the big Michael Vick dog fighting contro-
versy? I just think its another way to project negative
images of successful Black ball players...nobody cares
about animals living in the street that walk around with
hair missing from their asses and missing ears...whether
or not this practice is legal or illegal I still think it
was blown out of proportion due to the fact it was Vick.
```

When I first heard the news about this, I was terribly shaken. It came from former Negro Leaguer and close friend of mine, Larry LeGrande, who resides in Roanoke, VA. He and I played for Goose Tatum's Detroit Clowns in 1958. For several years now, he and I have communicated consistently about the nation's social affairs and also about the world of sports — something he loves now about as much as he did then, when we rode the same bus together across the country. For the past decade — during the college football season — Mike Vick has been a main topic of his, being that Vick was a resident from Newport News and played for Virginia Tech, a school located 30 miles from Roanoke. After the story broke — and in following Larry's account of it — a Black male appeared on TV with his voice disguised and face unrecognizable admitting that the dog fighting took place on Vick's property.

Additionally, supposedly saying that his dogs took part in the activity. It was thought that he made these statements because he had run afoul of the law prior, and his testimony would lessen his chance of him receiving a stiff sentence. If this is true, I am reminded of a farmer who had three daughters, who had a parrot. Each time he planted corn, crows would swoop down and eat it shortly after coming up from the soil. On one such occasion, he decided to settle this with his shotgun, but on the same day his daughters decided to let the parrot out. Subsequently being a bird, the parrot decided to join the crows. The farmer – in shooting in their direction – went out afterwards to see how many he had killed. Upon reaching the site, he found three dead and the parrot lying wounded nearby. Saddened by this incident, he hurriedly picked up the parrot and headed home. His daughters, seeing him with the wounded parrot, admonished him badly for being so cruel, but before he could explain what happened, the parrot cried out, "Bad company…bad company…bad company!!!" This is what happened in Vick's case.

Ultimately, I would like to sympathize with him, but I am definitely unable. I'm not a fan of dog fighting nor cock fighting, etc. My feeling is that those who enjoy these cruel acts are cold-hearted. Remember Birmingham, when dogs were sicked upon Blacks??? Vick placed himself in the limelight for a bad image to be projected of him, and Bob Hille – in the Sporting News magazine – took advantage of it by saying, "Okay, are you surprised by this dog thing? After all, isn't Vick the one who taught the Falcons to roll over and play dead?" In this sense, I'm really thinking he's speaking about Peyton Manning. Had not those wide outs made circus catches and another player had a great interception, he would still be in search of his first Super Bowl victory. Given this same opportunity prior, he flunked because of being too slow of foot to get out of the pocket. Subsequently, he made every excuse conceivable about the defense breaking down. Had Vick been bottled up in the same situation, he would have come outta there like a shot. Otherwise, the only answer I have favorable for Vick is, "I'm sorry. I don't support immorality. You made your bed hard…now lay in it."

Week of June 27, 2007

Hey Joe: With the 4th of July just around the corner, I'm wondering what our nation has to celebrate in 2007. We've started a tremendously unpopular war in Iraq, our grip as a military and economic superpower is slipping away, and reality TV seems to be the only thing that binds us together anymore. Should we tone down the booze, fireworks and flag-waving this year?

Sincerely,

Brent Rowley - Chicago, IL

In retrospect at a young age, I could hardly wait until it was time for the 4th of July and also Christmas. But growing up Black in our society, I eventually learned that both were frauds. Before then in reference to the 4th of July, my parents would give me money or I would hustle for it myself to purchase fireworks in celebration of something I had no idea about the meaning of its history. Not until the Civil Rights Movement did the true meaning of this holiday surface. Then names such as Frederick Douglass, Benjamin Banneker and so forth began to crop up, but nothing is more scintillating than to read Frederick Douglass' version of "The Meaning Of July 4th For The Negro," a speech delivered by him at Rochester, NY, July 5, 1852.

As for Christmas, nobody has been able to describe Santa Claus better than comedian, Dick Gregory. In explaining the situation, he says, "Now you know.it has to be fantasy for a fat white man in a red suit to be in the Black community with a bag on his back late at night bellowing, 'Ho, ho, ho'." Then realistically, you'd have thought he was Don Imus. Better yet, our parents - after working menial jobs - paid for the toys we received and lied to us about Santa bringing them. In so many instances today, I constantly hear about the man-less Black family, the destruction of the Black family and so forth. Well, it seems to me that our mothers and fathers years back didn't help the situation by giving credit to somebody else for what they did. Don't you think this was damaging to kids that thought their parents did nothing for them at Christmas???

Sometimes I drift off into a dream world when pondering over such things and its remedy. Like Black spokespeople who have tried the rest but now should try the best. You know, like a high profiled battery of Black intellectual lawyers, who would file a lawsuit against the U.S., The Declaration of Independence and The Constitution for the damage done to Blacks for over 300 years. See, it would only prove that The Declaration of Independence consisted of a group of people who broke free from another potentially controlling group in order to do their own thing in controlling Blacks. The Constitution bears witness to this.

Excluding all other things that solidify the case, only the interest for the free labor that Blacks' forefathers performed would be asked for. Instantaneously, each adult Black male and female would become millionaires. More money than this has been pumped into this unpopular war, otherwise, the money that would be given fulfills the promise of 40 Acres and a Mule. Up until this point, the Black masses - offspring of those forefathers - have only received ADC, otherwise known as Aide for Dependent Children - while at the same time ridiculed. In addition to the Black family being destroyed during bondage, there is also a catch in receiving ADC. This is that a Black male companion is disallowed to live in the household. The true reality shows are those that feature these millionaire presidential candidates, who claim to be so patriotic and whose millions - in all probability - stem from Black forefathers' work. But my definition of ADC means A Dedicated Citizen, who - in addition to all other contributions - had to fight the government to get into the military to fight the enemy in helping to protect the country. That's what is called PATRIOTISM.

Week of July 5, 2007

Hey Joe: Are you alarmed that the recently crowned Miss Missouri, Hazelwood resident, Lindsay Casmaer, is an Ivy League graduate (U. Penn) with a degree in neurobiology who works as a Washington University researcher? What gives: pageants are suddenly smarting up?

Anonymous

I'm not really a pageant fan, but I'm glad you brought this to my attention. I applaud Casmaer. What she has done is so refreshing in proving there is more to her than just a body. I applaud you also for paying such close attention. Since the show American Idol aired, all sorts of similarities have surfaced, and the judges – in trying to emulate Randy Jackson, Paula Abdul and Simon Cowell – have become increasingly sickening. TV shows like So You Think You Can Dance and America Got Talent are gimmicks that generate big money. Casmaer – without the slightest notion – opened a can of worms by exhibiting mental skill. If there is truth in the words "role model," then she is a shining example.

I've never cared for pageants, and this dates back to when Black ladies were disallowed entry. I've never thought swimsuits, or such attire, was necessary for a lady's ability to be judged. Now, with the bikini thing en vogue, ladies are only a step away from being stark naked, just to win the approval of some old geyser in order to prevail. My idea about this??? Sheer exploitation!!! Evolving from it are strip joints and massage parlors. Currently, it floods TV right before the watchful eyes of children, who we claim to love so much. I'm sure that every lady that finds herself in situations, which require the bearing of skin, has a reason for being there. The bottom line??? Money!!!

I'm wondering if one day women will galvanize. Presently, I don't believe they know their power. Without women, this country would go down the drain. Who wants to be around a bunch of "hard legs" all the time?!?? Whether they realize it or not, they have been short-changed by men in positions of power and reduced to sex objects. If women had been given a fair shake, then there wouldn't be such a big outcry over Hillary Clinton running for the presidency. If women secede from the church, it would mean the sounding of the death knell. Then, what would happen to organizations like the Moral Majority, or – in other words – religious right, who target homosexuality as its pet peeve while remaining mum about men, who endorse women to parade around naked before them in these so-called "pageants"?

Seems to me that this wing of Christianity would use its "morality" to see that these young ladies keep every stitch of clothing on during their competition. Otherwise, industries like Viagra, Cialis and Levitra will continue to soar financially, due to the sexual dreams of these old geysers. Casmaer has demonstrated that she is a brainy individual by her choice of study. I'm sure the other young ladies that appeared on stage with her are quite brainy too, hopefully in social sciences, especially after being so closely monitored. If so, they have more experience than the judges, who have no more than opinions. Exclusive of bikini outfits, these young ladies – after undergoing the experience – are prepared to teach disciplinary traits to politicians, clergymen and judges, who are out of sync with promoting a higher standard of morality. If successful, it might save young ladies in the future from feeling comfortable while performing naked before audiences in order to make a living.

```
Week of July 19, 2007

Hey Joe: Do you think it's good or bad that 18 Metro East
districts will start school in July? Aren't summer vaca-
tions beneficial for both students and teachers?

Mr. Thinking Cap - Mount Vernon, IL
```

Years back, seemingly teachers and students had a pretty good report. Now – seemingly for decades – all hell has broken loose. Just recently, students from one school held the mayor's office hostage in protest of a state takeover of city schools, which they felt would affect their chances of graduation. Ultimately, a trip was made to Jefferson City, MO to ask lawmakers to help in securing their point. I couldn't have been more sympathetic. I truly believe that one should have a voice in deciding his or her destiny. In reference to the teachers' and students' early return to the classroom, I certainly would like to hear from both sides what they have to say about this. After all, the students are employers and the teachers are their employees. If you think this is untrue, let all the students disappear from the classrooms.

Now, I'm not too familiar with the reason for this early return, therefore, I would not be unable to render a fair opinion, but some of these things I've been hearing such relating to busing, "deseg," charter and magnet schools (etc.) – especially in the St. Louis area – seems as if days long gone. Obviously, they aren't, and children suffer the consequences. I remember St. Louis Public Schools – like Beaumont and Central – being viewed as charter or magnet schools. This was when they were lily white, and the school board controlled by whites. At the same time, Blacks attended Sumner, Vashon and Washington Tech; they were forbidden to compete against whites. Sometimes I wonder why the Negro Leagues get such attention based upon the travels and denials encountered, when the same denials were accorded Blacks socially right in their own back yards. East of the Mississippi River (on the Illinois side), Black kids were bused from East Carondelet – right across the street from Dupo High School – through East St. Louis to attend Black schools in Brooklyn and Venice – the latter of which had a school "provided" for Blacks. Athletically, these schools played in the IL-MO League. After integration in 1968, "white flight" took place. Venice School is currently closed. After East Side High was integrated, it became predominately Black. This is the same situation that occurred at Beaumont, Central and the likes. I supposed the point I'm trying to make is that these institutions were/are components of the so-called "educational system," but the credentials teachers have received only apply to math, English and reading, etc. without covering everyday history. Therefore, students will never learn the social aspect of life. In other words, teachers who claim they are educators are really unfocused, and students will never learn the truth. To sum it up, seemingly teachers and students have been on long vacations, so now it is time to go to work.

```
Week of July 26, 2007
Hey Joe: A while back you ran a story on The Prince and
how he got snubbed by Bud Selig and some of his MLB cro-
nies by not receiving his pension for his service to the
Negro Leagues. I wanna ask The Prince has he settled that
dispute yet and what he thinks about former pro football
players' current fight with the NFL Sounds very similar
to me. Tsk! And they call these sports "pay for play."
LOL!!!
David "Jellyman" Abdul - University City, MO
```

No, I've never received a pension, but there is MORE to this story than has been revealed. In reference to football, it is my thinking that players lacking 10 years have been denied pensions, which makes it a bit different than former Negro Leaguers' perspective. Though I admire every football player who has the courage to stand and not falter to power, while in pursuit of what they feel is rightfully theirs. At least I believe their case has generated more national attention than that of former Negro Leaguers. This title alone separates its players from those who played football, which consists of different nationalities. Former Negro Leaguers means exactly that. Had there been justice, there would have been no such distinction.

My first knowledge of former Negro Leaguers receiving pension occurred in 1997, almost two years after I attended the first Negro Leagues reunion in Kansas City, MO, home of the Negro League Baseball Museum, approximately 50 years after the beginning of the destruction of the Negro

Leagues, a project that most Blacks initially thought was all positive. Even Jackie Robinson authored a book called Baseball Has Done It. Now, at this very moment, white baseball moguls are wracking their brains trying to figure out how to encourage Black American-born players and fans back into their ball yards, following the shellacking imposed on them throughout the white farm system and "Majors," which is currently loaded with Latin-speaking Blacks. No other person could be more proud than I to see these modern day brethren attain heights that they have reached. Notwithstanding the fact that it was the Negro Leagues that guaranteed their advancement – first, because it provided them a place to play and secondly, because American-born Black players chose football and basketball over baseball.

However, the first group of players to receive pensions were those who played before 1947, at which time was designated as the cutoff date. The annual amount for pensions was $10,000.00 – beginning with the first check until death. In 2004, Bud Selig lied to the nation about additional money for needy former Negro Leaguers, who played parts of at least four years. Later this was retracted to mean "four consecutive years." The only notice I received concerning these pensions was his statement, which I read in a local newspaper. I'm almost sure many other players were ill informed also. By the time I contacted Selig's office, it was already decided who would receive pensions, finalized with the assistance of Robert "Bob" Mitchell of Tampa Bay, FL and a one-year player with the Kansas City Monarchs, whose shakedown was $500.00 per player, which was in addition to the pension he finagled for himself.

In another year, Mitchell and the other players he shook down will be pension-less because of the four-year expiration date – leaving numerous players without ever receiving pensions. Then, Selig would have finished what white baseball moguls started in 1947, which was the destruction of the Negro League's history. Though he – with his Governor George Wallace (former governor of Alabama) mentality – could never have done this without help from Mitchell, who is Black, the NAACP Defense Fund, the National Civil Rights Organization and the Negro League Baseball Museum – organizations that accepted monies from a so-called Civil Rights game between the St. Louis Cardinals and Cleveland Indians. The irony about this type of game stemmed from an idea stolen from me, concerning a game to provide pensions for former Negro Leaguers, and these organizations were previously informed.

Week of August 2, 2007

Hey Joe: The movie "Evan Almighty" is out right now and Morgan Freeman plays God. Slate magazine describes Freeman as being in "full-on magical Negro" mode. Do you think this is a role Blacks should avoid playing in the future? Here's a description of "magical Negro" from Wikipedia:

The magical Negro is typically "in some way outwardly or inwardly disabled, either by discrimination, disability or social constraint," often a janitor or prisoner. He has no past; he simply appears one day to help the white protagonist. He is the Black stereotype, "prone to criminality and laziness." To counterbalance this, he has some sort of magical power, "rather vaguely defined but not the sort of thing one typically encounters." He is patient and wise, often dispensing various words of wisdom, and is "closer to the earth."

The magical Negro serves as a plot device to help the protagonist get out of trouble, typically through helping the white character recognize his own faults and overcome them. In this way, the magical Negro is similar to the Deus ex machina; a simple way for the protagonist to overcome an obstacle almost entirely through outside help. Although he has magical powers, his "magic is ostensibly directed toward helping and enlightening a white male character." It is this feature of the magical Negro that some people find most troubling. Although the character seems to be showing African-Americans in a positive light, he is still ultimately subordinate to whites. He is also regarded as an exception, allowing white America to "like individual Black people but not Black culture." To save the white protagonist, however, he would do anything, including sacrificing himself, as Sidney Poitier portrays in The

Defiant Ones, the prototypical magical Negro movie.
Anonymous

I'm not a movie buff. I began to learn from a young age that most were only illusions, but because of never being acquainted with the phrase "magical Negro mode," it really struck my fancy. As a result, I became inquisitive about it only to find that it was a comedy. Before learning that, I was busy holding my breath due to Morgan Freeman being a favorite actor of mine. And, I had been accustomed to seeing how Blacks had been portrayed as buffoons in movies, as I was growing up, which in all probability was the reason I got turned off. Freeman and numerous other Black actors and actresses refuse to buy that yesteryear jazz today. They immediately distinguished dignity from humiliation.

Black actors and actresses of yesterday had no choice, which isn't too much better today. Those like Eddie "Rochester" Anderson, Mantan Moreland and Steppin' Fetchit only took roles that were thrown at them – for instance (in most cases) reacting after being frightened. I recall one movie scene in which a Black dude outran a car driven by a white man. Once the car pulled even with him, the white man remarked, "I must be stopping." The Black dude exclaimed, "Naw, suh…I'se jest slown down to catch my wind." Hattie McDaniel was a prime example in the role she played in Gone With the Wind, which starred actor, Clark Gable. When Jackie Robinson joined the Dodgers in 1947 and stole second base, it induced an elderly white woman to scream, "I told you so, I told you so…no sooner than Nigras are allowed to play, they're gonna start stealing."

However, Blacks such as those aforementioned were jewels to the Black masses. They were heroes – in another sense stars. Their gifted antics relieved stress in time of need. They taught Blacks how to laugh at themselves while undergoing duress, as well as joke about how they were treated like saying, "If you are White you're right, if you are Brown, stick around but if you are Black, get back" – laughable quips that at times served better than medicine. This is why the basketball wizardry of Reece "Goose" Tatum of Harlem Globetrotter fame made him so fabulous. Goose was my idol, which – in baseball – led me to become known as Clown Prince Joe Henry.

The description of the "magical Negro" as outlined in Wikipedia, an online non-standard version, reads like a work of fantasy. Freeman in the movie, Evan Almighty, only played the role of God. The white protagonist made himself God. Unlike Aladdin, who could summon a genie from the magic lamp to fulfill his desires, the white protagonist – through conversion – created slaves out of human beings by forcing them to obey him against their will – ultimately producing an African-American Negro Colored Black, which coincides with the phrase, "Only the names change…the identity remains the same." The raw reality about this is wherever there are slaves, there are slave masters, who – in order to pacify their conscience – have to resort to negative propaganda to dehumanize so-called slaves. Over past decades, numerous studies have been conducted on Blacks to learn their physical and mental cultural status. I am unable to recall one such study conducted on whites. The magic of this is how Blacks used psychology, philosophy, sociology and economics to overcome their dilemma. Imagine people of America chasing truth in literature, such as history and The Bible, etc., as opposed to fantasy akin to Harry Potter. Isn't it time to rethink moral values???

Week of August 9, 2007

Hey Joe: Is it ever all right to hit a woman? Let's say, if she hit you first?

The Good Reverend Isaac - Tallahassee, FL

I live by the adage "Let Your Conscience Be Your Guide," of which I broadly speak, but in this case mainly about women. Thus, hitting ladies isn't the proper thing to do, though I suppose millions throughout society would like to know exactly what is proper. My prescribed method is a steady diet of Christian traits – not with intent as professed Christians claim – but as Christian trait bearers. The church in America has failed. The reason??? No conscience. God is being peddled on the basis of tithes – the more one gives, the larger the financial reward in return. However, thank God for The Bible and those who are true to it. Even with those of good will, society is still corrupt, but imagine having lived in it without The Bible – the country would be barbaric.

To left:
Prince Joe in 1958 with Detroit Clowns' Reece (Goose) Tatum

Below: The Prince meets Goose Tatum

No greater sin could have ever been committed than that of a clergyman who sits before a TV audience and proclaims to prophesy about people who – according to him – have certain illnesses that are being removed as he speaks with God, and the donations they give to his institution will seal the deal through his prayers. In other words, the Blessings of God have a cover charge. I've always been under the impression that the source of God's three basic laws are (1) There shall be no other gods before Me, (2) Love and (3) Obedience. According to The Bible, man's narrow-minded dictates have destroyed the Laws of God. Just recently, Michael Vick – with all his wealth and God-given talent – chose to follow man's corrupt idea of sport in dog fighting, a most brutal entertainment. Now, he is at the point of his own destruction. This is what happens when God is omitted.

For some selfish reason, man feels he has a monopoly over women and if they fail to yield to his desires, it affects his ego. Ultimately, he resorts to physical violence as his way of subduing them. Men gaining control over women through force is nothing new. If so, there would be no need for the numerous women abuse centers scattered across the nation. The control thing concerning them dates back to The Constitution. Those who feel they must be in control are insecure people. I doubt if the average person realizes that a love affair between man and woman works two ways, which consists of two loves – a physical as well as spiritual. If one party makes a habit of betraying the physical aspect, which is based upon intimacy, there is no conscience. The other party should become strong enough to sever the relationship before hatred develops, thus salvaging the spiritual love. A person can't be forced to do what they don't want to do. Jerry Springer's TV show is a prime example of not addressing the issue properly by having women to beat men while security guards disallow men to strike back, therefore, placing them in a helpless situation. But what happens once the guards are removed? We're right back at square one. Women should be taught the right way. Since the church and Springer fail to convey morality, Dr. Phil is their last hope.

```
Week of August 16, 2007
Hey Joe:  I  heard  you  attended  one  of  the  Gateway
```

```
Grizzlies' games over in Sauget last Friday. How did you
enjoy it?!
Beverly - Sauget, IL
```

Until Friday before last, I'd always wondered why radio broadcasters wore headsets. Joe Pott, resolved that. He is radio broadcaster for the Gateway Grizzlies, a team in the Frontier Baseball League. Before meeting him, several things occurred. As a former Negro Leaguer, I was invited there in honor of the Negro Leagues, and, MAN, WHAT AN HONOR – beginning at the desk of Adam Cooper, the charismatic park coordinator. Upon meeting him shortly after arriving to the park, he was wearing the jersey of a New York Cuban uniform, which completely surprised me, because I had no idea this would occur. What was so coincidental about it was that when I left home, I had with me a newspaper article from 1950, which talked about me collecting three hits against the New York Cubans when I played with the Memphis Red Sox. I also brought along a picture of me with the 1952 Mississippi Ohio Valley (M.O.V.) All-Star Team and a large poster advertising a game between the Indianapolis Clowns and New York Black Yankees in 1955. When I received the newspaper article, it had been enlarged to the size of notebook paper.

Before leaving the office, I struck up friendships with Paul, the team photographer; Dwayne Isgrig, historical researcher of the St. Louis Browns; and Chris Gibson, son of former pitcher, Bob Gibson. Prior to meeting him and/or even knowing he was a member of The Grizzlies, I happen to have been watching a segment of Channel 5's TV sports show one night when he was being interviewed, which was my source of information regarding him athletically. Being that he was the only Grizzly I was familiar with, once in the office, I made a special request to meet him. While carrying on conversations with different other members of the Grizzly family, suddenly I was approached by this mannerable young man, who extended his hand and introduced himself as "Chris Gibson." Offering my hand in acknowledgement, I asked him if he would push me to the mound in my wheelchair to assist me in throwing out the first pitch. With a smile on his face, he nodded and said, "I sure will."

Later, I found myself outside the park in a golf cart being chauffeured by a gentleman named Jason – with Adam seated in back. We took off and eventually entered the field through a large gate near the centerfield area. Moments later, another huge gate was opened displaying the beauty of the entire field from our centerfield view. While sitting there, I thought – since I'm already in the cart, it would be much easier for Jason to drive straight through the centerfield grass en route to the pitcher's mound, then Chris would be spared from pushing my wheelchair there. I echoed this idea to Adam. He answered by asking me if he understood me to say prior that it was difficult for me to walk without my cane. After I acknowledged this, he said, "Remember…we didn't bring your cane and if we go out on that field, we would have to outrun the groundskeepers to keep from getting injured." We finally reached our destination near home plate. En route, I waved at the fans of which I was told was the largest crowd of the season. Almost surrounding us near home plate was Chris, his manager and several team mates, all wearing a variety of Negro League uniforms. On the third base side stood the Chillicothe Paint, the Grizzlies' opponent for the evening. After Chris professionally handled my request of him and upon us reaching the mound, I raised my right hand as if to deliver the ball to the plate, but he took it out of my hand and delivered it for me.

After meeting Commissioner Bill Lee, I found myself being transported to the radio booth to be interviewed by Joe Pott. Once he adjusted the headset, everything was blotted out but his voice. In his field, it was the greatest I'd heard since the days of Mel Allen, Red Barber, France Laux and the likes. I was the only fan in the park surrounded by nothing but stars. But just think, had it not been for my grandson Sean – along with three of his children, "Yusey", Aquil and T'Asia, I probably would have missed the event. My great grandchildren kept asking me, "Papi Joe, when are we going back???"

Week of August 30, 2007

Hey Joe: Do you know if there are any Blacks on the Cardinals baseball team?

An-Ony-Mous

The question asked brings back memories of 1953, when I took Tom

Red Sox Hit Hard

LITTLE ROCK, April 16.—The Memphis Red Sox of the Negro American League pounded out 16 hits Sunday afternoon to defeat the New York Cubans, 10 to 4. Isaah Harris, Red Sox lefthander, limited the Cubans to eight hits and struck out 12. Joe Henry, Memphis second sacker, collected three hits in four tries. The Red Sox and Cubans will meet in Memphis Friday night.

Austin and Jehosie Heard to The Glass Bar, a fancy hotel and nightspot located on Lawton Street in the city. Austin was the Cards' first Black player and Heard was a former Negro Leaguer that I played against. At the time, Heard was with the Baltimore Orioles, formerly the St. Louis Browns, who were in town before the season opened to play a one game city series.

However, Preston Wilson, an American-born Black, started the season with the Cards but since has disappeared. So what's new??? Dating back to the pre-Jackie Robinson era, this is the Gashouse Gang, a fabled bunch of ballplayers with a sordid history – a team that at one time – in addition to having players with names such as Pepper Martin, etc. – fielded a combination of brothers like The Deans, The Coopers, The Boyers and The McDaniels. I could've answered the question whether the team has an American-born Black player by simply saying "NO," but I felt that I would be cheating somebody out of some other interesting things, especially in relation to the Cards' last season and now.

By them winning the championship last year, I see the image of Tony LaRussa being blown up bigger than life itself. Every time I hear him immortalized, I think of Josh Gibson, the former Negro League slugger, who played in the Mexican winter league at times. It was rumored that there one day, while sporting better than a .500 batting average by hitting singles, doubles and triples, he was called into the office by management, where he was told, "We no bring you here to hit singly, doubly, triply. We bring you to hit homerun!!!" The spokesman said before adding, "If you can no hit homerun, you be on plane." He used his right hand to indicate a plane taking off and climbing into the air, while humming a sound like its engine. In LaRussa's case, the homerun was a World Series, and prior to last year I thought he would have been run home, especially after Walt Jocketty tried to buy him a World Series team several years prior.

Obviously, management was more interested in his personality. Maybe it was recognized when he was hired almost 13 years ago that he possessed a 1947 mentality, which still exists. During the past two seasons, it should have been revealed that a baseball game is only that, excluding the Major League hype. Any player with ability and a desire can play it with an equal opportunity without a so-called "genius" as a guide. Robinson proved this in 1947. Then, it was said that he could play no higher than Class C. It was also said that if The Dodgers allowed him to play, the "niggas" following him would tear down existing ballparks. But because of his fan-drawing appeal – and other Blacks that followed – check the ballparks around the country today. It's no secret that LaRussa has exhibited his preference of players. My concern about him was satisfied this year, especially when I heard that he was asleep behind the wheel and then embarrassed one of the game's best players before the nation by not allowing him to play in the All-Star Game. This to me is strange mental behavior, but he could go out in style if he converts Chris Duncan into a third baseman – the easiest position in baseball – give the center field job to Rick Ankiel and cover left field with another one of his talented players. Then, cut Scott Rolen, Jim Edmonds and himself loose, so new faces could take their place. By doing so, all the dissention – which he instigates – that currently hovers over the team will disappear.

```
Week of September 6, 2007
Hey, Joe; What do you think about Kia Vaughn suing Imus
for his "nappy-headed ho" comment? She says he slandered
her good name, but come on!  Donald Trump's called me way
worse, and I haven't sued his rich-ass, nappy-headed self.
I think Kia's just gunning for easy cash and further clog-
ging our court system with her greed.
"Ro" - New York City
```

I think there is a book in this question, though I wouldn't be interested in writing it. I love the philosophy of George Washington Carver in that he said, "God gave him the ability free to do all the things he was able to do, so why charge a fee for them?". Therefore, if I can pass on information to the public free, I am satisfied with that. Anyway, I take for granted that Kia Vaughn was a Black member of the Rutgers' Women's Basketball Team – a school where Paul Robeson, a Black athlete, actor, lawyer and crusader for right, did everything but build it (the school). Though Vaughn – being at this institute of supposedly "higher learning" – has a great idea in suing Imus.

At this point, however, Rutgers – like every other Black or White college or university – hasn't reached the stage of higher learning. It – like the rest – is just a step above high school. Neither it, nor college or university, has deemed it mandatory to teach students about the great continent of Africa nor the great deeds that Blacks have contributed to America. History has recorded that Blacks – once upon entry – were reduced to a nationality of amorals, accumulating such names as "slave", "Negro", "colored" and "Black". Oddly, the latter was chosen by Blacks as a sense of pride. Beforehand when Whites used the word to address Blacks, it meant anything other than pride. In 1868, due to the 14th Amendment to The U.S. Constitution, Blacks became American citizens. The title "African-American" would eventually become the standard identity for Blacks but failed to rectify dehumanization of them. Concisely with history to back it up, a member of this group could be addressed as an "African-American Negro Colored Black". Nothing could be more slanderous. This is where Vaughn currently stands.

However, even with her college background, by the way the lawsuit was filed against Imus, it lets me know that she isn't familiar with The Constitution and in all probability neither is her lawyer(s). This is why I said earlier that she had a great idea. Had they been taught about it at the high school and college (or university) levels, the lawsuit would've been filed against The Constitution with Imus as its accessory. The Constitution – centuries before him – had slandered Blacks in every manner and gave people like him the same privilege. Oprah Winfrey and Gale King should take heed to this.

I recently watched Winfrey's show broadcasted from her Chicago studio related to the whole thing. On hand, was a collection of Black dignitaries, such as rappers, historians and so forth – all dealing with the pros and cons of the issue. In Atlanta at Spielman College stood Gale King, Winfrey's sidekick, with supposedly a group of Black female alumnus. From the locations of Chicago and Atlanta was a national hookup that aired the subject as it was discussed. Forgotten was Don Imus. The subject was focused on Black rappers calling Black women "ho's". I knew then that most of the people at both places didn't know The Constitution. Although it was never intended to work in reverse for Blacks under its Bill of Rights ratified in 1791, Black rappers were granted Freedom of Speech. Oprah and her bunch should attack The Constitution. When Black rappers fought among themselves, Whites classified it as "Black-on-Black crime". The Constitution is a document containing White-on-Black crime and needs democratizing. If I recollect correctly, Don Imus has been awarded a $20 million lawsuit settlement. While the court system clogs prisons with Blacks, it serves as a haven for White millionaires. I doubt if Vaughn's lawsuit will get to first base.

Week of September 13, 2007

Hey, Joe; Are you an optimist or a pessimist? You seem like a nice enough guy, but you sure do complain a lot.

If having a firm belief that right will overcome wrong, then I'm an optimist. If I call shots in support of my belief, maybe it is taken as complaining. My perception of pessimism would have to be directed at the news media. Seemingly, it feeds off morbidity – sorta like bad news is good news and good news is no news. A complainer to me is a selfish, faultfinding individual, who lives a miserable lifestyle and finds a way to convert good into something dismal, such as if asked how one is doing. The reply is usually, "Awe…I'm alright, but it could be better." Or, if addressed with "It's a beautiful day," the answer is, "Oh, yes it is, but just a little bit too hot (etc.)." The word "but" always plays an essential role as a means to an end – sorta like me seemingly being a nice enough guy but complains a lot.

Now, this part of the question trips me up, because either I'm a nice guy or I'm not. What must be understood is that the column I write is entitled "Ask A Negro Leaguer", meaning a Black – among other things is asked controversial questions and the differences between Whites and Blacks are often brought up and aired. Based upon my answers is how I'm judged. My position on this??? Optimism!!! And I refuse to think I am right all the time, because it would be unrealistic. Though I've drawn criticism from both Blacks and Whites – those who feel that my opinion should be voiced on their behalf. The year is now 2007, gone is the cry "Liberty for All". Though, during the American Revolution, Crispus Attucks, a Black, was the first killed while fighting for the cause of that principle and at the time, he was not free. And neither are Blacks and Whites free now from the labels "inferior" and "superior" – an issue long sidestepped that needs to be addressed. If continuously ignored and not rightfully approached by both parties in order to be resolved, it will hang above the country like an albatross. If change is to be realized, the time is now.

Recently, I did an article on Mike Vick. No matter how great his accomplishments, I voiced my concern about how vicious dog fighting is and how disgusted I am about his involvement – even went a step further to say that he "made his bed hard" now he must lay in it. At this point, though, because of how he stepped up and accepted responsibility without implicating anyone and even apologizing to the nation, I love and respect him more than before. Apparently there are others who feel differently. They want him totally destroyed. Like dogs trained to destroy each other, people that teach hatred are just as destructive.

Vick's confession should set a precedent. In spite of his crime, a compassionate news media could make him a drum major for "right", minus a severe penalty. Had the Commander in Chief exhibited his honesty, there would be no Iraq conflict, otherwise, he would have been standard bearer, and the people following his lead could provide the necessary steps for right to overcome wrong.

Week of September 20, 2007

Hey, Joe; It seems to me that if pro sports are so overly consumed with steroids or so-called performance enhancing drugs as well as dog fighting issues, they should also investigate substance abuse (alcohol) as well. I mean, the Cards fired their hitting instructor, the manager was cited in Florida for drunk driving, a player was killed on the highway and now a current player (Scott Spiezio) has left the team. All of these things are someway or another related to alcohol use, misuse or abuse and these "big wigs" keep getting slapped on the wrist or "the powers that be" seem to turn the other cheek. Things seem very hypocritical, racist and classist in the country.

```
Oh, I forgot...Anheuser-Busch is a big contributor to the
Cards' franchise, so I guess you can literally get away
with murder if the government can "see" (or tax) you but
if you ain't part of the good ol' boys' club, you get a
high tech lynching through media pundits. I'm sorry for
venting but what are your thoughts, sir??? Thanks for your
time.

Ray - Long Island, New York City
```

First and foremost, everybody needs an outlet to voice his or her concerns. Secondly, so-called "sports" of the professional calibre are nothing but "BIG BUSINESS", which are big contributors to politicians' campaign funds. If I recall, the bigger the funds are they are matched with government money. Seems to me that the public is getting pimped by the very people chosen to represent it. I'm not a betting man, but I'd be willing to bet that steroids are prescription drugs, thus casting them into the lot of "BIG BUSINESS". Obviously, dog fighting isn't, although it's been around before the Dead Sea got sick.

The connection of Anheuser-Busch and The Cards goes way back. Though it seems to point out more recent things relative to the subject – like Enron Park in Texas and Miller Park in Milwaukee. George W. Bush was owner and/or co-owner of the Texas Rangers before the park was named Enron, which occurred before he became President, followed by the big Enron scandal. MLB Commissioner, Bud Selig, was owner of the Milwaukee Brewers at the time the park was named Miller, so baseball – for better than the past decade (especially owners of the Rangers and Brewers) – falls into the category of "If you scratch my back…I'll scratch yours". The steroid issue, led by Selig and a few members of Congress, in an attempt to clean up baseball, sheds light on it. Rather than go after the drug industry, they found it more convenient to focus on baseball players, which includes Barry Bonds.

In reference to The Cards, I remember their owner, Fred Saigh, during the 50s when he was found guilty of income tax evasion. When facing the judge, he was told that it would cost him $5,000. It was rumored that Saigh said, "I have that right here in my pocket." The judge supposedly added,

"…And also 5 years." Then finished up by asking, "Do you have that in your pocket?!??" Of course you know how things worked out. Barry Bonds and Michael Vick are two wealthy Black men, which makes them prime political ploy, especially if done to keep the "color line" intact with bad publicity – like subtly saying, "No matter how great the accomplishment, a Nig…um…I mean, a Black is still a Black."

```
Week of October 4, 2007
Hey, Joe; What do you think about the rift between Fire
Chief Sherman George and Mayor Francis Slay???
Woodsy - Hotlanta
```

History provides an answer for any issue. In this particular case, my mind reverts back to 1950, shortly after I joined the Memphis Red Sox. One night in a small Mississippi town and while the team was taking a pre-game warm-up, I experienced a strange turn of events prior to both teams' line-ups being called by a White male announcer, who occupied the P.A. system. The incident that took place was in reference to the heights of our pitcher and catcher, which were quite contrasting – the catcher…very tall and the pitcher…very short, which obviously was quite noticeable on the part of the announcer. Following his introduction of our team's regular starting line up, he made a startling comment to the mostly White overflowing crowd regarding the size of the two by blaring over the mic, "Ladies an' gene'men…the battery fo the Memphis Red Sox tonight will be a big niggah catchin' an a li'l niggah pitchin'."

In 1975, I started a manuscript with its title named after the announcer's rude assessment of the catcher and pitcher. I thought it to be appropriate to point out the changing times within the Black community, as well as most Blacks emulating Whites once in a position of power – as a result, drawing much consternation from Blacks thought to be of a lesser degree and who felt they were being treated the same as they were by Whites. Strangely, a few years after I started the manuscript, my grandson, Sean, having been with me since he was a baby, started pre-school and developed good study ethics. After hearing me speak about writing a book so often, he undertook the idea of writing himself one, starting before his feet could touch the floor, while sitting in a chair. About 15 minutes later after compiling a log of pages together – each bearing chicken-like scratches – and finalizing it by clamping a front and back cover, he jumped out of his chair and said, "I've written my book." After high school, he wound up at Lincoln University in Jefferson City, MO on an academic scholarship and later transferred to Western Illinois University in Macomb, IL – leaving there with credentials commensurate to teaching and writing. Currently, he has me on numerous spots throughout the Internet with his soon to be released Princoirs: The Official Memoirs of Prince Joe Henry. Up until this point, he has typed every single article I have written for The Riverfront Times. What's so amazing about it is that he has done it over the phone, because I can't type a lick; it has never been my cup of tea. Our success??? Unity!!!

Anyway, vice versa – no matter what the stature or position, the title, "A Big Niggah Catchin' And A Li'l Niggah Pitchin'" reflects a statement designating as to why Black disunity. Reverse the title to "A Big Niggah Pitchin' And A Li'l Niggah Catchin'" and apply it to Chief Sherman George, a man with an impeccable background in firefighting and Charles Bryson, a Black who has been duped into accepting a position previously held by a White, who engineered the controversy involving the mayor and others then resigned leaving it in the hands of one Black to discipline another. The outcome in paraphrasing the aforementioned title would read like this, "A Big Niggah Pitchin' Orders And A Li'l Niggah Catchin' Hell." Sadly, Chief George must undergo such trauma from a man, who – once offered the job by his White appointer – should have said, "No thanks. You started the confusion, now resolve it and then give me the job." The end result??? Black and White dissension. As a footnote, Chief George had nothing to do with the faulty equipment that caused the loss of two lives.

[Editor's Note: The following was not printed in The Riverfront Times, however, it was answered as per a reader's request via e-mail.]

```
Hey, Joe; What do you think about Supreme Court Judges???
Judge Dredd - Sin City
```

Based upon arguments staged by Democrats and Republicans over the selection of a judge conducive to their parties, it's politically oriented. The real turning point that caught my interest in judgeship appointments occurred when Thurgood Marshall, a Black, was seated as an associate judge of the U.S. Supreme Court in 1967. His efforts in the case of Brown v. Board of Education brought down the wall of segregation (separating Blacks from Whites) within the school system and earned him the title "liberal". Clarence Thomas – picking up where Marshall left off – was regarded as a "conservative". His hour of infamy took place when Anita Hill, a Black female, broke the news about him allegedly making sexual advances at her during the time she worked for him prior to his being appointed Supreme Judge. Most humiliating was the stand he took against affirmative action, a planned designed to upgrade Blacks academically, etc.

The terms liberal and conservative denote differences and should never have been permitted in a court of law. Judges are thought to be just – at least this is the general consensus, but an experience I encountered in a St. Clair County (Illinois) courtroom in 1993 completely destroyed my confidence. Following a jury's decision of $2.75 million in the city of St. Louis for a personal injury claim, which was awarded to my disabled daughter, Denise (now deceased), in a case entitled "Henry v. Union Pacific Systems, et al" (Cause No. 892-08883, Division 1). Once the case number became 90-P-551 in the Circuit Court of the Twentieth Judicial Circuit, $625,000 was stolen with an invalid employment contract.

At the time, the law firm representing her was Brennan, Cates & Constance. Judy L. Cates was the lead attorney. Cates, a former prosecutor and president of the Illinois Trial Lawyers Association, is rumored to be running as a candidate in the 5th District for Appellate Judge. However, there were three parties involved in the aforementioned case; they were: Missouri Pacific Railroad, Montgomery Elevator Company and The Bakewell Corporation. Attorney Jeffrey Hammel was my daughter's Guardian Ad Litem before my grandson, Sean, and I became her co-guardians. At this juncture in April 1991, Hammel was dismissed and paid for his services.

Though Cates – in October 1992 enroute to stealing the first $20,000 – used Bakewell's petition, which I didn't see until 1996, as an out-of-court settlement without my knowledge. In doing so, she resurrected Hammel, waived me and the case was heard before Judge Hillebrand. She followed a similar procedure with The Montgomery Elevator petition for $605,000 – only this time, on November 20, 1992, she forwarded a statement of counsel (supposedly the contract), a notice of a hearing date and a petition to adjudicate to the county clerk's office. I never saw these documents until 1997, after the death of my daughter. The notice of hearing date was directed to Jeffrey Hammel. I received The Montgomery Elevator petition on Sunday, November 22, 1992. It revealed that he was a part of the master plan to hijack the $605,000 and also authored a trust fund. On December 2, 1992, the case was heard before Judge Jerome Lopinot. I was waived. Upon receiving the petition after the hearing, there was a notary by my signature, which I signed November 22nd, the date it was delivered. The statement of counsel consisted of Cates asking the judge to approve it.

Afterwards on January 26, 1993, I found myself in the St. Clair County courtroom of Judge Robert Lechien, following a rash of scandalous lies designed by Cates to have me removed as guardian. If anything, I should have been taken to court by them to prove my guilt. Anyway, Judge Lechien denied me a continuance to prove my innocence. Prior to, my attorney, Brian Konzen, filed a petition for a declaratory judgment regarding a house involved. Seeing that I had no chance, I resigned. Cates eliminated my grandson, who automatically became his disabled mother's guardian, and had Hammel appointed. After Denise's death, I gained access to a sizable majority of her case file, which I purchased for $107.75. Despite four documents indicating that Denise was mentally incompetent because of Multiple Sclerosis, Cates had her to represent herself regarding the declaratory judgment. Justice is all I seek – something I have been denied of from every nook and turn. Additionally, information gathered from transcripts, another $150,000 was added to the $625,000. I've never seen a petition from Missouri Railroad Company nor learned who signed for the house that Cates' father, Sidney Katz, had a hand in.

Week of November 1, 2007

Hey, Joe; What's with the Michael Devlin plea deal, Joe? Do you think it's a good thing or a bad thing that Devlin's misdeeds won't come to light?

Anonymous

My favorite maxim reads like this: "There is so much good in the bad of us and so much bad in the good of us, that it behooves none of us to talk about the rest of us." Devlin's misdeeds have already come to the light, although not in detail. Though, the manner in which he has been paraded around in public from one courthouse to another has displayed him as a buffoon. Obviously, he preferred it this way, otherwise, he would not have plea bargained for a lesser charge than committed. By doing so, he spared everybody involved, especially the state and character of the kids. Contrary to popular belief, the good thing about it is that his crime was committed against the state, which subjected him to state punishment. Additionally, he could have killed the children, but he didn't. As is, he will spend the duration of his life incarcerated.

The bad thing is…had he been a member of the priesthood, he would have been protected until eternity. Revealed in this institution is the ineffective representation of The Bible by the so-called Founding Fathers. According to the Heritage College Dictionary, Bible is defined as the sacred book of Christianity, a collection of ancient writings including both the Old Testament and the New. Better than 2,000 years after its perfection, America became a nation and chose it as her standard religion, along with The Constitution. Under its 1791 ratification of The Bill of Rights, five freedoms were guaranteed – the first being Freedom of Religion. With its approval, doors to the world of vice opened, beginning with separation of church and state.

Had the Christian doctrine been followed, there would have been no such thing as "religious freedom". God granted man free will, or in other words "Freedom of Choice", however, those who choose Christianity and fail to heed His Commandments, The Bible makes it perfectly clear that the end result will be unfavorable. The outcome of Michael Devlin is a prime example of double standard. Leviticus 24:22 explains it more succinctly: "Ye shall have one manner of law, as well for the stranger, as for one of your own country, for I am The Lord your God."

As for the Founding Fathers, the answer is found in Matthew 23:9: "And call no man your father upon the earth: for one is your father which is in Heaven." Because of following their method of religious freedom, The Bible was violated – Revelation 22:18 and 19 : "For I testify unto every man that heareth the words of the prophecy of this book. If any man shall add unto these things, God shall add unto him the plagues that are written in this book. And if any man shall take away from the words of the book of this prophecy, God shall take away his part out of the book of life, and out of the holy city, and from the things which are written in this book." While the state punished Devlin, in the case of priests, the church was given autonomy. By the mere fact that the church as one refuses to speak against such sin, all are equally as guilty.

Week of November 8, 2007

Hey, Joe; Who do you think is the most influential Black person in St. Louis???

Personally, my choice is Sherman George. I've followed him for a number of years. During this period of time, he has exhibited nothing but class even during the latest controversy surrounding him. He has displayed his usual mild-mannered character, but underneath it all the position he took against those with intent to transform him into a turncoat reminds me of words in the song, "My Way", song so eloquently by Frank Sinatra – especially the words that say "For what is a man? What has he got – if not himself, then he has not. To say the things he truly feels and not the words of one who kneels." Charles Bryson and Francis Slay don't fit this mold. Both caved in to third party desires.

I'm not familiar with the role Bryson played before being given the job to "discipline" George, but he must be aware now that it has created a storm of discontentment among many Black and White St. Louis citizens, who started a move to collect enough signatures to have Slay recalled. I'm also unfamiliar with how many younger Blacks are knowledgeable of Malcolm X's version of "House Nigga, Field Nigga". If not, the role assigned Bryson is a perfect example.

Seemingly, Slay is accustomed to taking advantage of situations. Less than 15 minutes ago, he seemingly emerged from a disagreement between then mayor, Freeman Bosley, and Clarence Harmon, which resulted in Harmon first supporting a White female candidate against Bosley for mayor until being talked into running against Bosley himself. Quite frankly, it is my firm belief that both Slay and Harmon have been St. Louis' two worst mayors. They also highlight some national polls' findings of St. Louis being among the nation's top racist cities. What other town in 2007 has Black and White unions to represent firemen under the same chief and fighting the same fires??? Better yet – from my understanding – it was the hiring policy of firemen mandated by an IQ Test that triggered the onset of the problem that introduced Slay and Bryson.

Seemingly, any test taken – written or oral – involving Blacks and Whites with the outcome based upon a determination as to which is most qualified, much consternation follows. In most cases, it is said the White candidate prevails. Case in point: affirmative action and the fireman test. Recently, a predominately Black St. Louis school lost accreditation because of the test factor. Maybe the words of John Wesley should be written into history rather than being left out. Wesley (1703-1791), a White male and a famous religious reformer, was the founder of Methodism and was also a prominent opponent of slavery. He denounced it because of its sinfulness. His words are, "The African is in no respect inferior to the European."

Slay demonstrated his insight into the future by supporting members of the White local union. Bryson demonstrated that he has no dignity and for a prestigious job and its title, he would immediately sell out!!! And, many people in St. Louis have decided that those who wish to keep St. Louis divided, they will help by trying to change mayors every other election until fairness prevails.

THERE GOES PRINCE JO HENRY . . . .

It Takes More Than A Fence To Stop Prince Jo

Prince Jo is one of the greatest stars and comedians in the history of the Indianapolis Clowns. It would take three volumes to describe his antics. His work will speak for itself, and is it any wonder fans hate to leave their seats even for a moment, afraid they will miss anything from a home-run to a nose-dive, by the Prince himself.

[Editor's Note: The following has been extracted from www.joepott.blogspot.com the original blog of Joe Pott, Broadcaster/Corporate Sales Associate for the Gateway Grizzlies Frontier League Baseball.]

STIRRING THE POTT

Just a spot to get me, Joe Pott, stirred up. Don't worry I'll try not to get too controversial. I work as the Play-by-play broadcaster and a Corporate Sales Associate for the Gateway Grizzlies, an independent league baseball club. A large chunk of my focus, especially in the summer, will be Grizzlies related. Read, enjoy, and comment if you will.

Tuesday, October 30, 2007

A Prince of A Man

JOE POTT

Here it is, this is the blog that I promised. I have told you previously that one of the best things about my job is the people I get to meet. This past season, I had the extreme honor of meeting and visiting with former Negro League player Prince Joe Henry. The Grizzlies did a salute to the Negro Leagues Night on August 3rd against the Chillicothe Paints. Hopefully people know the story of Prince Joe, but probably not everyone.

Joe is a Brooklyn, IL native who played roughly four full (parts of eight) seasons in the Negro Leagues, beginning with the Memphis Red Sox in 1950. Injuries forced him to leave the game in 1952, but he resurfaced with the Indianapolis Clowns in 1955. His nickname comes from some of things he did while "playing" with the Clowns, like turning his back to the pitcher before spinning around when the pitch came. When he hit a home run he would slap the catcher's hand, slap the umpire's hand, even have a conversation with a fan before circling the bases. He once came to the plate in the middle of the summer in a full tuxedo, tails and all. He was Clown Prince Joe Henry. Or Prince Joe. When it was decided in the early 2000's that Negro Leaguers would get a pension from MLB, Joe applied, only to be denied, numerous times, for various reasons. I won't get into the full story, though I will include some links to a couple of really nice stories regarding that issue.

The reason I wanted to write is because of what Prince Joe did for me. He transported me to a time I can only now read about. We talked for two half innings (one of them a long inning) on that humid, hazy August night, and it wasn't enough. I usually keep guests for a single half inning, yet I could have spent hours visiting with Joe about the things he saw, the players he played with, and what he called a better education than you could get at any college in America.

He told me the Grizzlies brought him back to a game he loved, and a game that he thought he was through with, yet I think anyone that had a chance to visit with Joe felt the same about him. Joe reminded all of us what the game is meant to be and why we work in this wonderful game. He was eloquent and nostalgic and just a true joy to visit with. Of all the interviews I have had the chance to conduct, this was my favorite. Hands down.

Prince Joe still lives in Brooklyn, IL. He suffers from rheumatoid arthritis and, I believe, he is confined to a wheel chair. Don't let that fool you, he is as sharp as I assume he ever was. He writes a column for a weekly newspaper, the Riverfront Times. It is called Ask a Negro Leaguer. Fans write in with questions and he answers. I haven't seen the column for a couple of weeks and I hope they haven't discontinued it.

I think there are plans to repeat our salute to the Negro Leagues next season with the Grizzlies. I am sure, if at all possible, Prince Joe will be part of our night. If you're a baseball fan and in the area, or you're a Grizz fan and you missed the first night, don't miss it again. It will be well worth it. Trust me.

Editor's Note: The following is from a teleconference Mr. Henry held with a fantasy baseball Internet group and its representatives. Initial contact was made with Dale Miller and later on with Mike Touchette.

I found a column in an online paper called "Ask a Negro Leaguer." I e-mailed Prince Joe Henry (the man doing the column and former Negro Leaguer) about a week ago and told him about Outlaws. The e-mail I sent is below:

Dale Miller - dale@fantasyoutlaws.com

Hello Prince,

My name is Dale Miller and I represent Fantasy Outlaws.com. We would love to have you come say hi to us all and tell us what you think of our site. The message boards can be found at http://www.fantasyoutlaws.com/forum/default.asp. We would love to post your weekly column on the boards there and in return we would list the link to your great column in our affiliates section and also include it in the actual post every time we post it. We would post your column in a sticky post so everyone at the site can easily find it and enjoy it and hopefully, together, we can spread the word to even more people about these great but sometimes overlooked stars of the past. Let me know what you think.

Today I got a response :

Greetings, Mr. Miller!!! My name is Sean, and I am the grandson of Prince Joe Henry. I handle all of his baseball-related affairs, etc. He has read your question and an answer will be forthcoming in The Riverfront Times within the next few weeks. Meanwhile, he would like for you to have his phone number and wants you to call him. He is very excited about talking to you. Please give him a call, Mr. Miller. Good luck with your site (and Gateway Redbirds), and you have a wonderful day. Thank you for your time and support, sir.

Respectfully,

Sean

Fantasy Outlaw Posts

I called Mr. Joe Henry today and talked to him for about an hour. I felt like a kid talking to someone who has seen and done so much. He isn't one to use computers himself, but he will have his grandson check in ever so often and said he would share some stories with us and that he would be happy to answer any questions we have. I listened in awe to his stories. Before joining the Negro Leagues he almost went to California to try out for a minor league team in the Pacific Coast League (I am pretty sure that's the name he said), but his friend talked him into joining the Memphis Red Sox instead. He mentioned that the first three Black players to play in the NBA all played in the Negro Leagues. He attended the only Negro League school ever and was known for clowning around and had the one and only "Double Duty" Radcliffe knock on his door once to get to know him. He is currently trying to get all former Negro League players a pension through MLB. They offered to give it to him after hearing he was going to the press over the issue, but they refused to give it to all the players so he refused and is fighting for all the former players. He thinks MLB disrespects the fans today with the high ticket prices and inflated concessions. He is a very well spoken man. He was very polite and told me to call him anytime. He loves that we will post his column and welcomes everyone to send in a question or comment to it. He said he is at our service and anything we would like to ask him about he would be happy to answer or share a story with us. He also told the Negro League museum about us and they will be contacting me soon. He seemed to be as interested in us as we are in him.

I will be posting his column here weekly and I encourage everyone to read it and maybe send in a question or two. Many great players played in the Negro Leagues, yet they get overlooked a lot. If you are a baseball fan you really should take the time to research the great history of the Negro Leagues.

– Dale Miller –

THU SEP 14, 2006 9:01 AM
ANSWERS WITH "PRINCE" JOE HENRY
 I am pleased to announce that we have our first round of answers with former Negro League All-Star, "Prince" Joe Henry. A very special thanks to "Prince" Joe Henry for taking the time out of his schedule to answer questions. As you'll see

throughout this interview, he's a very interesting and intelligent person. I would also like to thank Joe's grandson, Sean, for coordinating the interview. Another big thank you to Tambourine Man for doing all the work with this interview. His dedication to bringing this important piece of history to GRB has been amazing. Here's a little bit about the "Prince's" background:

Memphis Red Sox 1950-52 (NAL)

Indianapolis Clowns 1955 (NAL)

Indianapolis Clowns 1955-56 (IND)

Detroit Clowns 1957-58 (IND)

Detroit Clowns 1958 (NAL)

Detroit Stars 1958-59 (NAL)

Detroit Clowns 1959 (w/ Goose Tatum, IND)

Injuries put an end to a two-plus-season stint holding down second base for the Memphis Red Sox in the early 1950's, but Henry resurfaced in 1955 with the storied Indianapolis Clowns franchise. Henry's showmanship at third base during two seasons in Indianapolis, a team that counts home-run king Henry Aaron among its alumni and is often compared to basketball's Harlem Globetrotters, earned him the nickname "Prince Joe." After sitting out 1957, Prince Joe was coaxed back to the diamond by Detroit Stars owner Ted Rasberry, who renamed his team "Goose Tatum's Detroit Clowns" after the famous Globetrotter and Negro League phenom. Recalling his days in the league he said, "As I look back, it was the best experience I ever had in my life... the Negro Leagues took me to just about every state in the country and Canada. I had an offer from Goose Tatum to go with him to Europe, but it was across the water and I didn't like to fly."

THU SEP 14, 2006 9:14 AM

I had the pleasure of interviewing Mr. Henry on the weekend of August 13, 2006. The interview took place during three separate sessions, and will be posted as such. As always, thank you to the members and staff of GRB for making this such a pleasurable experience! Additionally, I'd like to make everyone aware that Joe's grandson, Sean, is working on Joe's memoirs. I'll keep everyone updated on the memoirs, which are slated for release next summer or fall.

Interviews with the Prince

Gateway Red Birds (interviewer Mike Touchette): It's my understanding that you were oblivious to the Negro League's existence up until the late forties. How did you get your start in baseball, and how did that lead you to the Negro Leagues?

Joe Henry: Okay. I was a softball player, 12-inch fast pitch softball. And it was my game. I loved it. I loved 12-inch fast pitch softball. And by playing it throughout the area here, I got quite a bit of recognition. This lasted up until Josh Johnson, who was a great catcher in the Negro League...

GRB: (Interrupts) I understand he was the backup to Josh Gibson, correct?

Joe Henry: No. I don't know anything but he [Gibson] played on a team that Josh was with. He was on the same team with Josh. Anyway, he used to watch me play this fast-pitch softball and he began to talk to me about how I was wasting my time. Then he said, "Why don't you convert yourself into a baseball player, because the opportunities are here now?" So I told him that I saw no future in baseball for me. And when I learned that he was a catcher in the Negro League and everything, I didn't know anything about the Negro League! The only thing I knew about the Negro League was hearing names like Reese "Goose" Tatum, who at the time of my knowledge of him, he was the original showman for the Harlem Globetrotters. From there, Abe Saperstein, the owner of the Harlem Globetrotters, was a promoter in the Negro League. So the nucleus of the Harlem Globetrotters came from within the Negro League. You know, guys like Ted Strong, Reese "Goose" Tatum, and there was Nat "Sweetwater" Clifton, and guys of that nature. Mr. Johnson really started working on me then, and it didn't sink in. Not until I heard about Robinson in 1947. During that period of time, I just didn't really have any interest in baseball. After Robinson, I thought about Satchel Paige going to Cleveland and I said, "Maybe I'll give it a shot." By doing that, I contacted A.S. "Doc" Young. Young was a columnist for the Chicago Defender, and my letter sent to him in Chicago was transferred to the west coast. That's where he was working from at that point, and he contacted me after he received the letter. So, I told him about myself, softball, Josh Johnson, and gave him Mr. Johnson's phone number. Mr. Johnson, at the time, was the principal at Dunbar high school in Madison, IL. Dunbar was a Black high school, the same as where I live here in Brooklyn and schools in St. Louis, Sumner, Vashon, Lincoln of East St. Louis, etc. So, Mr.

Young contacted Mr. Johnson and Mr. Johnson came down to tell me about what had happened. That was the beginning of me trying to get some directions about playing baseball. Mr. Johnson, being a former member of the Negro League, knew Homer "Goose" Curry, and Curry was the manager of the Memphis Red Sox at the time. And there was a discussion between Mr. Johnson and I about what would be the best place because Doc Young told him to tell me to pack my bags and everything. Just have fare to California, and once there he ["Doc" Young] would take care of the rest. He had it all arranged whereas I would get a tryout with the Los Angeles Angels of the Pacific Coast League. Then Mr. Johnson said, "Well, Memphis is much shorter, and I also know the manager of the Memphis Red Sox, Homer. Why not go to Memphis?" So during that time, Mr. Curry had the one and only Black baseball school, and so I went to that school. After I completed that school there for about a couple of weeks, he took me to Memphis with him. That's the way it all started.

GRB: That's how you got your start with the Memphis Red Sox?

Joe Henry: That is absolutely correct. I didn't know a thing about baseball. I'd only played about one or two games of baseball when I decided on converting myself.

GRB: So you just naturally picked it up pretty easily then?

Joe Henry: I don't know how easy it was. Heh, I was under the impression that the Negro League meant nothing but Black Americans. But once all the players reported for spring training, in the year of 1950, there were Panamanians, Cubans, and Puerto Ricans…Just a conglomerate of different nationalities thrown together.

GRB: So did you have to fight for a roster spot to make the team in spring training?

Joe Henry: No. Not right off, because from going to that school, then working out back in Memphis at Martin Stadium, I pretty well had "Goose" Curry up in the air over me about my play during the school, and the part of spring training prior to all the rest of the guys reporting. But, I found that once they reported, all that publicity and everything that I was garnering prior to that… Heck, I was afraid to get on the field with those guys after I started watching what they represented as a baseball player. I saw guys doing things that I'd never witnessed at Sportsman's Park in St. Louis among the so-called Major Leagues.

GRB: Pretend you're back in your playing days with the Indianapolis Clowns, and walk us through an average day in the life of a barnstorming ballplayer.

Joe Henry: Well, uh, I didn't really consider myself to be a barnstorming ballplayer. I considered myself to be a player in the Negro League, and the white kids considered themselves to be a player in the Major Leagues.

GRB: So what was an average day in the life of a Negro League player then?

Joe Henry: Beautiful! It gave me an opportunity to see America, or most of it, firsthand. By me already being a history buff...every opportunity that I got, once travelin' the country where some prominently named Black person was from, I would always try to visit the site to get more information about how they arrived at that point in their life. With the Indianapolis Clowns, when we played ball in Hazlehurst, MS., that was where Richard Wright, the great novelist, the author of Black Boy and other books grew up.

GRB: How would your day start?

Joe Henry: Well, we would do just like if I were home, ya know. At that particular time, everyplace that we were scheduled to play was like home. We got a whoppin' two dollars per day to eat with, and we would take that two dollars, and it was just as if we had 25 dollars apiece to eat with everyday. We would perform miracles with those two dollars, because that was the norm. Food was so cheap in restaurants. I mean, you could get a pretty good steak for about 35 or 40 cents!

GRB: What time would you normally arrive at the ballpark to get ready for the game?

Joe Henry: Oh, not until that night. So many times we'd play a game, and were headed for the next township where we would be bedded down, and whenever we felt like we wanted to go eat, we would go eat. And when it was time to go to the ballpark, the bus would be awaiting us. From the hotel, or wherever we were, there was a time where we were supposed to go to the ballpark, and all the guys would get their little carry-on with all their necessities. Ya know, soap, toothpaste, toothbrush...you could carry it around real handy-like, and just take that to the bus. Once we'd go to the park, after the game, we'd take a shower and use whatever we needed to try to primp ourselves up. That was it. Then the bus would take off back into the heart of the town. At that particular time, Mike, the area in which Blacks lived was referred to as the Colored section. So that's where we would go back down to eat. Then, if we were going out to the next town, right after we'd finished eating we boarded the bus and took off.

GRB: And the same thing the next day?

Joe Henry: Same identical thing. It was repetitious. It was beautiful. It was a wonderful, wonderful life. That's why the Negro League, at one time, was patronized as the bus league, because we were steadily traveling. And I must say, with some of the greatest bus drivers you'd ever want to ride behind.

GRB: Were they funny guys?

Joe Henry: You mean the bus drivers? Well, they were all dubbed as "chauff." That means, uh, an abbreviation for chauffeur. And do you know that many of the buses when I was out there, were of the flexible type – the equivalent of the Greyhound bus. During that time, these guys drove the bus night and day, but weren't permitted to drive a Greyhound bus. For instance, If that bus would break down en route to the place we were headed, all that chauffeur needed was the tools. I have seen a motor taken out of the bus and put together before the game was over that night. Now this means starting at a time before the game. And after they got the proper things to fix that bus with, they would fix them and be ready to roll again. So they were doing something that the Greyhound bus drivers couldn't do.

GRB: In addition to driving the bus, they were also mechanics.

Joe Henry: That is absolutely correct. There was a case about one bus that one of the older ballplayers told us about, where several players got so mad at the bus driver for keeping that bus in shape. They just played a little game and shot a few bullets in the motor. "Let's kill this sucka', so we can get another one!" That's how good those bus drivers were. They not only drove the bus, but there were several that could fix the bus. In Memphis, at a mechanic shop, about four of the bus drivers drove for different teams in the Negro League.

GRB: Oh, really?

Joe Henry: Yeah, all of them were mechanics! And I mean super drivers! That's right!

GRB: Where were some of your favorite places that you visited across the country?

Joe Henry: There were many places, like in Daytona Beach, that's where the college was. The college was named after a great, great, Black lady. I visited the college, and visited the gravesite of the lady, Mary McLeod Bethune. And there were other places. I would go to the spots where these people were from. I was really in a learning process while out there. One of my little buddies that clowned along with me when I was with the Indianapolis Clowns was from Daytona Beach. "Spec Bebop"(chuckles) was a midget. We used to tease him all the time, sayin', "That's the biggest midget in the world!"

GRB: Names like Josh Gibson and Satchel Paige are well known to baseball fans of the modern era. Would you mind throwin' out some names of the Negro League players who, in your opinion, might deserve more recognition for their abilities?

Joe Henry: To be honest with you, I know how things are marketed. Like Ted Williams in the Major League, guys like that. This is the same way the Negro League was marketed. Guys like Satchel Paige and Josh Gibson…I couldn't even begin to tell you of the players that I met when I went to Memphis in 1950. Then, I learned of so many other guys by meeting them. They were playin' in the Negro League before Robinson, and after Robinson's entry into the Dodgers organization. I met so many of these guys while they were still around, and some at an advanced age. Like Oscar Charleston, a great, great, great centerfielder… He was manager of the Indianapolis Clowns when I first met him. Guys that I read about that worked out before Robinson, or with Robinson, trying to get into the white baseball league. Like "Showboat" Thomas…There are just so many of them. I did have the opportunity to play against the Chicago American Giants in 1950 and '51. That's when guys like Ted "Double Duty" Radcliffe, who died recently, [and] Ted Strong, who was really the first Black in the NBA [were still playing]. That's when it was the South Bend Studebakers or the Chicago Studebakers, but that was the team that was playin' then in what was the NBA. Later, in the early fifties, three more came on to play in what is now the NBA. These three guys happened to have been Earl Lloyd, Chuck Cooper, and Nat "Sweetwater" Clifton, the guy that I would play with in 1958, which was my last year with "Goose" Tatum. "Goose" Tatum came back that particular year, or the next year, to try to boost attendance because Jackie Robinson's entry into the Dodgers organization destroyed the Negro League at that time. After 1947, the league began to go downhill. When I got to Memphis in1950, there were 10 teams still in the league. Teams like the

Homestead Grays and teams like...I never got an opportunity to play against those teams.

GRB: They were already dissolved by the time you got there?

Joe Henry: Yes, or they were already playing out East.

GRB: These athletes that you're talking about, like "Sweetwater" Clifton, they represent, in a way, the genesis of the two-sport athlete. You know how everyone points to Bo Jackson and Deion Sanders...

Joe Henry: (Interrupts) Ya know what, Mike. It's very comical to me when national news gets a hold of something like that, when in essence the Negro League was full of that. It was never ever advertised. There were football players, basketball players, and track stars all combined into one. That was no great big thing within the Negro League. You were subject to see anything happen. Guys playin' ball that may have been a heck of a ballplayer...That same guy could be boxing professionally. There was nothing but talent among those guys, ya know. In 1950 and '51 when I was with Memphis, you had guys coming out of the Black colleges. There were football players, baseball players, basketball players...Robinson played anything and then played golf! This man was super talented! And that's how so many Black players among the Negro League were of the same caliber. That's why I say that it was an experience to meet these guys with that much ability to perform in any of these categories. Here in Brooklyn, there was only a basketball team and a football team, and the coach kept tryin' to field a complete football team.

GRB: So you hadn't been exposed to that great talent, that level of athlete?

Joe Henry: Just like I say with being Black, you knew all about these things but it was no big thing! It was just like, if this guy feels like playin' football today, he could play it. If he feels like playin' basketball, he could play it. He's multitalented, ya know. I remember when Gene Conley of the Boston Braves ended up with the Boston Braves and the Boston Celtics. There was a great big hullabaloo and Black people, in that instance wondered, "What is so great about this?" Ya know, it was no big thing to them. Only when you come on the stage in the so-called Major Leagues, they reach and grabbed it then bam! It's the same thing with Lou Boudreau. He played shortstop for the Cleveland Indians and managed at the same time. Ya know what? He was a hell of a basketball player who came out of Illinois here! Had he been playin' in the NBA or somethin' like that at the time, then shortstop in baseball, they'd have made a big issue out of that.

GRB: What are your thoughts on the St. Louis Browns?

Joe Henry: Well, this is after the Browns had left St. Louis to go to Baltimore and became the Baltimore Orioles. Before that happened, after my second year with the Memphis Red Sox, I went over to workout because the Browns held a tryout school over there at Sportsman's Park. And there were at least a hundred people over there. So I went over there and worked out, and I was told by one of the coaches…I think his name was Freddie Fitzsimmons or something. He pulled me to the side, and he told me, "You are the best prospect we have out there on that field, but we don't have a minor league club to send you to." The Browns were so bad, that when I went over there to work out with them and was told that, I said, "Well hell, I thought the Browns were a minor league team!" They were the worst team in and out of baseball. They would choose a one-armed white outfielder over one of those guys in the Negro League. Then, Bill Veeck purchased a little midget to send him up to the plate.

GRB: Eddie Gaedel, right?

Joe Henry: That is absolutely correct. The comical thing about the Browns is that in 1947 when Robinson went to Brooklyn and Paige went to Cleveland, Willard Brown and Hank Thompson went to the St. Louis Browns. The Browns were so poor in attendance, because of being so bad, that they were lucky if a hundred or two hundred people would show up. What I'm doing right here is exaggerating a bit (chuckles), but I'm trying to point out how terrible the Browns were. Do you know that Willard Brown had been known for years in the Negro League as a power hitter along the lines of a Josh Gibson? Hank Thompson was one heck of an infielder. They cut Brown loose because of his age, or so they say. But that happened because he didn't hit a homerun every time he went to the plate to make the turnstiles go around, trying to fill up that ballpark over there! Then, they let Hank Thompson go! Hank Thompson went right from the Browns to the New York Giants and starred the next eight years!

GRB: So the Browns didn't know what they had on their hands?

Joe Henry: They cared less because they wound up with Paige. They really publicized Paige. Here's a guy moseying along and he had a big ol' comfortable chair where he would relax while the game was goin' on, or until he was called on.

I mean, he was used mostly as a selling point.

GRB: Publicity.

Joe Henry: That is right! But every time they'd hand him that ball, even being at the age he was, he was still a bad son of a gun! Let me make this clear, Mike. There was a difference in the way Black athletes, or Blacks period, saw themselves. They knew that they had been kept in obscurity. They knew what they could and couldn't do. Sadly, at that particular time, it was thought that Blacks could not excel on the same field as whites. Jackie Robinson got all this attention for what he was doing because he was told by some of the so-called baseball experts that he couldn't ever play Major League Baseball, and that he would be lucky to make a Class C team. Most whites, at that time, shared the same feeling that a Black person could not excel on the same field with whites. Every time I think of all this kind of stuff, in a so-called civilized society, it is really insane to me! And I'll tell you why I feel this way. Hey when I was playing 12-inch fast pitch softball, we whipped white teams up and down through this area...Jerseyville, and all of those different places. So when Jackie Robinson was going into the Dodgers organization, and I heard all the talk that he's incapable of playing ball with the white boys, it started making me think, "Am I crazy or not? What's so much different about the white boys that went up the ladder in the so-called majors, and the guys that played softball against us?" This was no big thing to me! It was no big thing to Robinson! Robinson was a whiz at UCLA. He knew what he could do. Let me tell you something else. That act that he and Branch Rickey put together was the biggest piece of psychology ever laid out in America. When Rickey was telling Robinson, "I don't want you as just a baseball player. I know what you can do as a baseball player. What I want is someone who can turn the other cheek." There were baseball team owners that hated Rickey's guts for doing what he was trying to do. Robinson knew that he could play ball out there. What was being said was a joke to him because he had already performed against white kids in college. He knew the attitudes of some of the white fellows that he played against while in college. It was a joke! The reason I'm saying this...I just wish you could be in my shoes, and look back over things, and hear some of the things such as, a Black could not excel on the same field as whites. It makes you wonder, "Where in the hell have these people been!" And this is terrible in a supposedly civilized world!

GRB: There are rumors that Branch Rickey wasn't as interested in actually integrating baseball but was more interested in the fact that he could sign a more talented Black player for less money than he could a good white player. Do you think there's any truth to that rumor?

Joe Henry: Look, you and I know that. You know that Rickey knew about great Black baseball players because he had some idea about the Negro League. But the point is, and is today, that the same thing that slaughtered the Browns, not much attendance, was the same thing that destroyed the Negro League, a loss of attendance because of Robinson going in with one of the white teams. Rickey's idea was to jam that park at Ebbets Field. If he jammed that park, it was going to start breaking down the thinking of so-called Major League baseball owners. Now when you look back there, and if you can sort out all of that history of Robinson not being able to excel on a field with white players...Look what Blacks did! It was said, at one time when Rickey was acting to bringing Robinson on the Dodgers... There was talk like, "If they bring him [Robinson] into this park, these niggers followin' him are going to tear down this ballpark!" Well, rather than tearing down the ballpark, if you look at these parks today, all of them have brand new ballparks based upon one of the biggest promotional events between Rickey and Robinson that the country has seen. It's just so simple. You can't be so far fetched and out of reality that you want to grab somethin' and say, "This guy can't do this because he isn't white." If you think about that, it is really, really, really, really comical.

GRB: Do you think that the modern Black athletes appreciate what folks like you and Jackie Robinson paved the way for?

Joe Henry: There might be a few, but most of them have gotten so caught up in the money and publicity that they don't have time to reach back into their great history to try to learn from whence they came. This is my negative feeling toward most of these Black players whether it be basketball, baseball, track, or whatever. They're makin' all kinds of money in track these days. And when I was growin' up, track athletes couldn't earn 15 cents. In fact, Jesse Owens, after winning in the Olympics, had to come back to America after causing Hitler to get up and leave the Olympic Stadium rather than shake his hand ...He had to come back to America and race racehorses many times at Negro League games. That was absolutely terrible. I really look back on things such as that, Mike, and it didn't make sense to me then. It doesn't make sense to me now. That is why I think the way that I do. And if this is supposed to be a civilized society, then people should not be hurt for standing up and telling the truth.

GRB: You were in a unique situation of having left the Negro League, only to return due to injuries that forced you to retire from the white minor leagues. What was the general attitude of the Negro League players who might not have been good enough, or never had the opportunity to make the jump to the minors or majors toward those players who did?

Joe Henry: Do you know that from the time Robinson was purchased by the Brooklyn Dodgers, every baseball player that was in the Negro League pushed him and rooted for him? I've seen things happen on the baseball field. After Robinson went to the Brooklyn Dodgers, there were guys comin' along like Aaron, Mays, and such. And the pitchers out there on that hill wouldn't do anything to hurt that player's chance.

GRB: So it was all camaraderie?

Joe Henry: In other words, they weren't goin' to let him get away on them scot-free. They were goin' to give him the best pitches that they had to deliver. If he was goin' to star on the pitcher then they were goin' to have to star by dealing with that pitcher's best stuff. But those pitchers would never go out of their way to knock down those who were goin' up. There was nothing but happiness among those players, because they felt that, "If he gets the chance, then I might get the chance." And the thought was, with Robinson moving up, that the things that were going on between Black baseball players and white baseball players...It'll break all of that junk up. I've read a lot of things about Black players getting mad all the way up till 1958. But back then, if there was word that there were going to be scouts in the park, they would spread the word like, "There's two or three scouts in the park tonight. Some guys from the Braves, so you'd better put on your very best brotha'!" That's why I consider the Negro League to be the greatest experience that I've ever had in my life. I had the opportunity to see class. I mean super class and everything that stemmed from around it.

GRB: So would you guys do any joking with each others like, "I'm gonna' hit a homerun tonight because I know there are scouts!" Was there anything like that goin' on?

Joe Henry: As I said, "You can show your wares, brotha', cause there's three or four scouts in the park! I ain't lyin'!" And if a scout talked to one of the players, the other guys were pleased because they always had this feeling like, "If he gets these chances, then I also have the opportunity of getting that chance." We knew that nothing was 100% all the time. I'm gonna tell you something, Mike. I feel that fans are getting kicked in the booty. Every time I get the opportunity to say things that other people would like to say, but might not have this type of opportunity, I say it. When they call this junk that they play today Major League Baseball, I still call it not Major League. It is all tied into a big business racket. What they should do, to really boil it down to truly being major, is cut those teams back down to 16 teams with eight in the American League and eight in the National League. With all of this money that Major League Baseball is being paid, the fans should be able to enjoy these games they attend with all of these high prices and everything. When you field a league with 16 teams of the very best, you can look for a battle every game that these teams play. Then, the fans would be respected in regards to the money that they're paying for a hotdog, ticket prices, and a playoff game. A man can't take his kids and wife to a ballgame. That's a hundred or two hundred dollars, or better. You know what? The fans have gotta' quit making jerks outta' themselves and realize that they're the boss! No fans, no team owners, no teams!

GRB: That's true, but you know that will never happen.

Joe Henry: You know what? Joe Lieberman, the Democrat from Connecticut, never thought that the people would get together there the way they did. He felt certain that he couldn't be beaten. Those people in that state let him know who the boss was.

GRB: He didn't even make it out of the primary.

Joe Henry: That is absolutely correct. These things that you say will never happen: they'll never happen if you don't try to make them happen. I'm a guy that never says never. I am a guy that feels that there are so many intelligent people in America that they can catch on, and when they decide, "We're gonna let you know who the boss is! We're gonna let you know that you can't walk all over us like you feel you can!" That's what baseball fans today have within their power to make happen.

GRB: When Jackie Robinson broke the color barrier in '47, he brought an exciting style of play that he'd learned in the Negro League along with him, especially regarding base running. What are your impressions of how the game is played today compared to the style played in the Negro League?

Joe Henry: Well, it was baseball that we played in the Negro League. Just like I say, there's always excitement goin' on in some kind of way, ya know. Willie Wells was supposed to have started the trend of wearing helmets because he had a miner's helmet. At the time, so-called Major League Baseball didn't have exciting base runners. There might've been one guy, or another guy that could steal a base here and there. Everything seemed like it was programmed. It became more exciting. Just like back then, you heard of Babe Ruth, Lou Gherig, Ralph Kiner of the Pittsburgh Pirates, and Johnny Mize of the St. Louis Cardinals. Guys like that were homerun hitters. There was a lot of difference because runnin' was always a part of the Negro League. I just can't pinpoint different things because in both cases it was baseball. There was just a little bit more added on to it. Ya know how they talk about when Robinson came with that little additional thing that he added to make it a bit more exciting? People like to see players steal bases the same as people like to see players hit homeruns. It was baseball. Both of them were baseball.

WED., SEPT. 29, 2006 – 9:28AM
GRB: Do you think the emphasis on power hitting has taken away some from the game today?

Joe Henry: I love power hitters! I really love it!

GRB: Whaddya make of Albert Pujols?

Joe Henry: Oh, he's a bad son of a gun!

GRB: Oh, yeah?

Joe Henry: Oh, yeah! He's a bad son of a gun! Let me tell you something. The money has changed the context of baseball today. All of those high-priced salaries and everything like that. Baseball was a game that, at one time, most of the players made about five thousand dollars a year. Players had to get extra jobs and everything. And in the Major Leagues, there were guys that jumped the league to play in Mexico when Blacks had been going there for years. Guys like Danny Gardella and Max Lanier. When I look back on the accomplishments and contributions of Black players like Curt Flood, sometimes I wonder if it was worth him sticking out his neck in order to break down the barriers that the baseball team owners had up. That's when the baseball team owners had a guy by the butt. If they didn't want you to play for another team, you couldn't play. When Flood started his fight, he was sort of dissatisfied with the Cardinals. And when they tried to pedal him off to Washington, he told them, "No way!" The thing that he started eventually broke that string of hope that the white baseball owners had over players. And there were a lot of guys that did not stand behind him. I think it was Carl Yastremszki that would not stand behind him. A lot of guys, they didn't have the courage to stand up. Look at these baseball players today. They're multi-millionaires. So now, after a guy signs a contract for 10 million dollars, there's a clause in there that states that if he gets cut, he'll still get a million or two! Well, he's a millionaire, so what in the hell does he care?

GRB: Do you think that some of those millionaire athletes might be in it for the paycheck, and not because they like playing the game?

Joe Henry: I don't think that a guy would want to suffer any embarrassment as a baseball player. Ya see, I've been watching A-Rod [Alex Rodriguez] recently. And he looks awful down because a lot of fans have turned against him, especially in New York. The average player, if he's any kinda guy with pride, wants to keep the love, that close rapport with the fans. And if he happened to be a guy like Ted Williams...That's a guy that I truly loved because he refused to be bent. I mean, you'd see the average player hit a homerun, and he'd begin and tip his hat as he'd round the bases. Williams didn't even know what that was. He'd jog around the bases and seemingly spit in the direction of the fans. This guy was so great that it's unbelievable for a guy with that much talent to stand up for what he really believed in. And I was a guy that really, really loved him.

GRB: He actually had a reputation as being somewhat terse with the media.

Joe Henry: Yep, and he'd let nobody twist him around. He was just one heck of a guy. And he was just so natural that he brought a lot to baseball.

GRB: He was definitely one of the greats.

Joe Henry: Yes, he was.

GRB: If you were given the chance to play in the game as it is now, Joe, would you jump at the opportunity?

Joe Henry: I don't think so.

GRB: No?

Joe Henry: Uh...uh. Every time I see a player slide, I hurt all over. It rings every bone in my body with this arthritis. I just don't have that much interest in baseball. In fact, I lost interest shortly after I went to Memphis. I just lost interest.

GRB: After you started your career?

Joe Henry: The history part became more important to me. And because of that history, I just lost interest in baseball. I was ridin' all around the country for free at the expense of baseball team owners. I was just enjoying myself. Even when I was with the Clowns, there was a white owner whose name was Syd Pollack...Even as I was puttin' on a show, after I was much, much, less than a 100% ballplayer, scouts were still followin' me! Ed Hamman, who became a part owner of the Clowns with Syd Pollack...When scouts would come around to talk to him about me, without my knowledge, he would tell them, "Aw, he's done! He's done! His arm's shot! He can't throw! He's gotta' walk the ball to first base!" (Laughs) He'd let 'em know right off the jump, "You'll never get him away from me! The man is almost broken to bits and stuff!" He'd let 'em know, because the scouts told me that! Ya know, the scouts for the New York Giants, the scouts for the Braves...

GRB: Even after that knowledge, did scouts still have an interest in you?

Joe Henry: They just though that I was puttin' on a show with all of those gimmicks that I originated. They thought, by the way I handled all of that, I could still play a hundred percent. So Ed would get to 'em, when they would look for the owner or somebody. And when I was mentioned, he'd say, "Hey, he can't play! He can't even throw the ball to first base! His arm's gone! His legs are gone!" That was comical to me when I knew about that. And Ed was so honest that he told me, "Well hell no! I was gonna tell 'em what was goin' on with you! I didn't plan for none of 'em to try to get a hold of ya!" That was real comical. Just like the Washington Senators, they wanted to send me to one of their top farm systems. It was the Florida International League somewhere. One of the teams in that league was based in Havana, Cuba. These people from the Senators told me that, should I come into the Washington organization, I would be ridin' in style. And I asked him, "What kinda ridin' would that be?" He said, "You'll be flying to Havana." So I told him, "Well, I wanna be perfectly honest to you, just like you were honest to me. Baseball is not my hobby. I like ridin' these buses." So that cut that off about that plane! There's no way!

GRB: You didn't care for flying at the time?

Joe Henry: No way! The Braves wanted to buy the whole Mount Vernon franchise just to get me. I had quite a few good experiences, ya know. It's good to bring up and relate to somebody who's interested in baseball, but I don't care much for baseball now. If the Cardinals weren't in the National League, I probably wouldn't look at a game. But every time I look at a game, it has to be something dealin' with the Cardinals.

GRB: That's the only team you pay any attention to?

Joe Henry: Mmm...hmm. But my interest in the Cardinals is for them to get beat! (Both laugh)

GRB: You don't particularly care for the Cardinals ownership at this time, do you?

Joe Henry: Not at all. No.

GRB: Would you mind sharing your feelings on that?

Joe Henry: The only time that I generated a little feeling toward the Cardinals was when Curt Flood, Bob Gibson, Lou Brock, Orlando Cepeda, guys like that... There's just something about that Cardinals organization over there that I don't care for. I haven't cared for a Cardinals broadcasting team since the days of [Charles] "Gabby" Street ("The Old Sarge") France Locke, Dizzy Dean, and Harry Caray. Ya know, Shannon sounds as if he has a whiskey voice or something. And when he says, "Get up, get up, get up"...All that kinda junk. And this guy, John Rooney, he's sickening. I've been tempted to name him "Motor mouth." I like to go back into the days of Red Barber and guys like that. They were so cool in broadcasting games that they just did something to ya. They would take a play and turn it into something so nice. A guy could run like Al Gionfriddo of the Dodgers. I remember one game, when a guy hit a drive toward the fence and Gionfriddo started off to retrieve the ball. And Barber went on to say, "And Gionfriddo is on the run. And he can run." That was so much class to me, ya know.

GRB: Right. Just a different style.

Joe Henry: Right. You don't gotta' tell what color drawers a guys got on and how often he changes his drawers. You don't gotta' tell that kinda junk. I'm gonna' tell you who I can't stand is that damn Joe Morgan! Aw man, it is so sickening that I just don't know what to do. I mean, Jack Buck was alright, but that's a dynasty there. It's a whole family of broadcasters! I really started out liking Joe Buck, but when they teamed him with this doggone Tim McCarver...It is sickening! I just loved that class, that real smooth class, ya know. All of that tellin' about everything that happened in a guys life...I just consider these guys to be butt kissers to hold their jobs. And this McCarver man, he's absolutely just sickening!

GRB: Do you ever listen to any Joe Morgan broadcasts?

Joe Henry: Oh, I can't stand that too long. I just turn the volume down. That's the way I do it with John Rooney and Rick Horton. I just turn the volume completely off and use my own knowledge of the game to try and enjoy it. This Rooney hollers louder than all get up when a guy hits a ball, "Way back, back!" He goes through all that and then the guy catches the ball. They have made a shambles out of everything. I used to love "Old Sarge" and "Gabby" Street. You're too young to know anything about them. They were nice. They'd tell a story or two, the kind you can enjoy. And then they'd talk about something else, like when Danny Street was trying to catch a ball thrown from the Washington Monument. It was so interesting the way they would do it. And then, I fell in love with Harry Caray.

GRB: You liked Harry?

Joe Henry: Yes, I did. I mean, he'd put you right there in the ballgame. He would dramatize it, like when a man would come up to the plate. He could make you see the game as he was talking about it.

GRB: Do you think he may have hung onto his broadcasting job a bit too long in the later years, or do you think he'd established himself as a Chicago icon?

Joe Henry: Well, I think he established himself anywhere there was a broadcasting booth because he was that kind of charismatic person. Ya know what? He would get into trouble for saying the things that he felt. If the Cardinals played like a bunch of chumps, he would say it! He was just a heck of a guy, ya know.

GRB: Why do you think that baseball has declined in popularity among today's Black youth, and how can baseball be brought back to the Black community?

Joe Henry: That's very easy! I can tell ya that! Things, especially in regard to Blacks, are out there to make some money. What people can't realize is that, since Blacks have been in America, and they were supposed to have been let free, the money was kept away from' em. When you go back into the history of Blacks and makin' money, you pick it up in the time of boxing. Blacks gravitated toward boxing because boxing had proven prior to be of financial security. And that's why so many boxers would go down the drain, but then you had so many that were successful. When Blacks began to get into baseball, they might be able play with one of those so-called Major League teams, or not! It was controlled to the point that you've got to be sent over here to Eau Claire. And after you spent time at Eau Claire, you might get sent to another farm team. Sometimes, you might go all the way up, you might not. And it was a long way of trying to make some money, but the money, at the time, was still good money. Then here came basketball and football. Baseball didn't offer all of the big bonuses and everything, especially to Blacks. After Curt Flood, they began to take the same type of avenue toward making some pretty good money. Then Blacks came along to jump towards basketball and football. Well, hell, if a player signed one contract and if he's successful, and could hang onto his money, he's gonna pile him up a lot of money. A lot of things went on back then, Mike. This sort of stuff that was carried on about how a guy had to move in order to be successful, there's still this kinda junk about basketball and football. About how a guy who played high school basketball could not come out of high-school and play in the pros. They tried to head that off at the high school level talkin' about proposition 48 and all that junk. This country is a capitalistic system. And a capitalistic system is one without conscience. Anything that the government can get some money out of, they're gonna lean toward that. It's just big business.

GRB: Would you mind sharing your boxing background?

Joe Henry: Who me? Well, I used to just train guys for the Golden Gloves in St. Louis. This was during the time that Sonny Liston and all those kinda guys were in the Golden Gloves. Kenny Silver and just so many guys that I rubbed elbows with, ya know. I was a pretty good boxer, but I couldn't hit!

GRB: Oh, you could dodge 'em, but couldn't hit?

Joe Henry: Yeah! I was fancier than "Sugar" Ray Robinson, and that's who I stole my style from. And that's who Muhammad Ali stole his style from, "Sugar" Ray Robinson.

GRB: What do you make of Ali?

Joe Henry: I think he is exactly what he said he was: The Greatest. You know what? He was exactly the greatest. I mean, whatever he got into that most in the country thought to be wrong...He had that type of personality to deal with it. And he was one of the greatest, not just in the ring; he was one of the greatest outside the ring. George Foreman stole his charismatic side, and look at the millions of dollars that he has made from it. Ya know, he was alright in the boxing ring as long as he didn't get in front of Muhammad Ali. All these things that people like to hear...They like to hear when a guy gets a whoopin' and not winning any fight he encounters. And so, Foreman turned into a pretty good showman on the order of Muhammad Ali.

GRB: Did you watch the infamous rope-a-dope fight with Foreman?

Joe Henry: Yeah, when they kept telling him, "Get off that rope! Get off the ropes!" His trainers, including Angelo Dundee, didn't want Muhammad Ali to fight George Foreman. And I couldn't blame 'em. During the Olympics, when George Foreman walked around the ring waving that mini American flag, that guy could hit harder than lightnin' could thump a stump! They kinda thought that Muhammad Ali asked for more than he could swallow. That's why he went into that rope-a-dope, and he did that to try and let Foreman wear himself out. Even Jim Brown, the football player, advised Muhammad Ali not to fight Foreman. Jim Brown was sitting at ringside, and could hardly look up to see what was happening to Muhammad Ali. And after Muhammad Ali let Foreman punch himself out, he could tell it. When he stepped in and delivered that sharp left hook and followed up, Foreman's knees wobbled all over the place. Then, Muhammad Ali looked out at Jim Brown and said, "I got this mother now!" That's right! It was all over then! But you see what all of that boxing did to him. It had a lot to do with his condition today. He was one of the cleanest livers that you'd wanna see. Then along came Don King, and he became one of the greatest promoters ever. He does a lot of talking and people love him because he can say comical things.

GRB: I understand Ali didn't care much for Don King, did he?

Joe Henry: I can't say that, but I've heard that sentiment expressed by several boxers.

GRB: It's obvious that you've competed against some very gifted ballplayers. To your recollection, who was the absolute best position player and best pitcher that you faced in your career?

Joe Henry: I couldn't really answer that because I couldn't even say that about Willie Mays when I played against him. Mays was just one hell of a baseball player! At that point, I couldn't speak in a way that he was going to go all the way and become what he became. That's the same as Ernie Banks. Banks was about 165 lbs, and he could hit the ball into the next community!

GRB: How'd you fare against Satchel Paige when you faced him?

Joe Henry: Oh, I only faced him one time when he was with the Chicago American Giants in 1951. I went to the plate five times, and struck out four without him throwin' as hard as he originally had.

GRB: Really?

Joe Henry: Yeah, he was just a smart, smart, smart man. Do you know that he and my manager, who knew each other very well, had a bet on me! My manager told him that he had a young kid from around St. Louis, and I was supposed to wear Satchel Paige out that day. And each time I struck out, and was headed back to the dugout, I heard Satch say, "Goooooose!" He was callin' my manager, but I didn't know what was happenin'!

GRB: So you didn't know that there was a bet goin' down?

Joe Henry: Uh...uh. The fourth time, after I struck out and was headed back to the dugout, he hollered, "Goooooose!" And I happened to look around as he was noddin' his head at me. Ya know, like sayin', "Is this the youngster from around St. Louis that's gonna' wear me out?"

GRB: So did you get a hit off him?

Joe Henry: I grounded weakly back to him. And he just went over, picked the ball up and tossed me out. But I was thinking about the fame that he carried with him. After the game, I was gonna' call my dad and tell him that I had faced Satchel Paige! I was gonna' exaggerate, because I was going to tell him that I hit a hard line drive back to Paige, and he had to do some heck of things to defend himself against a ball that was hit as hard as I hit it! Then when I got in the clubhouse to start preparing to take me a shower, "Goose"[Curry], my manager, was sittin' in a chair watchin' my every move. I saw him over there and I said, "Hey Goose, how ya doin?" And he was looking at me with his eyes frowned and he said, "Not worth a goddamn!" So I said, "What's wrong with you?" He said, "Boy, you can't hit a damn thing!" Yeah! So I said, "That's why you're upset with me?" Then he said, "Damn right!" I said, "You can't get upset with me, Goose. Look at all of these guys years back that he was striking out before I even knew anything about him." And, uh, that kind of broke up that closeness that my manager had with me. Because he saw in me, a person who could go as far as they wanted to go but it was up to me. So he stopped speakin' to me a little bit there. What happened in Rickwood Park in Birmingham, Alabama...he got beaten by two or three white policemen, who worked as security at the park, because he argued a called pitch with the Black umpire. And the umpire turned and beckoned for the white Birmingham policemen, and they ordered Goose to get back into the third base coaching box. Goose was tellin' them that he had three minutes to do that. Shit, they started whoopin' him right there at home plate. They led him away from home plate bleedin' and out the side entrance of Rickwood Park. I stood atop the front of the dugout crying like a kid when I was watchin' that. Now these were policemen that were tied into "Bull" Connor, who was the commissioner of police during the time that Dr. Martin Luther King and the group went into Birmingham. They were shot with fire hoses, attacked by dogs, cattle prods, and all of that.

GRB: How did Goose recover from that?

Joe Henry: Well, he came out all right.

GRB: Just a little shaken emotionally?

Joe Henry: Yeah, ya know, he bled a lot. But I thought that I could get back in close friendship with him. We were in Fort Wayne, Indiana and he was sittin' in the clubhouse with half of his uniform on. Ya know, the socks and all that. So I tried to say something to him to make him feel real good, because he was in his fifties then. So I said to him, "Goose, you know, you are really built." I could barely hear him say, "Yeah." And then I made it a little better and said, "How much do you weigh?" He said, "Well, it's according to who I'm up against. Against a white Birmingham policeman, I don't weigh anything." Then he said, "But I weigh a ton on yo' ass!" (Both laugh) I thought, "To heck with it. I can't be buddies with him anymore." So I left him alone.

GRB: Didn't you guys become friendly in later years?

Joe Henry: Uh...uh. He just treated me like a ballplayer. At first, he just thought the world of me as a ballplayer. But see, there were some pretty, pretty, pretty, women in Memphis. They came from Booker T. Washington High School over to the park and everything. And so, I met a couple and was gabbin' and talkin' with them. Then Goose happened to come out to the park at the same time, when one of them was standin', talkin' to me, smilin' and goin' on. So Goose passed me and said, "How ya doin', Joe?" I said, "Oh, Goose, I'm alright." He said, "Yeah, I see it! But I wanna let you know one thing!" Then he said, "Any ho' will wear out a pole!" Yep! (Both laugh)

GRB: What were some instances of running into the Jim Crow laws while you were traveling with the team?

Joe Henry: Uh, Blacks, at that time, had come to be what was considered marooned. You knew where you were. You always understood who you were. It became a way of life. Therefore, you were ever cautious.

GRB: Were there any veteran players that showed you any tough love? Ya know, did any of them tell you, "Look, you don't do that when you're traveling with this team!"?

Joe Henry: If you're from up this way, any place that's supposed to be considered the North, you know where ya are! When you get there, a certain lifestyle begins to takeover. You know that you're required to say yes sir and no sir. That's something that I never really went all out to say. I was about like guys when I was growin' up in this community. If two guys start wrestlin' and one gets a better grip on the other, ya know, if one gets an arm around the other's neck and really starts squeezin 'em. In order to get loose he had to holler "calf rope." Well, the average guy didn't want to show weakness by sayin' "calf rope." There were times when an opposing guy would bend their arm around the other's neck. And by the mere fact that the guys did not want to say calf rope, he could wait too long and darn near get choked to death! By the time that he realized that he was near being choked to death, he would try to say calf rope and couldn't get a word out of his mouth. He would make a gurgling noise.

GRB: Just some gurgles?

Joe Henry: Mmm...hmmm. Shit, if there wasn't somebody standin' right there by him actin' as the referee to say, "Let him go! Let him go! You chokin' him to death! You killin' him! You killin' him!" If you didn't have somebody to do that, well, there would have been deaths. But the average guy, like me, when a guy would get his arm around my neck tellin' me to say "calf rope," I'd say, (Hollers) "Calfrooooope!" (Both laugh)

GRB: You weren't gonna' give 'em a chance to let you not holler!

Joe Henry: Hey, no sooner did I feel his arm around my neck and he'd tell me to say Calf rope…(Hollers) "Calfrooooope!" And then I'd feel his grip loosen. Hell naw', I ain't that tough! (Both laugh)

GRB: What was your size during your playing days? How big were you?

Joe Henry: About 185 lbs.

GRB: How tall?

Joe Henry: About 6 feet…5'11 and a half.

GRB: That's a pretty good build! I bet you could've taken some guys down with ya!

Joe Henry: They used to call me the Arm and Hammer man. You know, like on those soda boxes. They had a guy on there with muscles and everything. Yeah, they used to call me that. The Arm and Hammer man. I was built pretty nice.

GRB: You'd have to be to compete at that level.

Joe Henry: Yeah, but when I contracted diabetes in 1976, I was weighing 218 lbs. and was pretty well put together. Now I'm down to 20.

GRB: You're down to what?

Joe Henry: 20 lbs! (Both laugh)

THU OCT 05, 2006 11:31

GRB: Describe yourself as a player, and please share how you got the nickname "Prince" Joe Henry.

Joe Henry: Okay, that's after I was injured in organized ball. The injury that I sustained happened to my left knee on a double play. A white kid in the Philadelphia Phillies organization went across the bag and caught my knee. And down I went.

That's when the injury occurred. After I was taken to the hospital and was supposedly ready to play again......Once I started playin', I began to favor my knee and still tried to throw that ball across the infield as hard as I had originally.

GRB: And you were a second baseman at that time?

Joe Henry: I was a third baseman. I got away from second base when with the Memphis Red Sox. All the rest of my playin' time was at third base. By continuing to play, I messed up my right arm. People always considered me to have a rifle-like arm. I used to tease around at third base, and knock balls down, and jump up get 'em, and hit the first baseman belt-high. It was nothin' but jumpin' across the infield. I messed up my right arm by doing that. So after I was out of baseball in 1954, I played in an all-star game with Mr. Johnson.

GRB: Josh Johnson?

Joe Henry: Josh Johnson. He had a team, and the team was named the Metropolitan All-Stars. We played a game at Stag Park in Belleville. Ted Savage was playin' second base. I played in that game and got about three hits that night, but I didn't have any hard plays. I could come in for a ball, pick it up, keep runnin', and then throw the runner out. I could throw it from the side or some other way to get it there. That night after the game, Buddy Downs, who was the traveling secretary for the Indianapolis Clowns...He talked to me after the game and told me how well I had performed. He started askin' me to come back to the league with the Indianapolis Clowns. After I told him that I was finished as a ballplayer, he said, "Aw no! Give us a chance first." So in '55, I decided to go to spring training with the Indianapolis Clowns. By that time the Clowns had gotten out of the Negro League and started traveling independently, like the Indianapolis Clowns, the New York Black Yankees, just like the Harlem Globetrotters did...Like I said, with the abilities that I had left, I could partly play the game as a modified ballplayer and put on a show! I just started originating all kinds of gimmicks and everything. I had the top hat and tails. Well, Ed Hamman, with some publicity that I didn't know about... It was in the papers, "Prince" Joe Henry.

GRB: So Ed Hamman gave you the name?

Joe Henry: Right! So I'm wonderin', "Where in the hell did this come from?" And Ed said that I felt like baseball was a gentleman's game and I strolled to the plate with the top hat and tails on. That's the way it started! I started playin' in the pants with the coat on, and they began to get worn down and raggedy. That's how I got that name, "Prince" Joe Henry.

GRB: What were some of your antics?

Joe Henry: I originated antics that "Goose" Tatum called when I was with him in 1958 on the Detroit Clowns; he called the things that I was doing "gems." I've got a great big write-up around here somewhere. The ideas and all that he came up with, like the tuxedo, top hat on, and strollin' away from first base once on base. The pitcher would try to turn to pick me off, but I would have a distance that was safe enough to know I could get back. Rather than try to slide back, I would just take a pratfall directly on my back towards the bag. I would kickoff with my spikes in the ground just like I was tryin to propel myself back to the bag with the top hat on touching the bag.

GRB: So the top hat was what would touch the bag?

Joe Henry: That's right! I did a lot of things. I had already started wearin' my pants down to my ankles. That came about because the softball uniforms were different from the baseball uniforms. They would be hangin' to your ankles. So I started wearin' my pants real low down to my ankles. I'd turn my back to the pitcher, and by timing his delivery when he turned the ball loose, I would swing around at the plate and take a cut at the ball. And there have been several times that I hit homeruns, and I didn't know the ball was going out! Then I would slap the catcher's hands, slap the umpire's hands, and go over to the stands and start a conversation with one of the fans and then jog around the bases. So I started that kinda stuff before Reggie Jackson even came into the picture. There were several things that I did, ya know. That's a hard job! There were newspaper clippings and things across the country that was rating me, "Next to the fabulous Reese "Goose" Tatum!" When I was with Goose, I'd pull all kinds of things. And I would always go right back to Goose, because Goose had taught me all those things. Then Goose would get in on the act with me. Like, he'd put a little nail into the top of a bat, and he would have a baseball fixed in some sort of way that it had a hole in it. He and I would get on the field and try the balancing act by putting the ball on top of the bat so it would stay there. And the people would get tied up in that. Every time it would seem that we were takin' that ball all the way up, they'd start clappin' and hollerin', but it would roll off. About that time, you could hear the crowd sayin, "Ohhhhhh"!

GRB: So they didn't know there was a nail in there?

Joe Henry: No. Then, after you'd do that several times, you'd try the same way, but you'd put the ball over the nail. And when you'd start goin' up, and the ball remained there, people would start clappin' and hollerin' and carryin' on! When you succeeded in keeping that ball on the knob of that bat, you'd just lean the bat across your shoulder with the ball still on it and start walkin' away!

GRB: Showin 'em the trick!

Joe Henry: That's right! I had a lot of fun doin' those things. It was just really, really, really nice. I got all kinds of publicity from the things I was doing, and people wanted to know where I'd come up with those things. I did many, many, many things, ya know.

GRB: Oh, yeah?

Joe Henry: Yeah! At that time, you weren't permitted to wear a mustache. So at 20 years old...Hell, I didn't have a mustache and my sister told me how to make a mustache. You'd take one of those wooden matches, burn it, then go get some water, and put the match down in the water. Then, from that burnt part, I'd just make me a mustache! I did everything that an ordinary ballplayer couldn't do. Those ideas that I thought up and put into motion, like hidin' my glove up under the inside of the coat. I might take a heck of a cut at the ball, and after takin that heck of a cut at a ball...I would do that purposely. And then, on the next pitch, I would slide my hand into the glove up under the coat so nobody in the stands could see it. So then, when the pitcher would turn the ball loose, I would snatch my arm out with the glove on my hand and catch the ball! And then, I'd throw it up into the air and fungo it!

GRB: (Laughing) Okay! As if you were hitting outfield practice. I know what you're talking about.

Joe Henry: Heh, there were so many things, ya know! I'd get a big ole' pair of women's drawers four sizes too big for the lady, and I'd get in an argument with the umpire. Then, the umpire would take off after me, and he's right behind me while I'm headin' for the stands runnin'. And by the time I'd get over to the stands, I'd jump into the stands where a lady was seated. Then, when I'd come back up, I'd have them big drawers in my hand holdin 'em up! And people just cried. They just cried.

GRB: Were the umpires in on the stunt?

Joe Henry: Well, he would only run me in the direction I was headin' to jump over into the stands. Ya see, when I'd jump over, I would go down to the floor out of sight of most of the fans. Then, when I'd come back up off the floor, I would have those big drawers spread out, showin 'em around to the people! Sometimes, I got a pretty big kick out of that myself!

GRB: I bet!

Joe Henry: I pulled that on one lady, and she reached up under her dress to see that she still had her drawers on! (Laughs) When I stood up and started spreadin' them drawers around, she looked at me and she said, "You'd better get away from me before I knock you out!" You would be surprised at some of those ladies. They wanted pictures and everything. It's a wonderful thing when a person has the ability to make people laugh.

GRB: Do you have any humorous stories from your playing days that you'd like to share?

Joe Henry: Uh, quite a few. Upon undertaking the showmanship with the Indianapolis Clowns, I happened to not be the only showman to keep people laughin'. You see, the Indianapolis Clowns had sideline entertainers. They had a pair of guys at that time. One was named Richard "King Tut" King and the other was Spec Bebop. He and Tut, a former baseball player, put on the show years before I arrived with the Indianapolis Clowns. My thing came after the injury, and after the fact that I'd acknowledged that I could not play 100% as a baseball player. That's where I came in. I decided that I would do certain things, and the top hat and tails were synonymous with the Indianapolis Clowns.

GRB: So you weren't the only one who wore those?

Joe Henry: Heh, no, I'd have to clear that up. Nobody ever did what I did in puttin' on a show with the top hat and tails, Bermuda shorts, the fisherman's cap..... Nobody ever did anything like that with the Indianapolis Clowns. For instance, whenever Goose Tatum, the former Harlem Globetrotters original showman, performed with the Indianapolis Clowns, at times he might put on the coat and tails, ya know. He might run out on the field, but after a play or two he would pull it off. That was it. The type of showmanship that King Tut and Spec Bebop did...You had two side performers like that. One was named "Hot Dog" Bobo

Nickerson. Then there was Ed Hamman, part owner of the Indianapolis Clowns. Anyway, these were sideline showmen. At one time, and this was long before I came to be an Indianapolis Clowns player, they had a one-man band sideline performer. I used to get a big kick out of some of the things that I was told by older guys when playing with the Clowns. The one- man band would holler out at the audience and ask, "Hey, have you ever heard of Paul Whiteman?" And when people hollered back, "Yeah.", he would answer, "Well, I'm Paul Blackman!" (Both laugh) It was all of these types of thing that pre-dated sideline entertainers like Fredbird and all of these different types that you hear of today. There was just so much entertainment along with Negro League baseball games that the people really had many things to enjoy themselves with.

GRB: What was the crowd like? What was the demographic makeup of the crowd? Was it mostly white people, mostly Black people?

Joe Henry: No, no. It was mostly Black people at all times. And it's a shame to say this in a supposedly civilized society, but whites in the ballpark were cordoned off! So where Blacks were in the majority, there were whites, but they were in a little section as when Blacks would attend something that would be viewed by predominantly white people.

GRB: Almost a role reversal in a way?

Joe Henry: That's right! There was no mixin' up with Blacks and whites together. It was like they said, Colored section. And when it was predominantly Black, white section. Yeah, that's typical.

GRB: Were there any good clubhouse pranks that you witnessed?

Joe Henry: No. I mean, guys were always pullin' little stunts and things that really went unnoticed. It was just to get a laugh right then and there, ya know.

GRB: That was it?

Joe Henry: (Laughs) I'll tell ya about a bus stunt from when I was with the Memphis Red Sox! My buddy, who joined the Memphis Red Sox the same time that I did in 1950…His name was Ollie Brantley; he and I were the only two kids to make the team, and we didn't start traveling with the team at that point. It was in Birmingham, Alabama where Memphis was playing, that the manager called back for Ollie and I to board a bus and meet the team in Memphis. Being kinda young, at one time we were walkin' around a town where we were to play, and we happened to walk upon a novelty store. In this novelty store, as we checked things out, we found a small bottle of stink perfume. So we decided while traveling that night to open that stink perfume and just wave it around in the bus. Because that's about all you had to do and then put the cap back on it! (Laughs) This was when there were different nationalities on the bus like Panamanians, Cubans, Puerto Ricans, and Black Americans. And one night, as we were ridin' along, the whole crew on the bus was asleep. It had kinda cooled off just a little bit while we traveled. So we took that stink perfume out, took the top cap off, and sprayed it around, just kinda shook it around a little bit. Then we put the cap back on right quick and acted as if we were asleep. That stuff started moving all over the bus and you heard a mixture of languages! They thought that somebody was just lettin' go! And Ollie and I would act as if we were sleepin' while we were doing everything to hold our laughing back! All of these people started complaining like, "Who's that nasty sap sucker that's sittin' back there and openly, without any kinda morals, lettin' go things like that?!?" (Laughing) And what was comical to us was that you could hear those side windows on the bus goin', "Plam, Plam, Plam" as they were opening 'em up, so that air could come through! (Laughs) After we finished the first time, and things cleared out, and the windows went back closed, we waited awhile until everything got settled down. And then we did the same thing! I mean, there was some cursing, and our "chauff" stopped the bus. Then he said, "Look, wait a minute! Whoever is doing this, if you've got to go to a restroom, I'll stop at a service station and get the bus filled up!" That's through the South, and whenever the bus was gassed up, we couldn't go into the restrooms. So that's the way we could get some patronage by the bus being gassed. And so, one guy on the bus said, "Ya know, I hate to feel like this, but whoever is doing this, point him out to me and I'll bust his ass wide open!" (Both laugh) I mean, Ollie and I just cramped from laughing so hard to ourselves and tryin' to keep it from everybody else!

GRB: And did they ever catch you?

Joe Henry: Nooooooo! The next day, we'd be walkin' around in the town we were playin' in, and we would be leaning on each other laughin', ya know! We were just about afraid to tell anybody about it, because we had just joined the team. And heck, we didn't know what would happen if they found out. It was little acts like that which were very, very, comical.

GRB: Some inside jokes there.

Joe Henry: Right! There was one thing that happened to me in Columbus, Mississippi. There was an umpire that didn't want to be bothered with that showmanship of mine, no matter how the crowds in the stands rolled over, howlin' and laughin' and everything. So this particular night, I decided to get some laughs off this umpire. And he let me know right off the jump, "Don't play that stuff with me!" That didn't mean anything to me! I would try to ease around up on him and every time he would put his hands on his hips. So he would stare, just stop and stare at me. So I would head in another direction, ya know, just entertaining the crowd. Later on I came back while he was tryin' to concentrate on umpiring, and messed with him again. And after I bothered him, he broke at me and I started runnin'! I ran from home plate and started slowin' down as I neared first base. Then, I heard the guys on the bench hollerin', "Run! Run!" (Laughs) Well, I happened to look around, and this umpire was right behind me! I carried him to that right field wall runnin'! And the guys were talkin' about how that tail of the tuxedo coat was standin' straight out as I was runnin'! (Both laugh) When I got back to the bench, even some of the guys on the other team were on the ground!

GRB: So he chased you all the way out to right field?

Joe Henry: Yes, he did! When he went beyond first base, he was serious, ya know! Had he caught me, the fans might've really had some entertainment! This guy had muscles. (Laughs) I'm tellin' ya, he was a big dude! And after he couldn't catch me beyond first base, he just stood with his hands on his hips watchin' me run! The people in the stands, I mean, they were crying! When I got to the bench, the fellas' on the team were crying on the ground from laughing so hard! I'm tellin' ya, we talked about that on the bus that night!

GRB: So when something like that happened, were you basically ejected from the game from then on?

Joe Henry: Who me?

GRB: Yeah!

Joe Henry: No! I was puttin' on the show, and that's what the people wanted to see! Ya see, I would do the showin', but the Clowns had a monster of a team. They had a powerful team. The Clowns, at one time, had won championships and everything. The Clowns had some dynamite teams. Let me say this: when I went to Memphis, there were 10 teams still in the league. Do you know that I saw, right there, the power of the Negro League? And for every one of those teams that were leftover, eight of those guys could've gone to those Major League teams. The Kansas City Monarchs; the Memphis Red Sox; the Birmingham Black Barons; the Baltimore Elite Giants......Junior Gilliam and Joe Black were with the Elite Giants at that time. Any eight guys, from any of those teams, could've gone straight to the Major League locker rooms and put on a uniform, like Ernie Banks did with Chicago.

GRB: Do you sense that the history of the Negro Leagues has been under appreciated? If so, what do you think can be done to preserve that history so that younger generations can learn it as well?

Joe Henry: Well, I think that the Negro League Baseball Museum has done one tremendous job. That is one history, preserved up to this point that will never die. I mean, it is something else. Ya know when they had their last voting about Blacks entering the Major League Baseball Hall of Fame, I wrote in one of my articles that I wouldn't vote for any single guy. For instance, Buck O'Neil or one of the other players...I cast my vote for the Negro League Baseball Museum to be placed in the Hall of Fame. And by placing the Negro League Baseball Museum in the Major League Baseball Hall of Fame, any Negro League baseball player could be acknowledged. Everybody would have been mentioned, in some kinda way, as a part of the Hall of Fame.

GRB: I understand you've attended some reunions at the Negro League Baseball Museum. How have those been for you?

Joe Henry: Oh, you mean in Kansas City?

GRB: Yes, sir.

Joe Henry: I'll tell ya what, I haven't gotten over attending those Negro League reunions.

GRB: Great memories?

Joe Henry: Oh, I mean, the time that was had......I met some of the older guys that I'd never met before. It was an experience that made chills come all over me. The last one in 2000 was very good. Charley Pride attended both. He's a former Negro Leaguer.

GRB: And a country musician.

Joe Henry: Right. Tommy Lasorda was master of ceremonies. I just can't name the different people. Hank Aaron was there, and Hank Aaron is an alumnus of the Indianapolis Clowns. There is so much history associated with the Negro League. I happened to be flippin' the television channels last night, and the Pirates and Cardinals were playin' in Pittsburgh. The Pirates wore the uniforms of the Homestead Grays, and the Cardinals wore the uniforms of the St. Louis Stars.

GRB: Do you like when Major League Baseball does acknowledgments like that?

Joe Henry: Well, it's a good advertisement for the Negro League.

GRB: In February of '2005, Mike Seely, who is currently a writer for the Seattle Weekly, did a profile piece on you and your struggles with the Major League Baseball Assistance Team (B.A.T.). Could you walk us through that process?

Joe Henry: Well, I had no knowledge of the latter pensions being given to the former Negro Leaguers. I happened to be reading the Belleville News-Democrat, and saw where they had a million dollars that they were going to give to former Negro Leaguer's in need. It was specifically stated, by Bud Selig, that this money was going to be given to guys who played at least parts of four seasons. That means, if you played one season, two seasons, three seasons, or the whole four seasons. And Major League Baseball began tying that up, in some kinda way, with four consecutive seasons. I still have that paper. After reading that, I contacted Bud Selig's office, which was being run by some organization called B.A.T., and inquired about what was in the newspaper. And I was told that it was true. So Jim Martin sent me an application, and nobody could've been as honest as I was, and I sent it back. After I received his answer, I didn't qualify. Here I am, a player in1950, two years after Robinson went to the Dodgers, who knew of guys who played before and after Robinson. The league continued in '1948, '49, '50, and '51. That burned me! That's when I got a hold of Mike Seely at the Riverfront Times, and he did that story on me. And it took off. Jim Martin learned that I was ready to expose that whole sham, and it was a couple of St. Louis Post-Dispatch writers that let him know. Jim Martin contacted these Post-Dispatch writers, and this was before I knew Mike Seely at the Riverfront Times. He told them that he was sending me another application to have me fill out, and then he would give me the pension.

And I told him, "No, I've got a letter that I'm going to give to you." So he told me that he wasn't in the business of correspondence, and that he was trying to give money to people who needed it. That application that I submitted lets you know about my financial background and everything. So he said to me, "You know, you're being belligerent." I said, "Call it what you may, but you will receive the letter." After I said that, he wanted me to fill the application out. I told him, "I feel worn out. You gave me your answer." So he was ready to give me the money for four years. I just told him, "Hey, just like Johnny Paycheck, when he sang Take this Job and Shove It; If you can't give a pension to all of these guys that played in the Negro League, and can prove that they played, take that pension and shove it!" That's when the battle started between Major League Baseball's Jim Martin and me.

GRB: Well, the funny thing about it is that if you hadn't left the Negro League to enter the minor leagues, you would've had the pension, wouldn't you?

Joe Henry: No. If there had been anybody more qualified than me, I couldn't find them. Ya know, after 1954, there were only four teams in the Negro League. They were the Birmingham Black Barons, the Memphis Red Sox, the Kansas City Monarchs, and the Indianapolis Clowns. And then the Clowns got out of the league after 1954. These guys that got the pension from Bud Selig and Jim Martin... They dealt with Bob Mitchell, a guy that supposedly played with the Kansas City Monarchs starting in 1954. After 1954, Ted Raspberry purchased the Kansas City Monarchs, and the guy [Mitchell] was playing with the team then. Hell, they tell me that when Ted Raspberry purchased the team, he sold every other ballplayer and even the bus. And nobody wanted this guy! Really, he didn't have any four years in. That's when Selig and them came up with the idea that 1957 was the end of the Negro League. That's how he got in there because he was still playing with the Kansas City Monarchs up until 1957. He played in '54, '55, '56,'57, and he wasn't due that money. If anything, he would've had one year in 1954, and he would have been excluded from the pension. They didn't follow suit. They didn't set parts of at least four years. At least he would've had one year, and then he would've been eligible for the pension. If the other years hadn't been added, he would've been out of there. Bud Selig didn't have any business telling anybody about when the Negro League ended because Selig didn't have any concern for the Negro League or its history.

GRB: Are there any other players that are in the same situation as you, who didn't get the pension due to the circumstances?

Joe Henry: Yes, and I was there playin' before any of these guys. Charley Pride made it very, very clear! He said, "I didn't want the money. I didn't need the money. But this one guy insisted that I take it. So I did and gave it to my brother." I'm just waiting for some good lawyer who wants to get his name out there across the nation. If a good lawyer were to take up the case, Major League Baseball would be too glad to pull pension money out of their back pockets and pay all these other guys. These men have played in the Negro League, and have been cut short because of Bud Selig cutting off the Negro League at a certain year. Thanks to everyone who took the time to read this interview!

END OF TRANSMISSION

In the Matter of the Organization) August 2, 1893.
of the Village of Brooklyn.) Return of Election.

On the eighth day of July 1873, a petition was filed to the County Judge, signed by forty legal voters for the incorporation of the platted town of Brooklyn, as a Village, under the Laws of the State of Illinois, and an election was ordered by the County Judge to be held in said town of Brooklyn, for or against the incorporation of said Brooklyn as a village on the 30th, day of July 1873 as appears in the County Record. And now the returns of said election having been made to the County Judge, he called to his assistance two Justices of the Peace, viz: Martin Heuert and Henry R. Challenor, to canvass said returns, the result of which was "For Village Organization" Sixty Six votes, "Against Village Organization" none, Which is by the Court, ordered to be entered of record.

State of Illinois)
) ss.
St. Clair County)   I Geo. E. Thomas Clerk of the County Court, do hereby certify that the foregoing is a true and correct copy of the original as appears of record in my Office, in Probate Record "F", page 194.

In Witness Whereof, I have hereunto set my hand and Official Seal, this 23rd, day of September, 1901.

Geo E. Thomas
Clerk.

WASHINGTON, WEDNESDAY, JUNE 28, 2006   No. 86

Congressional Record

United States
of America

...RATING THE 133RD ANNI-...SARY OF THE VILLAGE OF ...OKLYN, ILLINOIS

HON. JERRY F. COSTELLO
OF ILLINOIS
IN THE HOUSE OF REPRESENTATIVES
Wednesday, June 28, 2006

...OSTELLO. Mr. Speaker, I rise today to ...colleagues to join me in recognizing ...rd anniversary of the incorporation of ...ge of Brooklyn, Illinois, the first and ...African-American town in the United

...d the year, 1829, a group of 11 Afri-...rican families, some free, some fugi-...es, crossed the Mississippi River from ...and settled in the area that would be-...rooklyn, Illinois. The community contin-...grow as it attracted both escaped ...nd free African-Americans from the St. ...rea and neighboring states. The thriv-...ement was platted and named, Brook-...837.

...g Brooklyn's early years, before the ...r, African-Americans had no ability to ...petition for the incorporation of their ...ity. With the ratification of the Thir-...mendment to the Constitution in 1865, ...rteenth Amendment in 1868 and the ...Amendment in 1870, African-Ameri-...ained the legal rights of citizenship. ...after these events, on July 8, 1873, ...ens of Brooklyn petitioned to incor-...An election was called and, by unani-...ote, Brooklyn was incorporated as a

The history of Brooklyn has roughly paralleled that of neighboring municipalities in the industrial area along the Mississippi River, across from St. Louis. Many of its residents readily found work in the stockyards and factories that flourished into the middle of the last century. As those industries left, so did the jobs that allowed the citizens of Brooklyn to provide for their families.

Despite recent hard times, the same spirit that led those first courageous settlers to establish this community still lives on. The village motto is, "Founded by Chance, Sustained by Courage," and those words inspire the current generation to seek new opportunities for their community. The "North Star" Corridor Economic Alliance Project is one example of a new implementation of the community's founding values.

Mr. Speaker, I ask my colleagues to join me in celebrating the 133rd anniversary of the Village of Brooklyn, Illinois and to wish them the best as they move forward in the years to come.

STATE OF ILLINOIS

Senate Recognition

The Illinois Senate
of the 94th General Assembly of the State of Illinois
acknowledges

Village of Brooklyn

In Recognition of
celebrating the 133rd Anniversary of its Incorporation
as the first and the oldest African-American government/town
in American and Illinois history,

and extends its congratulations and best wishes to all its citizens
on this momentous occasion as they celebrate their heritage
as "A Pioneer in African-American Cultural Self-Determination".

Offered by: Senator James F. Clayborne, Jr.

State Senator

Emil Jones, Jr.
Senate President

Linda Hawker
Secretary of the Senate

No. 94-5766

July 8, 2006

OFFICE OF THE MAYOR

The Historic Village of Brooklyn, Illinois · MS. RUBY COOK – MAYOR

Proclamation
(Honoring)

Mr. Joseph Henry
(Historic Negro League Professional Baseball Star)

Whereas, Mr. Joseph Henry, native son of the Historic Village of Brooklyn, Illinois, has distinguished himself and the Village of Brooklyn, in American History, and

Whereas, Mr. Joseph Henry has distinguished himself as an outstanding professional athlete in historic Professional Negro League Baseball, and

Whereas, Mr. Joseph Henry and the Henry Family have made a life-time of invaluable civic, cultural and community service contributions to and for the Village of Brooklyn, and

Whereas, the office of Mayor declares this day forward, July 8, 1999, an Annual Day of Celebration for the Historic Village of Brooklyn, Illinois, and

NOW, THEREFORE, I RUBY F. COOK - MAYOR of the GREAT VILLAGE of BROOKLYN, ILLINOIS, do hereby proclaim July 8, 1999, as "MR. JOSEPH HENRY DAY" In the Village of Brooklyn; the year of our 126th Birthday.

IN WITNESS, WHEREOF, I HAVE HEREUNTO SET MY HAND AND CAUSED TO BE AFFIXED, THE SEAL OF THE VILLAGE OF BROOKLYN, ILLINOIS, THE EIGHTH DAY OF JULY, NINETEEN-HUNDRED AND NINETY-NINE.

Ruby Cook

MS. RUBY COOK – MAYOR
VILLAGE OF BROOKLYN, ILLINOIS

Editor's Note: Here is the letter by Mr. Henry to BAT after being denied pension.

September 13, 2004
Baseball Assistance Team (BAT)
c/o James Martin, Executive Director
245 Park Avenue
New York, NY 10167

Dear Mr. Martin:

Recently, after reading a newspaper article captioned "Pension Fund Set for Negro Leaguers," I contacted your office regarding the contents therein, which consisted of Major League Baseball (MLB) providing more than $1 million in pensions to former Negro League players through a new charitable program. In further reading the article, I learned that the fund was earmarked for 27 players, who performed after the advent of Jackie Robinson in 1947. Commissioner Bud Selig – in announcing this news to the nation – stated he was pleased that MLB was able to come to the aid of former players in need. He added that MLB and Baseball Assistance Team (BAT) would conduct the order of business in this new venture, which follows a similar affair set up in 1997 to benefit players who played before 1948. Upon conclusion, Selig conceded the new fund would benefit additional players who spent "parts" of at least "four seasons" in the league starting before "1958."

However, after contacting your office and being told I was required to submit an application – which I did – I eventually received a rejection response concerning the personal information I disclosed in my application that left me completely in dismay. It is hard to reconcile how MLB, an organization that Negro Leaguers pointed in the right direction of becoming Major League calibre after entry, would belittle itself by hoodwinking the American public by using electronic and print media to convey how "benevolent" it presently is towards former Negro Leaguers, following the destruction of this once powerful economy within the Black community.

Despite such catastrophic consequences – a predicament beginning in 1947 – I applaud MLB for the unconditional financial help provided former Negro League players beginning in 1997. Unfortunately, I am unable to say the same about the latter goodwill gesture that – as far as I am concerned – smells of scam. As a former Negro Leaguer – having begun my career in 1950 with the Memphis Red Sox (two years after Robinson entered the white baseball leagues) – I am appalled by the line of questioning found in the application I received, which was regarded as a "Grant Application" of which, I suppose, is tantamount to that designed for an ex-convict.

Though I left Memphis after the 1951 season to enter so-called organized baseball – with conditions similar to those Robinson encountered when entering the Dodgers' organization –according to Selig, in the newspaper article, the new fund would benefit players who spent "parts of at least four seasons in the Negro Leagues," which automatically made me eligible. In short, however, Selig's press release to the nation regarding the latest fund designated as to provide assistance for 27 players, did not exemplify the initial effort of considering former Negro Leaguers, period.

In reference to the first group to receive pensions – those who played before 1947 – it is my understanding that these players received quarterly pensions of $2,500 amounting to $10,000 annually. This was later changed to $833.33 monthly without duration in time. This I thought was truly genuine, especially since such names as Joe Black – whom I played against in 1950 – along with other players I heard about, worked diligently with MLB personnel to see this project reach fruition.

Conversely, the same cannot be said of the latest proposition regarding funds obtained to supposedly help existing players. Based upon Selig's statement and the disapproval of my application by you and your committee, the plan is saturated with loopholes that deny numerous former players' participation in its being. If my recollection is correct, of the times I attended The Negro League reunions in Kansas City, Missouri staged by The Negro League Baseball Museum (NLBM), not only did I see and meet former players before my heyday, but also players whom I played with and against, as well as those even remotely associated.

This position on the part of personnel at the NLBM demonstrated the true meaning of "Liberty And Justice for All." This pattern followed the tradition of the Negro Leagues, whose doors – during its time – were open to all members of Latin persuasion, as well as white owners and promoters, eventually to even patronize women. Unlike personnel at the NLBM, who – without discriminating – exhausted its list by inviting every former Negro Leaguer to both gala affairs, which included players long prior to Robinson and those who played until the league officially ended in 1960 or 1961. Apparently, MLB and BAT representatives shrunk whatever list they had to 27 players to share in the $1 million.

Obviously, as in my situation, numerous former players were not properly informed about the plan by either MLB or BAT. My knowledge of it stemmed from me reading the article published in the Belleville News-Democrat, a local newspaper, dated Tuesday, May 18, 2004. This led me to call your office regarding its authenticity. Following contact with your office, then after receiving and filling out the application you forwarded – only to hear later that it was not approved because of my income exceeding my expenses, I felt was quite ludicrous. This feeling is based on the fact that I am a former Negro Leaguer of the early fifties (mainly 1950 during a time when 10 teams were yet prevalent) who not only played with and against an overflow of players – both before and after Jackie Robinson dating back to 1948 up to 1950 – having names the likes of Junior Gilliam, Joe Black, Willie Mays, Ernie Banks and even the venerable Satchel Paige, just to name a few – notwithstanding firsts like Willard Brown (St. Louis Browns), Sam Hairston and Bobby Boyd (Chicago White Sox), Curt Roberts (Pittsburgh Pirates), Ernie Banks (Chicago Cubs) and Elston Howard (NY Yankees).

It is also because I am a player, who – after sustaining a career-ending knee and arm injury during a two-year stint in the Mississippi Ohio Valley League in 1952 and '53 – returned to Hank Aaron's alma mater, the Indianapolis Clowns in 1955. With a bad knee and arm, I played the game while originating every on-the-field gimmick ever witnessed on the surface of a baseball diamond. From this undertaking, I became known as "Prince Joe Henry," baseball's clown prince. As a result of this transformation, notoriety surrounding its showmanship soared to a national high. I am also a player who, after completion of the 1956 season with the Indianapolis Clowns, decided to sit out the 1957 year only (in early 1958) to receive numerous offers from the Clowns and Ted Rasberry, a stellar Black owner of the Detroit Stars about returning to baseball.

The choice was made in favor of Rasberry's team because of it being in the league, which was transformed into Goose Tatum's Detroit Clowns. "Goose," along with Nathaniel "Sweetwater" Clifton, composed the fun-making trio aimed at bolstering attendance, being that both he and "Sweetwater" were former Harlem Globetrotter Basketball stars. "Goose" was the team's original showman as well as a former player for the Indianapolis Clowns, while "Sweetwater" was one of the first of three Blacks to enter the National Basketball Association (NBA). However, after the '58 season, he decided to call it quits. But in 1961, while retired, I received a telegram and letter from Tatum and Satchel Paige about performing with them on Paige's team. Although a very humbling experience to be approached for such an assignment by two of the world's greatest showmen ever, the offer was declined.

As time progressed from 1959 into the early 90s, an idea shared by several former Negro Leaguers became a reality. It surfaced in the form of a baseball library, better known as the "Negro League Baseball Museum" (NLBM), located in Kansas City, Missouri. There, housed in this structure, is a history relative to some of the greatest Black baseball players ever to set foot on American soil. Before advent of the NLBM, many of these players were unheard of by the American public, due to being denied the opportunity to showcase their wares in white baseball circles because of skin pigmentation.

But with the ever-growing popularity of the NLBM, recognition was accorded to former Negro Leaguers, whose image became a household icon. Along with this belated fame, rose an industry of books, collectors, hobbyists and an assortment of Negro League memorabilia, etc. Additionally, MLB team owners capitalized on this notoriety by staging games, whereas their respective teams wore uniforms symbolic of teams in the Negro League. Often, former Negro Leaguers were in attendance. Sadly, in spite of this financial market, former Negro Leaguers have only received a meager amount of profits. Though, in relation to MLB, it too has seized the opportunity to project its image in a positive manner to the American public, this by making it appear as if the organization is a financial donor to the cause of former Negro Leaguers. However, other than supposedly collaborating with BAT in securing the initial group of former Negro Leaguers' lifelong pensions, those of who played before Jackie Robinson, by lending the MLB name and logo to groups such as Major League Baseball Properties (MLBP) and BAT, during the last two outings in their so-called charitable contributions to former Negro Leaguers, have badly damaged MLB's reputation by misleading the American public.

Prior to Selig's recent statement about $1 million being targeted for the aid of 27 players in need, in late 1998 a glimmer of financial hope invaded the minds of many former Negro Leaguers, after receiving checks from MLBP in excess of $300. The checks, purportedly money from royalties due to sales of Negro League memorabilia, was said to be an ongoing event to take place every six months – this move following the initial group's lifelong pensions beginning in 1997. In the year 2000, following dissipation of the initial amount of money, which took place in approximately three additional checks, I – like numerous former Negro Leaguers – received a last check from MLBP amounting to $3.26. This embarrassing "donation" by MLBP motivated me to cast it aside as useless, only to reactivate it following recent disapproval of my application.

During the years in between, my physical structure deteriorated to merely a shell of what it once represented. Exacerbated by the crippling effects of chronic arthritis – specifically "osteo" and rheumatoid – which has reduced my mobility to such an extent that I need the aid of a wheelchair, walker, or cane. Most recently, Southwestern Bell Communications (SBC), my telephone provider, exempted me from having to pay for 411 calls to receive operator assistance due to the arthritic condition of my fingers, which disallows me to manipulate the telephone directory.

Several years prior to reaching this state, I was introduced to high blood pressure and diabetes, illnesses I experience now along with arthritis. Thankfully, after joining the military in 1946 – the year Jackie Robinson joined the Brooklyn Dodgers' organization – the Veterans Administration has been my primary care provider with me only co-paying for most medications. Otherwise, I would be six feet under in debt. Many former players – who did not receive any of the fund money – having similar problems, were not as fortunate as I, because of not having a military background – those like Sam Taylor and Ira McKnight, etc. In reference to housing, for approximately 30 years, I have dwelled in a quite fashionable mobile home. Fortunately, until employment retirement in 1991, I was able to keep it intact. Since then – beginning with monthly social security benefits exceeding $600 along with a pension of $521.25 – I became a recipient of better than $1,100 per month. By 2004, due to occasional increases in social security benefits to $882, in addition to my pension, my monthly income escalated to over $1,400 per month. Meanwhile, I was compelled to manage money frugally by living down to earth, at times "robbing Peter to pay Paul," while at other times doing without.

Because of such a strict budget, I was unable to properly care for my place, as I so desired. Regarding the "Grant Application," inserted therein was a section requiring the signature of applicant(s) to grant your organization (BAT) permission to investigate the truth about answers given pertaining to bank accounts, real estates and autos, along with being asked to itemize utility bills and medical expenses, etc. – in other words, a conglomerate of requirements so aggravating it would discourage the average subscriber. Reluctantly, I acquiesced. However, after adhering to your policy – only to have the application rejected due to being so candid – I became very disgruntled, especially when informed that according to your charter and by-laws, I was outside the perimeter of qualifying for that which was being offered because my income exceeded my expenses. To make matters worse, it was indicated that a minimum of three years was necessary for me to be eligible. Thus, I found myself in a no-win situation, beginning with your statement regarding the "required" minimum of years. By declaring such provision, you contradicted Selig's position relative to "parts of at least four years." In so doing, I was automatically eliminated.

Additionally, Selig – by stating in his press release that the fund would benefit 27 players who started before 1958 – substantiated my no-win situation, because during that year I played for "Goose Tatum's Detroit Clowns" with teammates such as Art Hamilton and Larry LeGrande, and playing against the likes of Ray Haggins, Charlie Pride, the Country Western singer, and others. Prior to my teammates while with the Detroit Clowns, I played with guys like Clarence "Choo Choo" Coleman, Lou Johnson and Johnny Wyatt, while playing against others like Mike Smith and Reggie Howard, a Negro League Baseball Historian. Nonetheless, had the year 1958 been included – which would have satisfied the minimum requirement – I would have been denied anyway, due to my income exceeding my expenses.

In summarizing the affair, the Negro Leagues consisted of more than 27 players. Based on your decision regarding me, Selig – in announcing the news to the public about the 27 players and $1 million – should have said, "Former Negro Leaguers applying for aid needs to be destitute." I say this because my yearly income is below poverty level, which renders me tax-free. Moreover, any player having at least one year in the league was as much a former Negro Leaguer as was Robinson, Mays, Banks and Aaron – all Hall of Famers. As for the 27 players who started before 1958, neither MLB, BAT nor any other source – without producing evidentiary documents regarding the last vestige of the Negro League – has the authority to determine the ineligibility of players beyond that point. To do so would set back the hands of time. As a matter of fact, before Robinson, denial was based on color. Now, this is over a measly million dollars. The only difference between the two is Blacks being pitted against Blacks, which has created a deep division in this once proud dynasty. For reasons aforementioned, if by chance I were offered four years compensation at $833.33 per month, I would readily refuse it. Even if offered $40,000 in a lump sum, I would do likewise. The offer I would seriously consider is a lump sum of $50,000, and that would be contingent on if every other former Negro Leaguer received the same – those who produce documented evidence validating their Negro League authenticity. At least this would serve as a rewarding end for every former player, beginning with those who held the Negro Leagues Foundation together until the arrival of Jackie Robinson and up to those who performed under its banner until vestige was wiped away.

Fortunately, many players of the initial group have received $50,000 and beyond, mainly because of having lifelong pensions. Unfortunately, several have died along the way – the latest being Wilmer Fields – who from my understanding worked with others to bring this project about. Falling in this category were several former players, who grew to become my closest friends; they were: Verdell Mathis, Casey Jones (a Memphis Red Sox teammate) Josh Johnson (who influenced me to play baseball) Lee Moody (Robinson's Kansas City Monarchs roommate) and Cowan "Bubba" Hyde. This closeness stemmed from the autograph circuit. In the case of these players, when the plan was initiated in 1997, no time limit was assessed, nor was there any strings attached. Contrarily – almost seven years later – the recent plan – barring application rejection – called for a four-year limit. Had my application been accepted prior without my knowledge of the controversy involved, in all probability I would have acknowledged the aid. Afterwards – due to conditions previously mentioned – I changed my viewpoint to $50,000. This amount, based upon five years, would shorten the financial gap between the initial group and the existing former players.

It would also void the previous four-year system of application eligibility to receive monthly benefits. Furthermore, it would heal the rift between the 27 players receiving funds and those who have been denied, and – not to omit – by using this method, it would test the sincerity of MLB by wiping the slate clean. In doing so, it could truly be said that MLB is a benevolent donor rather than a pretentious deceiver. Thereafter, every player receiving money – if spared by death prior – could share it proudly in one small way or another with children, grandchildren and greats, so they – from generations hence – may keep the great legacy alive. This, without doubt, MLB can indeed do.

It must be remembered that MLB at one time was only so-called "Major." Not until Negro Leaguers became participants did the previous title change. During this era, salaries were so meager that white players like Danny Gardella, Vern Stephens, Mickey Owens and Max Lanier jumped the league to play for more money in Mexico, where Negro Leaguers had been welcomed for years. However, after becoming a part of the so-called "Majors," the Major League title was eventually legitimized, because the best players possible competed. Once the barrier was broken, the presence of other Black players – offspring of the Negro Leagues – was felt. One such person was Curt Flood, who – in addition to being a sensational baseball player – was the orchestrator of breaking down the barriers white team owners had established to control white players indefinitely, similar to how Blacks were controlled by whites until the arrival of Abe Lincoln. With the crumbling of this kind of rule, followed by bargaining of free agency, MLB transcended just being "Major"…It became big business.

Therefore, MLB should take a page out of the book of Joe Louis, the late great heavyweight-boxing champion. Louis, while in the military, defended his title on separate occasions for the Army and Navy relief funds without discriminating. MLB can do likewise, because it has the vehicle, which would be to stage a charity baseball game for the benefit of former Negro Leaguers. Subsequently, it could sit back in the sun and bask in its glory. Otherwise, I am requesting copies of your charter and by-laws and the list of players receiving monthly benefits, the list from which they were chosen and their respective applications. If I am not ashamed to reveal my application nationally, then you should not have anything to hide. I applaud former MLB Commissioner Fay Vincent for mailing checks in excess of $200 to every former Negro Leaguer he could locate, following the publishing of his book relevant to the Negro Leagues. By doing this, he did not discriminate.

Respectfully,
Joe Henry
JH/srm

cc: Bud Selig, Commissioner - Major League Baseball (MLB)
Negro League Baseball Museum (NLBM)

THE GLORY DAYS

Copyright 2004 Tri-Statedefender.com.
Reprinted with publisher's permission.

BY WILEY HENRY

He was good and should have gone to the Major League, a teammate said of "Prince Joe Henry." But after a stint in the Negro Baseball League over a half-century ago, the 74-year-old ex-ballplayer hopes to get a smattering of the $1 million that Major League Baseball is offering ballplayers who can prove they actually played and who are in need of financial assistance. Unfortunately, the league rejected Henry's application.

Long after Rube Foster founded Black baseball in 1920, nobody learned how to play the game better than the cadre of Black athletes who cut their teeth in the Negro Baseball Leagues. In a segregated society where Blacks were relegated to menial jobs and unsavory conditions, there was a sense of camaraderie on the diamond where these athletes proved their worth with innate athleticism and talent by enduring the hardships that befell many of the ballplayers during the turn of the century and throughout the history of Black baseball.

Reckless violence and wanton discrimination against Blacks, even during the 1800s, was the order of the day, and justice was fleeting or nonexistent for athletes of a darker hue. However wretched life was then, Joe Henry, who played off and on between 1950 and 1959, made the best of it with athletic prowess and showmanship. For the man who was dubbed "Prince" Joe Henry, those were glory days, where cross-country excursions with other Negro leaguers provided ample opportunity to socialize with high-caliber ballplayers, noted musicians, entertainers and other famous persons of the day.

"Those were the best days of my life," Henry recalls. But, then, after the Negro League filed dissolution papers in 1960 — according to Larry Lester, a historian who was contracted by the Major League Baseball Hall of Fame in Cooperstown, N.Y., to research the history of Black baseball — many Negro leaguers grew old, weary and, of course, penniless. Their best days were behind them. Henry hasn't complained about his role in the Negro League. However, he has continued to fight for his place in history and a mere pittance of as much as $10,000 annually over four years that Major League Baseball (MLB) started doling out in 1997 as quasi-pension payments to ex-Negro leaguers who qualify. This was good news to Henry, who first learned about the pension after reading a May 18, 2004, story in the Belleville News-Democrat (Belleville, Ill.). Henry says he's met the criteria for payments of approximately $1 million that is being administered by the Baseball Assistance Team (BAT), a charitable arm of Major League Baseball.

According to James Martin, executive director of BAT in New York, N.Y., more than 30 ex-ballplayers have received help from the charitable group since May. "No one is rejected if they qualify," he notes. Henry begs to differ. He says he sent Martin a letter stating that he was unaware of the pension, but nonetheless qualified. Martin sent an application; Henry filled it out and sent it back. In a letter dated July 20, 2004, Henry's application was rejected. The reason? According to a story in the Riverfront Times, an alternative weekly newspaper in St. Louis, Martin said this about Henry: "For BAT to provide assistance, a financial need is required on behalf of the applicant. In reviewing your application, your income exceeds your expenses."

Martin says the pension is paid to ex-Negro leaguers who played between the years 1947-1958. The money, he says, is financial assistance that can be used for just about anything, including medical and mortgage payments. Although there is no minimum or maximum amount a ballplayer can receive, his income cannot exceed his expenses and the applicant must have at least parts of four years in the league and prove it with newspaper clippings, mentions in books, or anything in print. "It's up to the applicant to prove he was a ballplayer in the Negro League," says Martin, noting that BAT, a nonprofit group, meets once a month to mull over applications. The money, he says, is considered a grant and is generally awarded within 45 days.

"The four years is badly misinterpreted," Henry protests. "This pension is for players who played parts of four years. If you played one to three years you're eligible for the money." Henry sent Martin a five-page letter to appeal his eligibility and to express his dismay. Again, Martin turned him down in a reply dated Sept. 13, indicating that Henry's playing career did not meet the program's criteria. Martin also points out that applicants must have played for teams who meet the qualification as organized ball clubs and not those who were considered to be barnstormers — a term denoting teams who performed exhibition games. All

Star teams that were consistent with Major League All Stars are qualified for the pension, says Martin, adding, "There were a dozen or more of these teams. Otherwise, there wouldn't be a way to control it (the issuance of money)."

BAT has been in operation since 1986 for the benefit of ballplayers. Although BAT's mission hasn't been any consolation to Henry, Martin concludes by saying that "anybody whose income exceeds their expenses, we wouldn't be able to help them." Henry is adamant about receiving the monthly pension. According to the Riverfront Times story, ex-Negro leaguers such as country singer Charlie Pride, who pitched and played outfield for the Memphis Red Sox, is receiving $833.33 a month for the next four years. Ten ballplayers altogether have confirmed they're receiving the same sum per month from BAT.

Tri-State Defender sportswriter William "Bill" Little, who played from 1955-57 as a second baseman and utility player for the Memphis Red Sox and as a catcher and utility player for the Kansas City Monarchs, says he was urged to apply. However, "I decided that I didn't want to go through the hassle because the need part would just knock me out," says Little, who also served the Red Sox as a batboy when he was an elementary student. Somehow Henry hasn't been able to convince BAT of his dire circumstances — which could make him eligible for the money along with his stint in the league. For three decades, the ex-ballplayer has solely depended on a fixed income of $16,839 a year -- a meager pittance culled from his Social Security check and a smattering pension he earned as a shop steward. Henry lives in a world within a 14-by-65 foot Windsor mobile home in Lovejoy, Ill., his hometown, where the town's population of 600 has lagged behind economically. Amid a few tattered furnishings, he finds quiet time to read, write and reflect on the arduous fight ahead. Despite his circumstances, Henry says, "Everybody should know the greatness that surrounded the Negro League." Now a 74-year-old man, he is battling diabetes, rheumatoid arthritis and high blood pressure and other ailments, and depends on the aid of a walker, cane and wheel chair for mobility.

Though old age has lessened his stride, the sharp-minded ex-ballplayer has fond memories of what was, and what could have been his fate if he had not been injured while playing second base for the Memphis Red Sox. That was decades ago when Henry's knee and arm injuries kept him sidelined until he made a last ditch effort in 1955 to play less than 100 percent at third base with the Indianapolis Clowns. "Bunny Downs, the traveling secretary for the Indianapolis Clowns saw me play with the Memphis Red Sox and asked me to play with the Clowns," Henry remembers. "I told Bunny I was hurt and my career was over, and he said to give it a try. That's when I had the idea to clown around," says Prince Joe, developing antics on the field akin to "Goose" Tatum, who played with the Indianapolis Clowns before he joined the Harlem Globe Trotters, better known in circles as the wizards of basketball.

Just like Tatum did, Henry entertained the fans amid the sound of side-cracking laughter. While at bat, he'd windup before the pitcher in a top hat, tails and painted red shoes, ready to smack the baseball into history. This was Prince Joe at his best, making do of a bad situation. Although Henry's days in baseball were numbered, he remembers from whence he started. "I didn't know anything about the Negro League (as a young man)," says Henry, who played for the Memphis Red Sox (1950-52), Indianapolis Clowns (1955-56), Detroit Clowns (1957-58), Detroit Stars (1958-59) and again for the Detroit Clowns (1959).

Henry entered the League as a young, sprightly 19-year-old with stars in his eyes. Before he joined the ranks of seasoned ballplayers, he studied the game. "I used to go to the Sportsman's Park in St. Louis at a young age. It was the home of the St. Louis Cardinals and the St. Louis Browns," he recalls. "We went in as knot holders (free). We were led to the stand in left field, an isolated area for Blacks. There was a place in the right field pavilion for influential Blacks. If a guy hit a home run, it would never go into the pavilion."

During the early '40s, when he was about 11 or 12 years old, Henry says he had no other choice but to admire the white ballplayers, such as Terry Moore and Marty Marion, who brought a measure of greatness to the game. He knew then that he wanted to play the game, having played 12-inch fast pitch softball with hissing speed. "We traveled up and down the line playing white teams. We beat the hell out of them and they beat us too," says Henry amusingly. But it was Josh "Brute" Johnson, a star Negro league catcher in the 1930s and '40s who witnessed Henry's talent on the diamond, who told him he was wasting his time, that he should pursue a higher calling. During that time, Jackie Robinson had broken the color barrier in 1947 in whom Henry had admired from a distance. "That's when I decided to try the Negro League," he says.

Eugene Crittenden, a "monster" basketball player and longtime friend of Henry's, also urged him to try out for the Negro League. After he joined the Memphis

Red Sox, he opted for a career in the Major League by way of the Negro League. Although Memphis was a pit stop for Henry, he fell in love with the city, he says, because the owner, Dr. W.S. Martin, treated the team like family. Martin and his brothers also built Martin Stadium on Crump Blvd. for the home team. But, then, during the struggle for civil rights, a dark cloud of hate hovered over the country, which caused violence to erupt, tension to mount, all spewing over onto the baseball field in a glob of Black and white mess. "The saddest time in my life is when I saw my manager, "Goose" Curry, get beaten by a white policeman in Birmingham after he protested a call to the umpire," says Henry, his voice punctuated with sadness.

"He (Curry) came down to argue a call with the Black umpire (in a game between the Sox and the Birmingham Black Barons), who beckoned for the policeman. And the policeman took him to home plate and beat him. Blood was streaming down." The violence didn't deter Henry from playing the game, although entry level Negro players were paid a smidgen of what Major League players earned: approximately $300-400 a month. The salary, of course, depended on the ballplayers star quality, he says.

After Robinson's history-making accomplishment, the gentle old man notes, Black baseball took a serious hit, a smack in the face with the best Negro leaguers causing an exodus to integrate the Major League. "When I got to Memphis in the 1950s, the Negro League was just about finished," Henry says. "There were about 10 teams left, and they were powerhouses who soon fell apart after Robinson. "If it had not been for Ted Rasberry, owner of the Detroit Stars who renamed the team "Goose Tatum's Detroit Clowns," the few teams left would have buckled sooner. He carried the Negro League on his back."

Henry is carrying a burden of his own. The game he played as a young man was fruitful, gratifying, and full of pleasant memories. But the life he's living today has not yielded the kind of payoff he feels he deserves as an ex-Negro leaguer. Ollie Brantley, a friend and former teammate of Henry's, was quoted as saying, "Joe Henry was a heck of a ballplayer. I thought for sure he was gonna get a shot to go play [in the majors]."

He didn't; but he came very close. Of the hundreds of Negro League ballplayers from over 40 teams who graced the diamond during its heyday, between 120-130 are still alive, according to Dennis Biddle, a former Chicago American Giants pitcher and president of the nonprofit Yesterday's Negro League Baseball Players Foundation. Before Major League Baseball commenced with the pension benefits and its criteria for receiving it, Biddle argued that MLB should have consulted his Foundation, which claims to represent the majority of ex-Negro Leaguers. Henry says Bud Selig, commissioner of MLB, who announced the new pension fund — which differs from the one set up in 1997 to benefit players before 1948 — expressed his pleasure that MLB would assist 27 players after Robinson's meteoric rise. The fact is Henry isn't one of those players getting the pension. Though teetering around or below the poverty level, he is barely making ends meet. He has not been able to hit a home run in his quest for payment since the glory days of Negro League Baseball.

From riverfronttimes.com
Originally published by the Riverfront Times 2004-11-17
©2005 New Times, Inc. All rights reserved.

Prince Joe's Lament

WHERE WAS JOE HENRY WHEN MAJOR LEAGUE BASEBALL COUGHED UP MONEY FOR EX-NEGRO LEAGUERS? IN THE DARK.

By Mike Seely

Joe Henry rises promptly at six o'clock every morning. His arthritis, as he puts it, "don't wake up till noon." A native of Brooklyn, Illinois, Henry lives just where he has for the past three decades: in a fourteen-by-sixty-five-foot Windsor mobile home (vintage 1975) on North Seventh Street, a short walk from Route 3 and the smattering of adult-entertainment establishments that serve as the downtrodden town's (population 600) lone economic engine.

Until 1991, the rectangular residence was, in its owner's words, "quite fashionable." That was then. Ripped upholstery is now: Henry, 74 years old and retired, makes do on a fixed income of $16,839 per year, thanks to Social Security and a small retirement pension gleaned from his years as a shop steward.

Clad in a white undershirt and jeans on a tattered couch in his dim living room, Henry, who suffers from diabetes and rheumatoid arthritis among other ailments, offers a brief assessment of Cardinals superstar Albert Pujols ("He's one bad-ass son of a gun"), then shuffles to his breakfast nook to pour himself a bowl of Quaker Oats. Prior to consumption, he pauses to recite a blessing: Lord, help me if you can, to eat all that's in the poor man's pan. If there's any more left in the pot, please serve it to me while it's hot!!!

Henry's day-to-day reality hasn't always been so stark. Strewn around this room are mementos from his days as an all-star infielder in the 1950s in baseball's Negro Leagues. Knee and arm injuries put an end to a two-plus-season stint holding down second base for the Memphis Red Sox at the dawn of the decade, but Henry resurfaced in 1955 with the storied Indianapolis Clowns franchise. Henry's showmanship at third base during two seasons in Indianapolis, a team that counts home-run king Henry Aaron among its alumni and is often compared to basketball's Harlem Globetrotters, earned him the nickname "Prince Joe." After sitting out 1957, Prince Joe was coaxed back to the diamond by Detroit Stars owner Ted Rasberry, who renamed his team "Goose Tatum's Detroit Clowns" after the famous Globetrotter and Negro League phenom. "Joe Henry was a heck of a ballplayer," recalls Ollie Brantley, a teammate from Henry's Memphis years. "I thought for sure he was gonna get a shot to go play [in the majors]."

But like many Black ballplayers of the 1950s, Henry didn't, for reasons no more complex than complexion. While Jackie Robinson's 1947 contract with the Brooklyn Dodgers signaled the end of the ban on Black players in the Major Leagues, it did not usher in an immediate era of integrated baseball.

"Segregation and the color barrier didn't turn over at twelve o'clock midnight on April 15, 1947," says Negro League historian Larry Lester, referring to the day Dodgers general manager Branch Rickey signed Robinson. "It was a gradual transition. It took a couple decades to balance out in the minor-league and major-league levels. When Jackie Robinson retired [in 1956], there were still three teams without a Black player."

That was the gist of Bob Mitchell's appeal to big-league commissioner Bud Selig's office after Major League Baseball in 1997 began paying $10,000 annual pension benefits to 69 ex-Negro Leaguers who played before Robinson broke the color barrier. Mitchell, a Tampa resident who'd played for the Kansas City Monarchs during the 1950s, didn't get much of a response from the commissioner's office. Undeterred, he contacted U.S. Senator Bill Nelson of Florida, who enlisted the NAACP in the campaign.

The effort paid off: This past May 15, the Washington Post reported that Major League Baseball, in concert with its charitable arm, the Baseball Assistance Team (BAT), would administer approximately $1 million in monthly quasi-pension payments (totaling $10,000 annually over four years) to 27 former Negro League ballplayers who'd been excluded from the original group of 69 but had played in portions of four or more seasons before 1958.

The next day Joe Henry read a brief wire story in the Belleville News-Democrat and sent a letter to BAT executive director Jim Martin, noting that he met the stated criteria but had known nothing about the program before picking up that morning's paper. Soon afterward Martin sent Henry an application filled with questions about his Negro League tenure and current financial situation.

In a letter dated July 20, 2004, Martin rejected Henry's application. Though Major League Baseball had mentioned nothing about financial need with regard to the program, Martin noted that Henry's expenses (which he'd estimated on the form at $1,000 per month) didn't outstrip his monthly income of $1,403.

"For B.A.T. to provide assistance a financial need is required on behalf of the applicant," Martin wrote. "In reviewing your application, your income exceeds your expenses."

"He can't afford any expenses," scoffs Lester, who knows Henry personally. "A lot of ballplayers live like Joe does. I know what shirt they're gonna wear at the next reunion, because they only have one."

Henry persevered, sending Martin a five-page appeal restating his case for eligibility. A September 13 reply from BAT turned him down again, this time asserting that his playing career didn't meet the program's criteria.

Anthony Avitabile, MLB's director of industry risk management and financial reporting, says that since the mid-May announcement, the league has added players to the new plan, bringing the number of recipients to 32. Avitabile declines to disclose recipients' names, nor will he comment about individuals who were deemed ineligible for the program. But the Riverfront Times has interviewed ten ex-Negro Leaguers (including Bob Mitchell) who confirm that they are receiving monthly checks for $833.33 under the new program, as well as three former players who appear to meet the plan's criteria but aren't getting pension payments.

Along with Henry, fellow former Clown Clifford Layton, who played from 1951 through 1954, is not receiving any pension benefits. Nor is Don Johnson, who played from 1947 to 1952 with the Philadelphia Stars, Baltimore Elite Giants and Detroit Stars.

The three men have more in common than their outcast status. All live on fixed incomes at or below the poverty line. And none has ever kicked any money to Bob Mitchell's Communication Network of Negro League Players, the entity through which Mitchell solicits donations from ex-colleagues to defray costs associated with his ongoing efforts on their behalf.

Meanwhile, all but one of the players interviewed for this story who say they're receiving the new pension payments speak of Mitchell in glowing terms. The lone neutral party, Ollie Brantley, is also the only one of the group who hasn't contributed money to Mitchell.

"Ollie gave me his ass to kiss," Mitchell says of Brantley. "The [other] ones who are getting the money give it to me. They know that if I hadn't done what I'd done, nothing would have happened."

Country music stardom was actually Charley Pride's Plan B. "I didn't intend to be in the Hall of Fame for singing," allows the 66-year-old Pride, who pitched and played outfield for the Memphis Red Sox, among other Negro League squads, in the mid-1950s. "I wanted to be the next Babe Ruth. My thing was baseball. I'm just glad the Lord blessed me with a voice to sing."

Pride is among the 32 ex-ballplayers receiving $833.33 per month for the next four years under Major League Baseball's new Negro League quasi-pension plan. What with royalties and concert appearances, Pride says, the payments are superfluous, so he uses the money to help his brother Mack, a fellow ex-Negro Leaguer who fell short of the minimum service requirement for the $40,000 windfall.

"I really didn't need it, but since they decided to do it -- I call it guilt money," says Pride, who has donated money to Mitchell over the years. "I look at it from the situation of Japanese internment: I think everybody who ever played, whether they played one game or two weeks, ought to get something."

The criteria for the ancillary plan appear to have been hammered out in late 2003 at Bob Mitchell's home in Tampa, during a meeting with Major League Baseball executive vice president Jonathan Mariner. Though Mitchell took a position much like Pride's, Mariner argued that the eligibility should resemble the 1997 plan, which required that players took part in four Negro League seasons. In addition, the league decided to make 1957 the last eligible year of service.

"The prevailing thought was that all Major League teams were pretty much integrated at that time," Mariner says now. Except they weren't: The Philadelphia Phillies didn't field their first Black player until 1957. Ozzie Virgil became the first Black Detroit Tiger in 1958. The Boston Red Sox were the last team to bring a Black player aboard, in 1959. Even after that, Negro League play continued until the early 1960s.

"I don't know what the criteria were for choosing 1958 as the cutoff," says Larry Lester, who is currently under contract with the Major League Baseball Hall of Fame in Cooperstown, New York to research and establish the definitive history of Black baseball. "The league filed dissolution papers in 1960, so that's my cutoff date."

Mitchell sought out Lester to help establish which players would be eligible for the new pension payments -- an inexact science at best, given the spotty archives of Negro League box scores from the 1950s. MLB's Avitabile says Mitchell submitted a list to the commissioner's office. "Mitchell, at one point, put together a list of players who played at any time, and years of service," Avitabile says. "We picked the names off the list Bob had sent with four-plus years. That's where we started from." According to Mitchell, that's where Prince Joe Henry got culled from the ranks.

"Larry [Lester] provided me the list that I went through to eliminate the barnstormers," Mitchell explains. "[The Indianapolis Clowns] were barnstormers. Their last official year was 1954." Through much of the mid-1950s, the Clowns traveled with the New York Black Yankees and played exhibition games for amused throngs nationwide. But Larry Lester says the team's last official year was 1955. That was Joe Henry's first season with the Clowns -- and his fourth in the Negro Leagues.

"They were in the league in '55," Lester asserts. Noting that the Clowns weren't sanctioned in 1956 and 1957, the historian adds, "I would also consider '58 to be legitimate, because they were the Detroit Clowns."

"It is important for people to understand that the Clowns were really the only clown team that was ever part of the organized Negro Leagues," seconds Bob Kendrick, marketing director for the Kansas City-based Negro Leagues Baseball Museum, which Lester co-founded. "They did a lot of barnstorming, but what Negro League team didn't?"

Jim Zapp, who played with Willie Mays in Birmingham in the late 1940s, is among a handful of Negro League players who were overlooked back in 1997. After being granted the full pension package retroactively about a year ago, Zapp cut Bob Mitchell a check for $1,200.

"I gave him $1,200, but he seems to want more," Zapp says today from his home in Nashville. "He seems to be kind of angry with me."

"Zapp's money was just like any other person's money," Mitchell retorts. "The appreciation don't rise up the way it should. I sent out 54 letters two weeks ago."

Those typo-pocked mailings, which Mitchell dispatches on official-looking stationery in periodic fusillades, serve a dual purpose: to provide former colleagues with updates on what he's been doing on their behalf, and to ask for money.

An excerpt from an April 2, 2004 appeal: "At this juncture, I urge you to move on the above in the 'most timely manner; All checks you write 'must' be sent to me for and to assure distribution and your cooperation [...] Remember, 'you' wouldn't have received a red cent accept for the untiring efforts I've put forth with much sacrifice as many of you just waited patiently for this soon to come day.

"Remember, when you get this money, the Lord giveth, the Lord can take it away. I am the vessel that He are using to Bless you…think on that, for some have secretly criticized my efforts with doubts…you cannot know what I do every morning at four o'clock…while you are still sleeping??? Legend, let the conscience that God gave you…while you are now living be your guide…for the conscience is the voice of your spirit. Acknowledge at your will."

"You can tell his elevator don't go all the way to the top floor," Joe Henry says of Mitchell.

While acknowledging Mitchell's crucial role in bringing the recent $1 million pension program to fruition, Major League Baseball's Mariner won't discuss the ex-Negro Leaguer or his Communication Network, which is not registered in the state of Florida as a charity or for-profit enterprise.

Former Chicago American Giants pitcher Dennis Biddle is less reticent. Biddle is president of Yesterday's Negro League Baseball Players Foundation, a nonprofit that claims to represent the majority of living Negro League ballplayers, whose numbers are dwindling by the day.

"There were 314 [ex-Negro Leaguers alive] in 1995," Biddle reports. "Now between 120 and 130 men are still living. Ain't that many guys left."

Biddle believes the commissioner's office should have consulted his group in developing the new pension program. "Major League Baseball has ignored me and the foundation that represents the players to go with some guy who's doing something for his benefit," says Biddle, whose group shares Charley Pride's view that all living Negro League players should be entitled to remuneration, length of tenure notwithstanding. "Bob is a member of our [group]. Bob should have turned it over to the foundation, but Bob was looking for self-preservation."

As far back as December 1995, Mitchell's unilateral lobbying caught the attention of legendary Negro League veteran Buck O'Neill, who as chairman of the Negro Leagues Baseball Museum's board of directors (a post he still holds) addressed a letter to all former players.

"Several players have been calling the Negro Leagues Baseball Museum concerning Bob Mitchell's request for money on behalf of an organization called the Communications Network," O'Neill wrote. "The creation of splinter groups, like the Communications Network, only serves to confuse people."

Count Prince Joe Henry and Larry Lester among those who remain confused. "Joe should be there," Lester says. "He played from '50 to '52 with the Red Sox and '55 with the Clowns. That would give him the four years right there. And then you've got '58. Joe Henry was obviously a good ballplayer, and I don't think there's any question that he played, and he played a lot. In fact, he played more games than almost anybody in the league."

Riverfront Times 'Letter to the Editor'

LONG LIVE THE PRINCE

Had he only been white. The article by Mike Seely on Prince Joe Henry ("Prince Joe's Lament," November 17) was timely and informative. Recognition of black baseball legends like Henry are few and far between. Henry's many contributions to the national pastime have been swept under the rug and forgotten. Now in his golden years, he suffers from financial neglect by the same organization that barred him from the game in the prime of his life. We will never know the quality of life he would have had if he had been a white ballplayer.

We need more investigative articles like Seely's that reveal the living conditions of men who played before the color barrier fell. I am thankful to Bob Mitchell for his efforts, and the Baseball Assistance Team (BAT) for considering his case, but why the Negro Leagues Baseball Museum in Kansas City isn't lending a helping hand is the bigger question.

Larry Lester – Kansas City

Editor's Note: The following is a personal testimony and sent to Mr. Henry. There are many correspondences sent to him on a regular basis, however, we were especially touched by this particular one and thought we would share it with the public. It has been reprinted by permission.

Dear Sir,

I am a 48-year-old Ordained Minister and Sergeant Of Police. I told you earlier that I work for the City Of Kinloch. Your article on Brooklyn, Illinois really inspired me. I am from Oakland, California, but I grew up within a township in Oakland that reminds me of both Kinloch and Brooklyn. I love my people and I always want to do whatever I can to help my people flourish. The youngsters in Kinloch think I am too hard, but if they grew up in the era that I grew up in they would understand that my only concern is to see them better themselves. When you called me the other day I really did not know who you really were. I looked you up on the Internet and found out that you are one bad dude. My father passed in January of this year and he was an avid baseball fan.

He used to tell me about the Negro League and about players like you who should have been granted an opportunity to play in the Major League. If I had told my Father that I had spoke to "Prince Joe" on the phone, he would have said, "Okay son, speak to me when you awake from your dream."

Anyway, the City Of Kinloch is the oldest African American City incorporated in the State Of Missouri. It is also the actual hometown of California Congresswoman Maxine Waters. Due to a buyout by Lambert Airport, most of the people in Kinloch sold their homes and Kinloch lost 75% of its population. The population is now four hundred and forty nine. There was a time when the people of Kinloch did not have to leave the city of Kinloch to have their needs met. There were grocery stores, funeral homes and plenty of doctors, dentists and mechanics in Kinloch. They had their own public schools also. I have met people who have lived twenty or thirty years and never left the boundaries of Kinloch. They actually had never been to St. Louis City.

President Roosevelt took his first plane ride ever out of Kinloch Field. The first experimental Parachute Jump in the world took place at Kinloch Field. Major Albert Lambert purchased the field (500 acres) and renamed it Lambert Field. We have a great mayor, Keith Conway, who has a vision for the city and a great police chief, Donald Hardy, who is a native of E. St. Louis and a retired homicide detective with St. Louis City.

In his Service,

Everett James

Constable For Christ Ministry
Rev. Everett L. James, BAPC; Rev. Hattie Hopkins, MA
Ordained Minister, Founding Pastor
Sergeant Of Police Faith Center Ministry
To Protect And Serve...Let Not Your Heart Be Troubled

MY MOTHERS APPOINTMENT
November 22, 2006

My mother was the type of person that would never miss an appointment. Although, because of her advanced age, she could no longer drive an automobile, she would be sure to call on one of her children to make sure that one of them would be available to drive her to whatever place she was scheduled to be. She loved her family doctor because he was so warm, friendly and down to earth. This doctor, who is also my doctor, would always greet her with a smile and ask about the welfare of other family members, calling each of them by their first name.

On the last appointment mother had with her doctor, he hospitalized her originally for rest. However, after administering several tests it was discovered that mother had terminal cancer and was given only a week to live.

When I went to the hospital to visit mother she had only one request...She asked me to read her a passage from the Bible found in the book of Romans. Mother had me read this passage to her several times over.

"That if thou shalt confess with thy mouth he Lord Jesus, and shalt believe in thine heart that God hath raised him from the dead, thou shalt be saved. For with the heart man believeth unto righteousness; and with the mouth confession is made unto salvation."

Romans 10:9-10

Isn't that something? This was not about religion, it was about a relationship. So many of us miss the point. Although my mother was a stern Christian, at the end of her life on earth only the basics were important. She believed in Jesus. She believed that God brought him back from death. And she spoke what she believed with her mouth. No jumping, shouting or turning flips. Just believing...Mother died with a smile on her face. It has been over five years and I have not shed one tear. Why? Because...I also simply believe.

In his service,

Rev. Everett L. James, BAPC

Prince Joe's Victory

BY CHAD GARRISON
Published – Riverfront Times (November 7, 2007)

After waging a three-year battle with Major League Baseball, Riverfront Times columnist Joe Henry has won inclusion in a pension program for former Negro League ballplayers. News of the decision greeted Henry last month, just days after he celebrated his 79th birthday. The $40,000 pension will pay Henry $833 per month over the next four years. But if you think Henry is grateful, think again.

"They did everything they could to find me ineligible," says Henry, who suffers from arthritis and diabetes and spends most days lying on a tattered couch in his Brooklyn, Illinois, trailer-home. "Now that MLB has finally given me a pension, they need to make right and give everyone who played Negro League ball a pension."

In 1997 Major League Baseball began paying retirement benefits to 69 ex-Negro Leaguers who played prior to Jackie Robinson breaking the color barrier in 1947. Seven years later, MLB's Baseball Assistance Team (BAT) opened up a separate pension for players of financial need who continued in the Negro League through 1957. In July 2004 the MLB rejected Henry's BAT application on grounds that the $1,400 he earns each month from Social Security and a small pension from his days as a shop steward outstripped his expenses. A second application was rejected when BAT discovered Henry's playing career didn't match the program's criteria. (See "Prince Joe's Lament," November 17, 2004.)

Henry, who starred as an infielder with the Memphis Red Sox and Indianapolis Clowns during the 1950s, says he'd given up hope of ever receiving his MLB pension. Then came a letter last month from Anthony Avitabile, the league's director of industry risk management and financial reporting. Avitabile says Social Security records unearthed by Henry's grandson, Sean Muhammad, prove Henry played the requisite four years needed to qualify for a separate MLB pension — also established in 2004 — known as the voluntary Negro League pension plan.

"The one year we could not verify was that Joe played for the Indianapolis Clowns in 1955," says Avitabile. "But now we have the employer's payroll from that year, and Joe's name is on the list."

Henry maintains his fight was never about money. Moreover, he vows to continue to "wage war" on Major League Baseball until other former Negro Leaguers are also granted pensions. "I'd give away half my money if it would go to other deserving Negro Leaguers," says Henry, who believes the four-year playing requirement and 1957 cutoff date for MLB's Negro League pensions deny dozens of players their rightful benefits. "The Negro League existed up to at least 1960. For Major League Baseball to say it ended in 1957, that's as wrong as two left shoes."

www.ingramcontent.com/pod-product-compliance
Lightning Source LLC
Chambersburg PA
CBHW080457110426
42742CB00017B/2911